Architecture of the World in Colour

WERNER HOFMANN AND UDO KULTERMANN

MODERN ARCHITECTURE IN COLOUR

MODERN ARCHITECTURE IN COLOUR

Werner Hofmann and Udo Kultermann

112 colour plates and 152 plans

 THAMES AND HUDSON

Translated from the German *Baukunst unserer Zeit* by Peter Usborne

English translation © 1970 by Thames and Hudson, London
© 1969 by Burkhard-Verlag Ernst Heyer, Essen

Colour plates printed in Italy by Istituto Geografico de Agostini Novara
Text printed in Holland by A. W. Sijthoff, Leyden
Bound in Holland by Van Rijmenam n.v., The Hague
I.S.B.N. 0 500 34042 0

CONTENTS

LIST OF PLATES

Architecture and 'mere building'

The word 'architecture' has a certain glamour about it, as architects themselves are well aware. The architectural profession likes to describe itself as practising the highest of the art forms, the 'mother of the arts'. This gives architects a sense of mission. Like every concept which has the authority of classical antiquity behind it, architecture is associated with high ideals. It demands respect. The mere mention of architecture evokes images of solemn or elegant shapes, symbols of dignity and majesty, of spiritual and temporal power: the tomb, the church, the temple and the palace.

Discussing architecture thus, sets it on a high, artistic level, but tends to make us forget that architecture also means building, and can be simply a means to functional ends – as is the case with bridges, department stores and stations. The Viennese architect Adolf Loos, who modestly but proudly insisted upon calling himself a 'builder', wrote in his essay 'Architecture' (1910), 'only a small part of architecture has anything to do with art; the tomb and the monument. Everything else, everything which is built for functional purposes, must be excluded from the concept of art.' More than half a century before this, John Ruskin had drawn an equally clear distinction. He considered architecture to be art only when associated with sculpture and painting, serving rather than dominating them. In the foreword to the second edition of *The Seven Lamps of Architecture* (1855) he wrote: 'The fact is there are only two fine arts possible to the human race, sculpture and painting. What we call architecture is only the association of these in noble masses, or the placing them in fit places. All architecture other than this is, in fact, mere *building*' (Ruskin's italics!). Ruskin could not believe that this 'mere building' could contain the seeds of a renewal of the art of construction.

Unlike Loos, Ruskin drew a distinction not between the functions a building was supposed to perform but between the ways that building materials were used. This attitude arose from a study of the new engineering structures that were prompting questions unanswered by architectural theory. Could the new building materials and functional structures really be regarded as architecture? Ruskin gave Paxton's Crystal Palace only limited recognition. He mistrusted iron, but admitted that if used within its own limits it could have an important role to play. He shrewdly recognized the inherent contradiction between iron and decoration, and therefore, logically, had to exclude buildings made of iron from his definition of architecture based on painting and sculpture. He insisted that architecture must be limited to non-metallic, traditional building materials. The architectural element of a building was something beyond its structure. It was the 'unnecessary' element. This inevitably implied that iron, more than any other material, was purely functional.

Ruskin was not alone in his opinion. The fatal split between the Beautiful and the Useful can be seen in the seventeenth- and eighteenth-century buildings designed from the outside in; where decoration, laid over the structural frame, takes on a value of its own. Historicism emphasized this division of architecture into distinct elements. When archaeological interest in Gothic and Classical architecture began to grow in the middle of the eighteenth century, the structural elements of a building were often regarded as being separable from each other as well as from the decoration. According to Blondel (1772), it was at that time widely believed that a perfectly beautiful church would have the nave of Amiens, the choir of Beauvais, the portal of Rheims, and the spires of Chartres. In 1825, Sir John Soane designed a church to suit three historical styles. The ground-plan remained the same but the client was allowed to choose his own decorative 'shell' to put on top of it. Schinkel did the same in his plans for the Werdersche Church in Berlin.

The history painters of the eighteenth century were also concerned with the problem of decorum. They no longer took it for granted. In about 1720, James Thornhill was commissioned to paint a picture of the landing of George I in Britain. The problem was, should he paint the scene as it really occurred, or improve on reality? He considered the alternative: 'There was a vast crowd which to represent would be ugly, and not to represent would be false.' Finally he decided against historical accuracy and sought to improve upon it. Once more beauty had triumphed over truth.

Half a century later the opposite point of view began to gain acceptance. The first signs of this are to be seen in painting in England, the country where iron was first used as a building material. French painters followed and improved on the English initiative. David believed that he was painting a factually accurate pictorial record, whether it was of the dead Marat or the battle of Thermopylae. In a note on his picture *The Rape of the Sabines* he wrote that his aim had been to portray behaviour in ancient times so accurately that if Greeks and Romans were to stand in front of his pictures, they would believe them to have been painted by an artist thoroughly acquainted with their own way of life.

In painting, the two extremes were absolute accuracy and idealization; in architecture, they were construction and decoration. The eclectics, who have suffered from the verdict of history, laid several different styles of decoration onto the structural frame of a building. This implied that decoration was transferable, while the structure underneath the decorative surface had an essential independence of its own.

There are similarities between this process of polarization and the new attitudes towards past and present which started in the Age of Reason and were spread by the French Revolution. 'By destroying tradition the French Revolution made people aware for the first time that the present could be looked at in the light of the present and the future, rather than the past' (Löwith). New historical consciousness led to new attitudes to the present. The idea that 'creations should be true to their creators' (Wackenroder, *Herzensergiessungen eines kunstliebenden Klosterbruders*, 1797), meant leaving Gothic to the Middle Ages and allowing a suitable contemporary style to develop.

It is no mere coincidence that the early engineering structures were the first evidence of this new, progressive attitude. They appeared in Great Britain, the country in which the new ideas outlined above were first discussed. In 1779 Abrham Darby III built the first cast iron construction: the bridge over the Severn at Coalbrookdale. The architectural establishment took no notice of this and other pioneering achievements, and avoided all contact with the new material which had no tradition and was therefore regarded as not quite legitimate. This attitude eventually led to the idea of architecture's being limited to decoration.

Ruskin believed that architectural form was unconnected with function. One of the consequences of this was that the functional forms of 'mere building' were not deemed architecture, but merely necessary objects. 'Architecture' as defined by

Ruskin was not 'necessary', and therefore needed some other justification. So he made 'architecture' into a vehicle for the work of painters and sculptors. In so doing, he is now considered to have diminished the concept of 'architecture', to the advantage of 'mere building'.

It was between these extremes that architecture fluctuated in the nineteenth century. At one extreme, there was artistic but superficial and pointless decoration; at the other, sober, functional form. At about the time the shed of St Pancras Station, London (Plate 4), was built, the exotic Neo-Gothic hotel in front of it was erected.

Ruskin and Loos were not of the 'academic' school. Loos allied himself with the anonymous builder against the art-architects of the Art Nouveau movement. Nevertheless, what Frank Lloyd Wright contemptuously called 'beaux-arts formalism' did influence Ruskin's and Loos' defensive and unrealistic concept of architecture. The eclectic academicians equated 'architecture' with functionless 'nobleness' (Ruskin), while stooping to superficial exploitation of earlier styles. All their energy and ingenuity was spent on devising artificially and unnecessarily complicated ground-plans, and laboriously detailed façades. Thinking in terms of space and form degenerated. Only dignified buildings were decorated in the respectable and deliberately limited sense implied by 'architecture'. All others were left to the 'mere building' of the engineers. Nineteenth-century bridges, stations, and exhibition halls were placed, consciously or unconsciously, outside the dignified confines of prestige 'architecture' but, as Konrad Wachsmann said, they foreshadow much that is typical of modern building. Regarded with suspicion by the forces of conservatism and driven into a no-man's-land, it is the constructions of those nineteenth-century engineers that begin to show new horizons of creative possibilities and developments upon which all the significant architectural events of the twentieth century were based, although they were always in conflict with accepted ideas. Just as the creative expansion of twentieth-century painting and sculpture broke away from the boundaries set by the old concepts of aesthetics, so the pioneers of the new building disregarded the distinctions arbitrarily drawn between 'architecture' and 'mere building'.

This wider definition of architecture was new only in contrast with the cramped drawing-board academicism of the nineteenth century which preceded it. But the abstract concept of 'nobleness' in architecture, which considered a station hall to be merely a 'shed' (Viollet-le-Duc) was in fact itself preceded by a different and wider concept of architecture which derived from the very beginnings of the 'mother of the arts'. In Greek, the word *tekton* meant not only carpenter, but also artist, producer, and finisher. The word *architekton* meant the 'arch artist' who originated the work. Vitruvius' *De Architectura* covers architecture in the broadest sense, using the word to refer to buildings of all types, from temples to harbours. In the tenth book he even uses it to cover mechanics. Alberti's *Ten Books on Architecture* (1485) treats the concept in the same way. Alberti defines architecture very broadly and discusses it in relation to its role in society and civilization. 'Alberti is not interested in drawing firm boundaries for architecture, but in broadening the concept by allowing it new objectives and tasks' (Max Theuer). Of course, he gives the most dignified buildings – temples and palaces – a position of central importance, and regards functional buildings, such as libraries, schools, baths, stables, harbours, bridges and canals, as less significant. But with his practical and humane approach to architecture, Alberti even gives advice on 'the destruction and deterrence of snakes, mosquitoes, bugs, flies, mice, fleas, spiders and similar noisome and pernicious creatures'.

In the Renaissance we find a conflict between matter-of-factness and the aspirations of the idealists. It was the latter who won, and it was out of their victory that 'beaux-arts formalism' eventually grew. The universal Renaissance hunger for knowledge, with its demands for objective standards, led to a fresh analysis of architecture and its spread into all areas of life. The practical men called for a complete change in man's environment, extending even to the landscape of both town and country, and at the same time the speculations of the theorists were treated with increasing attention. The comparatively naïve, pre-scientific 'customs' of the Middle Ages were swept away by the new demand for systematization and codification. The new research into basic principles derived its orientation from the classical age, and it was there that Renaissance theory and practice found their formal guide-lines and ideal prototypes.

Renaissance architecture took the column as its central motif. The column could be used almost anywhere, and in being able to give, as it were, unity to diversity, it fulfilled the aspirations of the age. Alberti, whose ambition was to put columns on every conceivable building, nevertheless conceived various degrees of architectural orders, suitable for different ranks of building. Thus he claimed a pyramid of values, with temples at the top and mere functional buildings at the base. It was this kind of thinking which led to the reckless eclecticism of the nineteenth century. Conventional forms came to be equated with architectural nobility. Every building has to conform to these conventions, which became accepted as values of their own, needing no functional justification. The romantic novelist Victor Hugo, a declared enemy of classicism, showed where these attitudes could lead in a passage in *Notre-Dame de Paris* (1831): One could find oneself standing, he wrote, in front of a building which might equally well be a palace, a parliament, a town hall, a racecourse, an academy, a warehouse, a court of justice, a museum, a barrack, a temple, or a theatre. It was, in fact, the stock-exchange.

So we can see that the Renaissance urge to highlight each element of form for its own sake, and to give it a clear and abstract definition, was the thin end of the wedge of the self-justifying formalism of later theorists, and the cause of the fatal division between the decorative shell and the structural frame of a building.

The classical movement in architecture was merely a part of the general process of compartmentalization and intellectualization which overtook all branches of art after the Renaissance. The only exception to this was Baroque, where individual art forms were not given complete autonomy, and which therefore managed to avoid the rational processes of self-examination with which the classicists contended.

In the symbolic art of the Middle Ages everything was conceived of as meaningful, from the different areas within a building, to the glass windows, the internal fixtures, and the decorative elements. This meant that the various parts of a building were integrated, and were not divisible into concrete and abstract elements. Architecture, sculpture, painting, and crafts existed, as it were, within each other. But late medieval naturalism and Renaissance 'compartmentalization' began the long lasting division between autonomous art forms, which were seen as existing alongside, rather than within, each other. Once painting and sculpture began to justify themselves by the accuracy with which they represented visual and empirical reality, they lost their abstract common denominator with architecture. Once they took the depiction of the real world or of heavenly events in worldly terms as their primary objective, the 'fine arts' (painting and sculpture) set up their own areas, and withdrew from their earlier symbiosis with architecture and decoration. The ultimate tangible results of this were free-standing sculpture and movable easel-paintings.

The seeds of the new 'idealism' were to be found in Renaissance realism. Detailed treatment of human anatomy and structuring of space according to the laws of central perspective, both instruments of formal integration, became the two main features of a movement which systematically attempted to imitate and represent nature. They were also the basis upon which a new empirical idealism of form was to be built. The classical theorists of the seventeenth century turned these ideas into laws, which subsequently constrained painting, sculpture, and architecture alike. The classicists drew a distinction between ideal beauty and factual but inadequate reality, and it was from this that the division of the arts into the superior and the inferior developed. The former became servants of the cult of functionless beauty, and the rest became tainted with 'function', and, as the word 'craft' itself seems to suggest, were virtually put beyond the pale of true art. This in turn led to the belief that the functional must be ugly and only the functionless could be beautiful (Théophile Gautier, 1834). A station hall was dismissed as a 'shed' because it was functional.

The development of architecture reflects, *mutatis mutandis*, the split which developed between the systematic search for an ideal world of fictitious beauty and inductive scientific research into the world of facts. As late as the sixteenth century the Florence Academy of Art was still 'a type of polytechnic school where mathematics was a compulsory subject' (L. Olschki) and the 'Arti del disegno' covered the various technologies of both art and engineering. But in practice a break was developing between architects concentrating on aesthetics and scientists on theory.

Unrecognized by the great architects, and without any interest of their own in the practical application of their theories to building, a number of the most important mathematicians and physicists of the seventeenth and eighteenth centuries concentrated on purely theoretical examination of the laws of mechanics and statics. For a long time there was no contact between these theoretical specialists and those who actually practised architecture. It was not until the middle of the eighteenth century that an attempt was made 'to apply the methods of exact science to a practical building problem' (Straub). This was when a crack appeared in Michelangelo's dome of St Peter's, which made a thorough examination of the statics of the building necessary. It is significant that it was a problem of restoration to which the discoveries of science were first applied.

The new awareness of the importance of science was paralleled by a new phase in architectural research during the eighteenth century which examined classical as well as the long despised Gothic styles. The decorated façades of revivalist architecture were the most obvious results of this archaeological reappraisal, as well as the most superficial. But of course we should not judge this new growth of scientific awareness simply by façades. Its searchings went much deeper than that, and were concerned with the central argument in architecture about form and function. The proponents of both the Gothic and the classical style – and some architects were at home with both – were really searching for prototypes of the great ideal of the age, which was shared in all spheres of political, social, and intellectual life: the rediscovery of original, organic laws. And it is this ideal which still inspires modern architecture.

Georg Büchner (in his *Death of Danton*, 1835) made Camille Desmoulins say, 'A country's constitution should be like a transparent garment which clings to the body of the people. Every twitching of a muscle, every swelling of a vein, should be visible through it.' Applied to architecture, this means a simple basic structure, bare and unembellished, which allows the internal structure of a building to be seen without embroidery. Gothic and classical styles were to show the way to this. For instance, Carlo Lodoli, an Italian Franciscan monk, attempted to free the classical elements of architecture from the decoration which had been imposed upon them, and to reduce them to their stereometric essentials. The logic of his functional rationalism demanded that the 'natura della materia' should be taken into account. (About 150 years afterwards, Wright was to write a book entitled *In the Nature of Materials*.) Lodoli rejected Baroque because it used building materials in an unnatural way, reducing architecture to what he called an 'arte plastica'. Augustus Welby Pugin, one of the leaders of the British Neo-Gothic school, maintained that there should be nothing unnecessary on a building. He believed that 'architectural skill consists in embodying and expressing the structure required; and not in disguising it by borrowed features'.

The basic agreement between these two theoreticians seems to conceal widely differing points of view. William Blake summed up the difference between them in his not unbiased comment, 'Grecian is mathematical form, Gothic is living form.' This goes to the heart of the matter, the conflict between Gothic and classical, which continues today. The classical is still, as it was 150 years ago, invoked to justify the 'natural logic' of stereometric simplicity and regular closed form. And it is always Gothic which is invoked to justify dynamic tension, symbolic form or the expression of the fullness of life by means of irregular, bizarre or vegetative shapes. In spite of the fact that theorists like Pugin and Lodoli were concerned to think out afresh the structural problems of building, their ideas stagnated in traditional vocabulary. Although they were aiming at the right objectives, they were unable to realize them in terms of form. Indeed, the chief characteristic of thinking about form and function in the decades around 1800 was that it refrained from the ultimate consequences. In 1795, Goethe wrote, 'If Architecture wishes to be counted as an Art, it must produce objects which are not only necessary, and functional, but which also make a harmonious impression upon the senses. This sensual harmony is both essential to every art form, and different one from the other. And it is something which can only be judged according to its own laws. These laws are determined by the material used, the function, and the sense upon which the end-product is intended to make an harmonious impression.' But would Goethe have been in a position to judge the Iron Bridge over the brook at Striegau, in Silesia (1797), according to his own 'laws', or the formal harmony of the Pont des Arts in Paris (1803)? Would he have realized how progressive both really were? Probably not, for his notion of harmony for the senses was based on the traditional theory of proportions, with Palladio seen as the leading exponent.

Goethe clung to this theory (which he called 'Fiktion'), to counteract the purists, who would turn everything in architecture, as in the other arts, into 'prose'. It appears that this was the first, albeit contemptuous, reference to the new tendency in architecture which Ruskin, sixty years later, dismissed as 'mere building'.

'Prose' meant the anonymous building which had no claims to style, the vernacular which developed outside the respectable artistic idiom. In the twentieth century, we find corn silos, warehouses, African and Balkan villages nestling on cliff faces included under this heading, all examples of a 'natural architecture' (Neutra). This was the type of building admired by Olbrich, Van de Velde, Gropius and Le Corbusier. By 1800, the simple naturalism of the vernacular was being classified as 'picturesque'. Marie Antoinette's village was built in 1781; John Nash put up Blaise Hamlet in 1811, and fifty years later came Philip Webb's Red House (Plate 2).

Goethe saw that it was not only in architecture that poetry was being turned back into prose, and he was probably aware that his ideas about what constituted the 'pinnacle of beauty' were out of date. Schiller probably insisted so firmly upon the value of 'the traditional approach, both in poetry and in sculpture' because he saw that these values were threatened. The relationship between art and reality was already developing along new lines, and the creative artists were adopting a hitherto unknown and shocking directness. Goethe criticized this when he attacked Diderot for praising the spontaneous, sketchy qualities of a painter's 'handwriting'. What was happening was that the media of pictorial expression were being allowed a degree of prominence and individuality never given to them before. These developments seemed to the classicists to amount to vulgarization. The same thing was happening in both the 'fine arts' and architecture.

What Goethe called 'Fiktion' was the equivalent of the 'nobleness' which Ruskin wanted to impose upon architecture. Both wanted to fence off aesthetics from the vernacular and refused to recognize that the needs and potentialities of the future made it essential to develop this 'prose' creatively. They shut themselves off from the view first expressed by Friedrich Semper about the Great Exhibition in London (1851); 'above all architecture must come down from its throne and go into the market place to teach there, as well as to learn'. Semper was probably the first architect of the various revivalist movements to welcome an engineer's solution to a new building problem as the best possible. He wrote that Paxton's Crystal Palace, which was built in six months out of iron and glass, incorporated the essential tendencies of the period.

The three basic styles of 'modern architecture'

The brevity of this introductory essay does not allow a detailed historical survey. This constraint has, however, the advantage that it offers the opportunity of concentrating thoroughly on one basic problem which is usually given too little emphasis, or is lost under a welter of facts. Every historical guide must begin with a definition of its terms and syntax, and can only be clear if it progresses from the simple to the complex. The question which the following pages attempt to answer is, How did the prototypes of modern architecture come to be created and when did they first appear? This puts all the variety of the last hundred years within our scope. Basic models or prototypes define the area in which an infinite number of combinations and permutations of form can take place.

The middle of the nineteenth century was a turning point of great historical significance for the development of the new architecture. In the space of a few years three buildings were erected, each of which amounts to a statement of basic principles: a cast-iron factory in New York by James Bogardus (1848), Joseph Paxton's Crystal Palace in London (1851) and Philip Webb's Red House in Kent (1859). In all of these are to be seen the beginnings of trends which have become central to architectural and town-planning practice and theory during the past hundred years.

Since Bogardus and Paxton used a new material, iron, a few notes on the history of iron in connection with building should help in understanding their achievement. Wood and stone were the two natural materials which were available to architects up to the beginning of the industrial age. In addition, there were tiles, which were not really natural building material since 'in the burning of the clay there is an attempt to change the natural characteristic of the building material' (Joedicke). And it was this which made iron and reinforced concrete artificial. Whereas wood and stone, which are worked upon only by hand or by machine, keep their original consistency, iron and concrete are produced by industrial processes.

Iron began to qualify as a building material only when it became possible to mass-produce it to a reliable standard of quality. One of the most important steps towards this was the intensified mining of coal in Great Britain in the eighteenth century; this made it possible to use coke instead of wood, which was becoming increasingly scarce, as a fuel in the smelting process. This was first tried by D. Dudley in the seventeenth century, but nothing came of it. It was rediscovered by Abraham Darby II in 1735. Henry Cort succeeded in improving the production and quality of wrought iron very considerably with his puddle process (1784). This production technique was replaced by Henry Bessemer's simpler and cheaper process in the 1850s, which Sydney G. Thomas managed to perfect even further in the 'seventies. Cast and wrought iron have different characteristics. Wrought iron has ten times the strength of wood under compression and one hundred times that of stone. Cast iron is twice as strong as wrought iron under compression but is less strong under tension. This explains why wrought iron has always been used for suspension bridges (the first of which was erected in 1796 in North America) and cast iron for arched bridges.

Iron has been defined as a linear two-dimensional fragile-looking material, in contrast to the solid, three-dimensional sturdiness of masonry. If one accepts that elegant linearity is iron's most rational form, it should also be accepted that these characteristics lead away from the solid, block-like, closed type of building, towards an open, linear, articulated frame. The frame principle can be seen in its earliest form in the tent and in its most ingenious form in the Gothic cathedral. What was new about the iron frame was simply the range of possibilities it opened up.

The contrast between masonry and iron construction reminds us of Blake's distinction. While masonry conceals the skeleton frame, and covers the structurally necessary parts with a decorative or stereometric cladding, cutting off the interior space from the exterior, iron construction allows the frame to be completely visible. It makes possible an open type of construction which allows interior and exterior space to merge. When Paxton built the Crystal Palace he left some trees inside, which had the effect of partially breaking down the usual divisions of space, turning the interior space into open, exterior space. This double openness, in the display of the structure and the lack of division between spaces, was regarded for a long time as a failing of iron construction. But this is criticizing iron for something it cannot avoid, and overlooks the fact that the loss of traditional values is outweighed by the establishment of new ones. The channelling of power into linear form offers a dynamic, weightless spatial experience and an intuitive insight into the transformation of mass into energy. It is here that the poetry of the new material lies.

While the traditionalists dismissed iron as, at best, 'mere building', a few people began to dream of a type of monumental architecture, the sole objective of which would be the creation of a spectacle by the release of different forms of energy. It would be the apotheosis of Progress, and at the same time like a tale from *The Thousand and One Nights*. The followers of Saint-Simon had a vision of the future in which functionless 'architecture' and 'mere building' were intimately combined. Less well known than their unexecuted projects for a Nile Dam and the Suez Canal, is the Saint-Simonists' interest in iron construction. In 1832 Enfantin criticized contemporary architecture for its lack of 'movement'. He wrote that 'permanence, stability and movement are the three essentials of a building'. The following instruction is like a manifesto for a dynamic and open-frame style of construction, and a manifesto which still remains partly unfulfilled today: 'the structure of a building should be like the molecular structure of the body. It should have both mass and open form, allowing for play and elasticity. The members of a building should be assembled like the molecules of a body.' He also accorded iron the leading role in the '*architecture sacerdotale*' of the future even though this was a time when iron construction was still in its infancy.

Enfantin hoped to achieve musical and optical effects of a completely new kind by taking advantage of the articulated character of iron construction. He recommended that iron tubes be used as supports and as organ pipes at the same time. 'The whole temple would then be like a full orchestra or a huge thermometer. Who could describe the extraordinary galvanic, chemical and mechanical effects which one could achieve by combining different metals and putting a fire in the middle of a holy building, which would be connected to thunderstorms by means of a lightning conductor?' This vision of a musico-architectural total work of art stretches our imagination somewhat. It involved temples with electric pillars, a temple made of giant magnets, temples of melody and harmony, holy places studded with lens-like openings through which light and warmth would flow. Science would transform the old idea of a 'world theatre' into both an object lesson and a fairy tale. Electricity and magnetism would represent the unresolved and the mysterious, while metals and priceless materials would represent glitter and gloss. Life on the sun was to be symbolized by light and warmth, life on earth by the arts. 'What an extraordinary Communion, what a moral Example for a whole people, what a Glorification of God, of his Messiah, and of Man!'

While Enfantin was dreaming his fantastic architectural visions, practical iron construction concerned itself with thoroughly prosaic tasks, usually involving the spanning of large distances. Since they could rely on increasingly accurate methods of calculation, engineers were able to increase the span of their bridges considerably. The span of the Severn Bridge (1779) was about 30 metres; the span of a bridge planned over the Thames by Thomas Telford (1801) was 183 metres. Telford built the Conway Bridge in the 1820s, a suspension bridge with a span of 127 metres. The principle by which suspension bridges were built was not adapted until relatively recently for use in modern suspended roofs, whereas iron arches quickly served for the construction of halls and domes. The most important buildings of this type, some of which no longer exist, were: the dome of the Corn Market in Paris (1809–11), the swimming pool of the Diana Baths in Vienna (1820), the smelting factories in Sayn-im-Rheinland (1824) by K. L. Althans, the Palm House at Kew (1843–47) by

D. Burton and R. Turner, the Reading Room in the Sainte-Geneviève Library (1843–50) and the Bibliothèque Nationale in Paris (1858), both by Henri Labrouste, the Crystal Palace (1851), Les Halles of Paris (1853–55) by Baltard, and Paddington Station (1854) by I. K. Brunel and M. D. Wyatt.

These buildings were all large, straightforward, well-lit spaces, built over geometrically simple and thoroughly conventional ground-plans, and they were all 'public' buildings. Haussmann rejected Baltard's original plans for a hall, in which he envisaged an elegant stone building, saying, 'all I need are huge umbrellas'. A requirement like this takes new aesthetic and functional properties for granted. Only an iron structure can really provide these, since its strength, unlike that of a masonry building, lies in what it can omit, and its charm lies in its lightness and its ability to reduce a building to bare essentials. Since iron buildings were usually made of standardized parts, these halls could be taken down as quickly as they were erected. So the counterpart to iron's discreet simplicity is the sense of impermanence and changeability it tends to give. The Crystal Palace, erected in six months, was later moved to Sydenham and re-built to a new design.

The impermanence of the structure of iron buildings also applies to their functions, which are often interchangeable, since the same hall can be used equally well for trade, study or traffic. The swimming pool of the Diana Baths in Vienna was in fact covered over and used as a dance hall. We should, however, recognize that multiplicity of function is the inevitable result of this particular type of construction. An iron building is an uncompromisingly simple and clean structure, and can obviously be used for different purposes, all of which are, however, concerned in some way with the 'collective' rather than the individual. Work, trade, travel, exhibitions, sport and study are activities which, in a democratic industrial society, are inevitably associated with satisfaction of the needs of large numbers of people. The simple spaces offered by an iron construction, itself functionally neutral, offer solutions to many of these collective requirements.

Parallel to the development of iron construction, which tended to produce arched and domed spaces, there was another school, concerned exclusively with the rectangular relationships between support and beam. In 1801 Boulton and Watt built a seven-floor cotton mill in Salford, in which the whole of the interior was constructed, for the first time, with iron supports and beams. The exterior walls were of masonry.

In 1848, James Bogardus, who called himself an 'architect in iron', supported the external walls of his New York cast-iron factory with pre-fabricated cast iron columns and beams, and filled the space between them with huge windows. The use of pre-fabricated parts made it possible to erect buildings very quickly, and even to transport these (as Semper put it) 'frames for furniture'. It is true that Bogardus invoked the Venetian Renaissance in his façades, yet they were similar to the façades of the 'skeletal' buildings which were to come later. Buildings with skeleton frames tended not to have prominent façades, and since they were built out of pre-fabricated parts, variations in grade between different storeys began to disappear. The structural functions were performed by a network of upright and horizontal beams which were given lightness and transparency by huge areas of glass. Bogardus considered using steel skeleton frames for houses, but he did not build any. For the time being, steel skeletons were used only for business buildings; such as multi-storey offices and department stores. With the exception of Saulnier's chocolate factory in Noisiel-sur-Marne (1869–74), this new technique developed exclusively in the cities of the United States of America.

The one-roomed hall and the multi-roomed cellular construction are extreme formal solutions which, in spite of their differences, are both suited to collective standardized functions, and are intended to shelter large numbers of people at once. The hall is used for meetings, traffic and exhibitions. The 'lonely crowd' which gathers in it has little cohesiveness, or, at best, the fleeting togetherness of the anonymous mass. In the office block, as Sullivan put it, 'one tier is just like another tier, one office just like all the other offices – an office being similar to a cell in a honey-comb, merely a compartment, nothing more'; consequently a man is merely an inhabitant of a cell. In the hall and the office block, the individual is in continuous contact with the collective, and spends his time in open 'public' spaces. He is surrounded by a network of communicating links with other people.

Two things seem clear: first, that extreme architectural solutions of this type are inevitable in our age, that they have essential functions to perform, and second, that they give the individual no opportunity for self-development, or, rather, cannot give this opportunity because of their one-sidedness. Modern architecture would be monotonous indeed if it were limited to buildings based on the two prototypes, the hall and the cubic cellular building.

It was in Great Britain, where industrial architecture originally developed, that this very problem was first recognized. At the same time as public exhibition and station halls were being erected, people began to realize that private residential buildings also needed rethinking. Here the architect's task is to achieve individuality, which neither the schematism of eclectic villa and palace architects, nor the uniformity of towers and halls, could achieve. The Red House, built in 1859 by Philip Webb for William Morris, attempts to move away from the impersonal world of industry back to the snugness of the country idyll. It has no standardized or pre-fabricated parts, and the interior contains only well-made craft products and works of art, in contrast with the mass-produced goods of the time. Only in two respects does the building fit in with the ideals of the engineer-architects; it does not use any borrowed styles, with the exception of a few Gothic references; and it is honest about the materials it uses.

So the Red House, being essentially different from cellular buildings and halls, can be taken as the third prototype of modern architecture. In order to appreciate fully the significance of this romantic revolt against the basic tenets of technological and industrial building, it should be realized that the engineer-architects had to pay for the monumental uniformity of their buildings by abandoning subjective form and romantic idioms. The proper use of pre-fabricated and standardized building units makes regular repetition of forms unavoidable. In halls, uniform shapes stretch into the distance; in blocks, elements are aligned vertically and horizontally. Simple, usually rectangular, ground-plans, and the rectangular patterns on the surface of the walls give the building uniformity and make it comprehensive and strongly homogeneous. The vertical cube of the tower presents as few surprises as the horizontal span of the hall. The whole building mirrors the unavoidable precision of its individual parts, and its system of forms, free of all embellishment, gives an impression of perfect harmony, but it is usually easy to see that it has been pre-fabricated, and that it could be (and often was) demounted as easily as it was put up.

The Red House does not share this ascetic purism. Webb believed in everything which the engineers had to abandon. He believed in a ground-plan not drawn up according to firm rules, but which could, in theory, be altered at will, and which allowed rooms to be arranged functionally, while seeming to extend into the environment; in the asymmetrical, non-uniform, structural frame, loosely arranged to take account of the different functions of the rooms; in the romantic charm of the irregular, the hand-made, and the organic, of which his client William Morris considered Gothic to be the prototype. And lastly, he believed that a building and its contents were intimately related and should form a single whole.

These are all principles which seem almost reactionary in relation to the progressive attitudes of contemporary engineer-architects. Nevertheless, they are essential elements in the development of modern architecture.

Semper said, in 1851, that the American house was something one could buy 'ready-made on the market'. It was not really a house, but a 'frame for furniture'. The Red House is not a neutral, uncommitted 'frame' suitable for any type of interior decoration or occupant, but a unique, subjective, dwelling which, with its interior, forms a complete work of art.

The development of the prototypes

In the 1890s, we see in the U.S.A. and Europe the outcome of the pioneer constructions of the mid-nineteenth century. The additive cell system, the single-room hall, and the irregular, multi-room ground-plan, were all developed and adapted, giving rise to a language which anticipates that of the twentieth century.

The two main attractions of the Paris exhibition in 1889, the Machine Hall, and the Eiffel Tower, formed the climax, as well as the conclusion to the phase of vast steel-framed space enclosures. At the same time, the Chicago School was producing the first version of the classic steel-framed cellular building. Webb's principles of organic, irregular, 'open' idioms were considerably enriched by the buildings of a new generation of architects, whose work extends beyond what is usually understood by 'Art Nouveau'. At the same time, reinforced concrete became available, although it was not widely used until the twentieth century.

Dutert and Contamin's Machine Hall 'incorporates the experience of a whole century of construction' (Giedion), and is a solution to one of the central problems of form arising from the trend towards homogeneous single-room buildings. The problem was how to construct the shell in such a way as to present a continuous flow of form uninterrupted by struts and supports. Gothic arches had already attempted to round off smoothly the modular units of the romanesque building, and to conceal the borderline between the wall and the arch, and pillar and beam. But architects still had to use vertical walls and flying buttresses. The engineers of the nineteenth century had to cope with the same problem. They were able to increase the span of their halls only gradually; in the case of the Crystal Palace, the widest span was only 22 metres. The Palace of Industry (1855) in Paris had spans of 48 metres. The Machine Hall had a span of 115 metres, which was larger than anything previously built. This was achieved by means of the triple-tied arch developed by Contamin. 'All the forces are concentrated at the apex and at the two bases of the arches by the ties' (Joedicke), while the load-bearing elements of the structure became thinner nearer the ground. This was something new and seemed very strange at the time. It gave the building an appearance of weightlessness and obviated the need for vertical walls. The line of force could now start at ground level and sweep upwards through the arch to the apex in a single curve. Structural techniques which until then could only be applied to the arch, could now be applied to the whole building.

The Eiffel Tower partly fulfilled Enfantin's vision of a brilliant architectural display full of movement. During the day visitors to the great exhibition saw a glittering, gilded pattern of metallic lines shining in the sun; in the evenings it was transformed into a pillar of light or a fantastic firework display. Eiffel turned Enfantin's suggestion, that buildings be assembled like molecules, from a poetic metaphor into practice. And it was this, rather than the light and firework displays, which was the really remarkable aspect of the tower. The knot-like joints of its metallic framework seem to weave a complex net in space which presents a continuously changing pattern to anyone who enters into its complex framework. It is an all-embracing and complete spatial experience in which the boundaries between interior and exterior space cease to exist. It was the first building which surrounded without enclosing. To enter its frame is to set in train a series of unforeseeable events.

Eiffel's 'molecular' arrangement of weight-bearing elements was the first statement of the principle from which, in our own times, Buckminster Fuller and Konrad Wachsmann have developed their systems of modular co-ordination of their de-mountable and transportable halls and domes (Plate 109). Nowadays hardened plastics often supersede steel. 'It is quite conceivable that the time will come when plastics will be the dominant and typical building material' (Wachsmann). One does not need to be a prophet to forecast that in the future this material will fulfil the demand for increasingly transparent, light, and temporary structural frames.

The contents of an age usually appear simultaneously in various art forms. If we take the technological venture of the Eiffel Tower, Eiffel can be said to have erected a functionless monument to the idea of work. Rodin at the same time was actually working on a sculpture called 'Tower of Work' involving a number of Dantesque figures. And the Chicago School was producing its office tower blocks, which, if not monuments to work were monumental functional buildings for working in. Various developments, including the invention of the lift by 1850, the need to concentrate ever larger groups of workers in single functional units, and property speculation, turned the cellular buildings of the middle of the century (in 1853 Bogardus was already planning a tower 90 metres high) into the skyscraper. The most obvious feature of the skyscraper is the repetitive pattern made by the floors on the exterior walls. The lack of differentiation between storeys means that the whole building makes 'a unit from top to bottom without a single line out of place' (Sullivan 1896) (Plate 26). Since the first skyscraper was put up little over eighty years ago, the problems of this type of building have stimulated almost all important architects to produce their own solutions.

At the time achievements in steel construction were reaching their peak in Chicago and Paris, a new and revolutionary chapter of architectural history was modestly beginning. The use of reinforced concrete was barely noticed at first. It is a technique which can be seen either as adding steel to masonry construction or vice versa. The purist will regard it as a compromise, the pragmatist will justify it by necessity, and the dialectician will welcome it as a synthesis. The chief characteristics of this new material were that it combined the strength under compression of concrete with the strength under tension of steel. Concrete, which is a mixture of water, sand, gravel and cement, was already being used at the beginning of the nineteenth century. It was only just after the middle of the century that the Frenchmen Lambot and Coignet and the American, Hyatt, quite independently of each other, had the idea of strengthening ceilings and beams with steel nets. In 1867, the Parisian gardener Monier was granted the first patent for the production of flower tubs strengthened with iron mesh. The first building made completely out of reinforced concrete was a curiously shaped villa by Hennebique, near Paris (about 1892). This was soon followed by A. de Baudot's church of St Jean de Montmartre, a postscript to Neo-Gothic.

Here we are back again in the conflict between classical and Gothic, between the right angle and the arch. These two buildings foreshadow the applications and the developments of reinforced concrete during the twentieth century. One application was the multi-storied cellular residential and business building, the other the vaulted place of assembly. The former is characterized by the right angle, and the latter by the weight-bearing arch.

During the first phase of the development of the reinforced concrete skeleton frame, in which French architects were heavily involved, we find that, just as was the case with steel skeletons, the weight-bearing elements (the joists, beams, girders and ribs) were visibly distinguished from the spaces between them, which were filled by bricks or glass. The inherent monolithic characteristics of reinforced concrete began to emerge only between the two world wars, as increasingly accurate mathematics began to allow the construction of homogeneous self-supporting shells. This shell technique of building is now dominant in public buildings. In their spherical roofs the difference between primary and secondary (i.e. load-bearing and space-filling) elements is abolished, and they combine material and functional economy with an exceptional lack of weight, making use of the almost unlimited possibilities of reinforced concrete to achieve daring spatial sculpture. If we look into the future, it is clear that, as far as public buildings enclosing large spaces are concerned, 'shell architecture will replace the skeleton. The spherical shell is obviously the proper form for reinforced concrete, in contrast to the steel skeleton, which is naturally associated with the right angle' (Kultermann).

We also find the third prototype of modern architecture at a new stage of development around the turn of the century. We have already seen in the Red House the essential elements of this style. We find buildings erected on a ground-plan, the form of which was determined inductively. These buildings would nowadays be called 'open', and they give an impression of variety and informality when compared with the tower, the hall, and the domed space. Their shape is too complicated and varied for the use of any pre-formed frame. They are based on variability, change, asymmetry, and expansion, qualities which preclude the essential elements of the two other prototypes: continuous repetition of geometric modules, straight walls, and the resulting ease of comprehension.

Around the turn of the century, a number of variations on Webb's theme were developed which are called Art Nouveau in books on the history of architecture. However, this expression was first used to describe certain types of craft products, which prevented it from being extended to cover architecture, sculpture and painting for some time. One wonders whether it is really possible to group together under one term the work of more than a dozen architects spread across the cities of both Europe and America. The majority of these people were born between 1861 and 1871 (Gaudí 1852, Berlage 1856, Voysey 1857, Horta 1861, Van de Velde 1863, Eckmann 1865, Olbrich and Guimard 1867, Mackintosh and Behrens 1868, Wright 1869, Hoffmann and Loos 1870, Endell 1871).

Does this really mean that we can talk of a connection between the whole generation? Or to put it another way, is there really a common factor connecting the many sided 'art-architect' Van de Velde, who designed houses, cutlery, clothes, and book bindings, with his rival Adolf Loos, who described himself merely as a builder? What is the connection between Gaudí's exaggeratedly sculptural form (Plate 33) and Hoffmann's straight-edged shapes (Plate 32)? Anyone looking for an answer to these questions would be well advised to use the ambiguous concept of Art Nouveau very carefully.

The leaders of architectural theory at the turn of the century had to fight on two fronts. They attacked passionately the elaborate façades of the historicists, while rejecting the puritanical vocabulary of the engineers. ('Architects and engineers are today marching along different routes. Nevertheless they have a common objective: victory over matter,' said Van de Velde.) Ruskin and Morris saw hand-made craft products as the antidote to bogus clichés and standardized pre-fabrication. With their belief in craftwork, these bourgeois optimists coined democratic slogans like 'art is for everyone'. The manifesto of the Vienna Secession claimed, in 1897, that there was no difference between superior and inferior art. But in fact these people still thought along conventional aristocratic lines. In practice, therefore, the movement was exclusive and ineffectual. Its uncertain attitude towards industrial design strongly limited the extent to which its influence was able to spread. It is therefore no coincidence that its greatest achievements – with a few exceptions – were concerned with the private dwellings of the élite or with theatres and exhibition buildings – public places in which a culture spiced with art could conduct its own celebrations.

But these architects did develop a new, greatly expanded vocabulary of form, in which can be seen evidence of their struggle against both the traditionalism of the historicists and the orthodoxy of the constructors. Although they used iron columns, ribs and brackets for both construction and decoration, internally and externally, they made them into playful, intimate and improvised shapes, avoiding standardization and replacing formal discipline with a new elegance. It is as though they wanted to raise the engineers' 'prose' to the level of 'poetry' or mix the two together. This explains their combinations of masonry and skeleton frame techniques, their combination of traditional architecture and functional innovation. They drew on a very wide range of different forms and materials. They unhesitatingly used, in the same building, three-, two-, and one-dimensional means of expression, and they saw no reason not to use iron, wood, stone, tiles, marble, ceramic, and glass together. But although they were driven to look for new ideas by the worn-out vocabulary of historicism, they were far from hostile to the past. Their approach to history was fresh, straightforward and productive. They rejected historical styles, but not their underlying principles. Thus we find Gaudí saying, 'we should not copy or repeat Gothic today, but develop it', and Otto Wagner calling for a 'free Renaissance'; while Loos admired Schinkel's classicism.

One look at the extremes of form used by architects of the time – curves and right angles, flat and arched surfaces – shows that classical and Gothic had lost none of their authority by the end of the nineteenth century. Ruskin's statement that 'all beautiful shapes are made out of curves' was true of Gothic, as well as looking forward to the sweeping and sometimes curvilinear form of the *fin de siècle*. This tendency was in accord with the requirements of the new movement for Total Art, based on the Gothic tradition, since it made possible the abolition of barriers between architecture, art, and everyday utensils, and evoked the romantic concepts of natural and organic growth. These ideals prompted architects to attempt to merge the individual parts of a building into one indivisible whole. In Gaudí's work, for instance, the furniture is almost fashioned out of the plasma of the building. This is the principle of 'interpenetration', clearly referred to in Ludwig Hevesi's description of Olbrich's Villa Friedmann: 'The doors are the same colour as the panelling and the furniture and are so much part of them that three doors in one small room do not disturb one. The cupboards and the doors in each room were made by the same carpenter. Cupboards, doors, sofas, benches, and beds are preferably joined together to form one combined piece of furniture, an indivisible "piece of room". In one of the guest rooms, for instance, for two people, both beds have a common head board out of which a double bed table is made between them. Of course with a house equipped like this, you cannot move the furniture out, because it is an organic part of the house' (1899).

The irrational ground-plan is the opposite extreme to the rational right angle. Where the right angle dominates, individual building elements are allowed to retain their individuality and are discreetly joined together. Here we find free and loose arrangement of different parts of the building as opposed to their forced subordination. Loos (in contradistinction to Olbrich) allowed furniture to be movable and to be the prime responsibility of the carpenter, but gave the architect the right to put in some fixed items of furniture, integrating them into the shell of the building and making it multiformed and irregular.

Curvilinearity was one of the distinguishing characteristics of the subjective art-architects who felt compelled to 'protest against every hint of rules or standardization' (Van de Velde, 1907). The right angle was the essence of objective form, and led to standardization. Many of its proponents actually preferred the anonymous industrial product to 'pseudo-antique or pseudo-modern decoration' (Loos, 1903).

This was what the arguments about form at the turn of the century were about. The fierceness of the controversy should not blind us to the similarities which can be seen in all the buildings of the period, including those put up by the supporters of both sides. The common factors, which are amongst the most important characteristics in modern architecture, are the 'open' ground-plan, the broken, articulated elevation, and 'three-dimensional planning' (Loos). The concept of 'interpenetration' covers all of these.

Consideration of the history of form will make this concept clearer. When the architectural theorists of the eighteenth century began analyzing the complex architectural structure of Baroque, they discovered that its basic element was the cube. In 1734–36 Robert Morris suggested, in his lectures, that buildings should be based on a series of cubes of equal size. This idea led in two directions. One direction was the attempt to achieve absolute, crystal-clear, form. The building was separated from the space surrounding it, isolated from other dominant or subordinate shapes, and presented as pure geometry. Taken to extremes, the result is a smooth, homogeneous, box. The other direction is the opening up of the closed cube, breaking it down into its component parts, and counteracting the effect of 'splendid isolation'. In other words, the vertical and horizontal space divisions as well as the interior and exterior walls are more independent, and the boundaries between interior and exterior space are abolished. This tendency was most clearly seen in its more extreme form in the German pavilion at the Barcelona World Fair (1929) by Mies van der Rohe. Here, not only were the boundaries between interior and exterior space abolished, but the individual space divisions overlapped. The main and subsidiary pavilions were open in several directions, and rhythmically connected by an articulating wall. The ends of this wall were covered by the flat roofs, but the longest part of it was in the open air. And so, without formally demonstrating it, the wall belonged to three different sections of space. In so doing, it lent strength to the architect's intention of creating an unbroken, fluent spatial experience. Instead of the closed box, we have an open transparent set of elements. The dismembered cube allows space to expand. Independent parts of the cube are not joined together but, like the different spaces, can be read in several ways while visibly retaining their individuality and their appearance of movability.

Mies van der Rohe's brilliantly executed interpenetration was modelled on Frank Lloyd Wright's concept of organic space (Robie house, 1909). This building develops the technique of multiaxial, asymmetrical arrangement which Webb had already used in the ground-plan of the Red House (Plate 2).

Another extreme example, Rietveld's Schröder house (1924, Plate 49), demonstrates interpretation of the elevation. The cube is broken down into layers of space and wall, laid on top of and alongside each other without regard for the horizontal alignment of floors. There are no additive exterior walls corresponding to interior spaces, but rhythmic interpretation of layers of space, with storeys interlocking by means of slabs placed almost at random, performing the same connecting function as the crosswall in the Barcelona pavilion.

By the turn of the century, we already find stepped wall design, in contrast to the uniform screen pattern and the smooth walled cube. Webb was a pioneer of this development as well. For this stepped articulation of the elevation corresponds to the multiaxial flowing ground-plan. The Glasgow Art School (Plate 22), the Palais Stoclet (Plate 32), Olbrich's Mathildenhöhe Building in Darmstadt (Plate 36), the Vienna Secession Building (Plate 25), and the theatre for the Werkbund Exhibition in Cologne by Van de Velde are examples of this. And we can add the staircase window in Horta's Maison du Peuple, which suddenly breaks the horizontal line and forms a connecting link between two floors.

Loos' 'three-dimensional plan' is a new step in the process of opening boundaries between spaces, in that it allows it to happen at different levels of the interior. The effect of the interconnection of rooms at different levels, which later became famous in Le Corbusier's Cité Radieuse, was to turn two rooms into a third, larger, room. The three-dimensionally planned Rufer house (1922) has precedents throughout Loos' earlier work, particularly his staircases. One can also see signs of this trend in the villas of Olbrich and in Hoffmann's Palais Stoclet (Plate 32). But these buildings lack a dynamism involving all the spaces in the building, a dynamism which, in Loos' work, applies not merely to the interior spaces, but carries the interconnections of the interior spaces through to the exterior of the building. The large opening is a further step in the process of interpenetration: the connection of the three-dimensionally planned interior with the terrace, thus extending the building into its environment.

Interpenetration is the main characteristic of the multiformal idiom, and at the same time the major advance which *fin de siècle* architecture has given us. Wherever this variegated style of architecture appears during the last hundred years, it belongs, whether directly influenced by it or not, to the same chapter of architectural history as Webb's Red House and Nash's Blaise Hamlet. If we discount various fringe styles, this line of development can be clearly distinguished from the other two 'uniform' formal styles, from both the closed multicellular cube and the single-roomed hall or dome.

The prototypes in urbanism

With the exception of Frank Lloyd Wright, a consistent proponent of 'organic building', the leading architects of the twentieth century have used all three of the prototypes described. They tried once the open, then the closed form, following the law of creative dialectic and the demands of the building tasks they were faced with. Sometimes they chose strict uniformity, sometimes variety and loose syntax; sometimes they adopted systematic repetition, and sometimes deliberately mixed idioms.

If we use the three prototypes to guide us, the breadth and variety of modern architecture, which is often regarded as confusing, need give no difficulty. Once one has developed a feeling for a few basic underlying themes, the descent of the countless mongrel forms and paraphrases of our times becomes clear. If one also takes the ground-plan as a key, the situation becomes even simpler, since the three prototypes make only two basic types of ground-plan. The first group (A) includes all 'regular' ground-plans, such as circles, segments and sectors of circles, ellipses, and polygons which can be divided into two symmetrical parts along at least one axis. On to these ground-plans can be built stereometric forms with either flat or curved planes; cubes and other right-angled bodies, cylinders, pyramids, domes and vaulted halls. The second group (B) includes the remaining irregular and complex ground-plans and spatial forms. Both types of ground-plan can be extended into the environment of the building. The difference between them is that group (A), which is in line with the ideals of Renaissance and Baroque art, includes symmetrical buildings, and these therefore tend to have prominent façades, while group (B) avoids any kind of symmetry.

Cubes, towers, halls and domes represent an attempt to achieve pure, self-contained form, following the classical, and often neo-classical ideal of absolute, simple form. The result is balanced, symmetrical building. The development of this kind of building has emerged in the work of Mies van der Rohe, Wachsmann, Nervi and Buckminster Fuller.

The 'impure' forms of the variegated style are quite different. They are characterized by group (B) ground-plans, all of which are variations on Webb's basic theme. They obey no unbreakable rules, nor do they strive for classical finality, but tend to explore the full range of formal and structural possibilities. In this style, the design is the product of an inductive process, a kind of dialogue between the different elements of the building, often resulting in an effect almost of improvization and spontaneity, as opposed to the predetermined uniformity of the other style. The vocabulary of this type of architecture is correspondingly large, and is often displayed in the contrasting and mixed forms which are typical of interpenetration. The sculptural nature of the new artificial building materials had a stimulating effect on this style.

Its vocabulary includes the straight line as well as the curve, the flat as well as the curved plane, the prismatically 'broken' and organically 'growing' building. Examples of this are Gropius' Bauhaus, Häring's Gut Garkau, Mendelsohn's Einstein Observatory, Mies van der Rohe's Lange house, Wright's 'Falling Water', Le Corbusier's church of Notre-Dame-du-Haut at Ronchamp, Aalto's student hostel in Cambridge (Mass.), Le Corbusier's Swiss student hostel in Paris, Förderer's Commercial High School in St Gallen, Scharoun's Berlin Philharmonic, Kahn's research buildings at the University of Pennsylvania in Philadelphia, Utzon's Sydney Opera House, and two of the most important buildings at Expo '67 in Montreal: the German Pavilion by Frei Otto, and Moshe Safdie's Habitat.

The characteristics of interpenetration are open ground-plans, sculpturally articulated elevations and 'three-dimensional planning'. These force buildings to reach out in all directions. This type of building has no specially designed façade, or distinctions between different storeys. Roofs tend to be modelled sculpturally, thus becoming an integral part of the building; they have none of the self-sufficient independence of towers, cubes, halls and domes, and are therefore always capable of development and adaptation. They are essentially open in all directions to their environment.

Wright described this kind of architecture, rather beautifully, as 'a kind of weaving'. Buildings of this type, with their multiple shapes and forms, merge easily not only with the landscape but with the vast groups and rows of buildings of the modern townscape. These urban architectural complexes are no longer concerned with individual units. They attempt to combine all functions, and have become huge conglomerations of connections between zones for living, traffic, recreation, business and pleasure. The 'environmental' architecture of Sant'Elia, which was inspired by the *fin de siècle* styles (Otto Wagner) but remained a Utopian dream, was the prototype of the enormous networks of tunnels and cells being planned by Kenzo Tange, Yona Friedman and others today. They are moving towards an ideal of a 'super-architecture', which includes everything in its sphere of creative influence. Their ambition is to express the tremendous variety of real life, to intensify it with their pulsating, all-embracing forms. 'Organic architecture', a phrase which is often used to describe this trend in modern architecture, derives from Frank Lloyd Wright, its most daring exponent. This phrase should be used with caution, like any generalization. It refers essentially to the inductive nature of the creative process. It refers only secondarily to concepts associated with romanticism and natural philosophy. The 'shape games' which Wright learnt to play in his Froebel Kindergarten show the extent to which multiplication and 'weaving' are the essence of this variegated, interpenetrating style. The road to 'super-architecture' is already signposted.

The strips of coloured paper, glazed and 'matt', remarkably soft brilliant colours. Now comes the geometric by-play of those charming checkered colour combinations! The structural figures to be made with peas and small straight sticks: slender constructions, the joining, accented by the little green-pea globes. The smooth shapely maple blocks with which to build, the sense of which afterwards never leaves the fingers: *form* becoming *feeling*. The box had a mast to set up on it, on which to hang the maple cubes and spheres and triangles, revolving them to discover subordinate forms. (Wright, *An Autobiography*)

So 'organic' architecture does not reject basic geometric principles, but draws upon them as a source of individual forms, or, as it were, 'letters' rather than as 'words'.

The central problem of our time is not concerned with the individual object or with artistically ambitious 'background' architecture (L. Kahn), but large scale town- and landscape-planning. And it is the variegated style of building which is most relevant here, for mixed forms and interpenetration contain the seeds of urban super-architecture. However, we should not overlook the fact that both the other two proto-types – tower and hall – do attempt to say something, as well, about the solution of town-planning problems of the future.

There are two types of solution to these problems, corresponding to the two groups of ground-plan (A and B). Wright expresses the central idea of the inductive-organic style of architecture when he refers to 'weaving'. He discovered that since everything remained to scale, the proportions of the project as a whole, whether large or small, were unchanged, and that in this way – as in a woven carpet – a firm fabric was created consisting of a number of mutually dependent, linked units. One could consider this 'design' to be a continuous, demonstrative protrusion of the various functions of house or town. Their many-sided interrelationship was to be understood as a never-ending process of change. This interrelationship between house and town, a single object and a complex of buildings, brought to mind something that Palladio had said four centuries ago: '. . . a town ought at the same time to be a large house and, vice versa, a house just a small town'.

Of course, the meaning of this depends on which type of ground-plan one assumes the 'house' to have. If we assume that it is the irregular ground-plan of the Red House, or even the 'open'-type house built by Wright, then one can reasonably claim Palladio as a proponent of 'organic architecture'.

But purists might also claim that the Italian architect's statement supported them. Their solution to the problem of the metropolis is deductive, and often smacks of megalomania and utopianism. The different functional areas of the town, far from being connected together, are forced into strict and uncompromising forms consisting of enormous towers, cubes and pyramids. The private and public areas of town are hidden behind a corset of rigorously geometrical superblocks. A town like this does indeed strike one as a 'big house', a geometrically predetermined super-architecture. This style puts all that complex architecture opened up for us back into huge, domi-nating forms (cubes, cylinders, pyramids). So in the field of experimental urban archi-tecture today, the compact superblock or superdome stands at the opposite extreme to the 'super-environmental complex'. The multi-level, multi-channelled environ-mental building stands pitted against the unalterable supershape, the inside of which houses different functions within different cells. The Dutchman Constant, in his New Babylon project, is thinking of a supershape like this, which settles itself, dominant and protective, over a labyrinth of functions. 'Technically, all that is involved is a simple framework' (this reminds one of Semper's 'frame for furniture'). 'A framework which is raised on columns above the earth means that traffic can flow freely at ground level . . . On the raised platform, a huge building provides for living accommodation and social activity . . . The highest terrace, which is the roof, can provide sports grounds and even aerodromes. In the interior of this multi-level building there is a large public area, which can be used for social activities (as well as private residential quarters). This area is broken up by movable walls and structures which can be connected by a series of stairs, steps and passageways . . .' Other projects also involve the self-sufficient multi-functional superblocks: Nishiyama's 'housetown', Jean-Claude Mazet's 'house for 100,000 inhabitants' and Nyblom's 'Round Town'.

These plans for the future sound Utopian, but are merely logical consequences of the development which began about a hundred years ago. The cellular tower already concealed many different functions behind the uniform pattern of its outside walls; the divisions between its internal spaces could be removed and it formed a functionally neutral frame for some future furniture. Equally striking is the connection between the geodesic dome which Buckminster Fuller proposed to put over the centre of Manhatten and Paxton's Crystal Palace. Both these enormous structures pay for the cleanness of their forms by being functionally neutral and uninvolved with their 'contents'. The superdome stands arched over the city's confused conglomeration of houses and streets without organizing it, and in so doing demonstrates the conflict between the platonic idea of pure form and real life. Just as splendid and uninvolved with what went on below, the Crystal Palace stood over a picturesque, chaotic jumble of foreign exhibits. So even the most daring contemporary ideas about form are part of the historical tradition whose origins and main lines of development have been described here, and they correspond intellectually and formally with the formulae worked out by the pioneers of the new building more than one hundred years ago.

Whatever its approach to town-planning – superdomes or superparks – modern architecture aspires to tremendous power, and there is a risk that a new total architecture will condemn mankind to the pseudo-freedom of the labyrinth and of the golden cage. Of course, the proponents of 'environmental architecture' are in favour of 'openness', but where does this process of 'opening up' go once it has control of the whole of the natural landscape? Of course, the geodesic dome allows the city the right to remain 'chaotic' but it conjures up a test-tube world and seems to encapsulate the American way of life in a New Jerusalem.

The disappearance of artistic boundaries

'We have arts without having any one real art' (Semper). This view is reflected in art historians' interpretations of the 'moderns' and warns us against ascribing a common style linking all art forms of the period. We do frequently find references to expressionist or cubist architecture but the question of the extent to which the development of modern architecture was actually connected with that of painting and sculpture is seldom or never asked. It is in fact possible to find connections, but only between structural principles, rather than style. The connections lie in the formal grammar and in the details.

Originally the new building materials and structural techniques which were discovered performed non-artistic roles and satisfied needs which 'architecture' arrogantly disregarded. For this reason they have been treated as independent developments. But they did not evolve in some closed-off, special area reserved for function. Like every revolutionary expansion, it was a process of undermining the old by the new. Looking at it from this point of view we can see that architecture in the last 150 years has been affected by the same changes of form as the other arts. Painters like Goya, Friedrich or Delacroix, as well as the constructors of bridges, stations, and exhibition halls, achieved what Semper called the key task of the art industry of the future: the destruction of the old traditional forms. This negative achievement was historically counterbalanced by the discovery of new and vital forms. These new developments did not postulate their independence from history, but they cannot really be measured by the dignified standards of traditional architecture any more than the above painters' pictures can be judged in terms of the dogmas of academic aesthetics. The connection between architecture and painting appears at first sight to be slender, but it is easy to see if approached in the right way.

Revivalist architecture relied upon the stock of forms built up by previous ages. Its typical architectural characteristics were superficiality and painstaking archaeo-logical diligence. In its efforts to use 'respectable' idioms, it completely hid, behind decorative cladding, what was going on inside the building. Thus a stylized mask concealed reality. The eclectic idealists did the same in painting and sculpture. Just as 'architects' (in the sense understood by Ruskin and Loos) only took on respectable building tasks, so they only dealt with respectable subjects. The present had nothing to offer them, and they fled into an ideal world of the past which they found in mythology and allegory. They depicted people in carefully chosen postures. The 'dignity' of content was matched by the painstaking precision of treatment. Just like the revivalist architects, these painters and sculptors hid the underlying structure and the creative process, striving for the smooth, polished surface, and perfection of every detail. The actors in their pictures were guests at 'the masked ball of style' (Nietzsche) arranged by architects dedicated to borrowed beauty.

This suggests that the occupants of the opposing camp have an entirely objective and realistic approach to the problems of form and content. This, however, is an oversimplification. In the engineer buildings of Paxton and Wachsmann, and in the works of Wright, Mies van der Rohe or Kenzo Tange, we find not only clearly stated objectives, but also unambiguous display of both the materials used and the creative process. Painters and sculptors rejected both the predictable smoothness of old masters and the lifeless schematism of 'ideal' beauty. Their reappraisal was inspired by sceptical realism, a desire to understand the essence of things, and a concern with the real values of form. Their important discoveries led to the development of self-consciousness and the often strange forms of modern art. This process has become more and more radical in the last hundred years. It is to be found in all two and three dimensional arts – painting, sculpture and architecture – and seems to have passed through the following phases:

Schiller remarked with some concern on the 'strict feeling for truth' of people who were not satisfied by 'pleasant shapes'. This feeling for truth led the engineer architects of the nineteenth century to use materials in a way which truly corresponded to their natural characteristics and not as a medium for ostentatious 'artistic' façades. Their realism was expressed in the vernacular and attempted to express life rather than poses. Their functional buildings have none of the pretension of revivalist architecture, nor do they stand on aesthetic islands, but are part of the life of modern industrial society.

One does not stand in awe of them, one simply uses them. Frank Lloyd Wright touched on another aspect of this 'strict feeling for truth' when he demanded in his polemic against the 'artificial' architecture of the revivalists that architecture should interpret man as he really is. And the engineer architects of the nineteenth century offered their contemporaries the possibility of expressing themselves and living in a modern, democratic environment, rather than behind a mask of the past. They cut them off from flight into the bogus world of superficial beauty to which revivalist architecture was always beckoning.

The great painters of contemporary life looked for their subjects in the city and took work and pleasure as themes for painting. Compared with the dignified subjects taken from myth and allegory, the subjects chosen by Courbet or Manet were as banal as the functional buildings erected for everyday use by the engineers. Just as their buildings drew their dynamic and their vitality from the honesty of their structure, so the impressionist painters attempted to reflect the ever changing life around them with their open and spontaneous brush-strokes. Both were concerned with opening up the hitherto enclosed form and freeing the structural kernel from its aesthetic shell. This movement away from the clichés of external perfection set form free as energy and as a visible process. It is obvious that the attention to the proper, and honest use of materials led to different results in architecture, painting and sculpture. Nevertheless, there are clear similarities. If we consider the last decade of the nineteenth century we find, in architecture, the development of structures made of standardized industrial parts. At the same time, the architects commonly grouped together under the title Art Nouveau were drawing on an immensely wide formal vocabulary and were producing their often surprising mixtures of closed, open, flat, linear and solid forms. Sometimes they improvised details, and sometimes produced apparently deliberate irregularities and astonishing combinations. Meanwhile, contemporary painting ranged from strict, standardized objectivity to subjective freedom and variety of expression. It extended, for example, from the impersonal and anonymous discipline of Seurat's pointillism to Gauguin's cult of the ornamental surface and line, and to Van Gogh's coarse brush-strokes.

Up to the 1880s one has to look for structural relationships between architecture, sculpture and painting at various 'levels'. The three art forms developed quite independently of each other till then, since the builders of halls and cellular towers aimed at undecorated structural purity, which meant that painting and sculpture could not be introduced into their buildings. Meanwhile the two 'fine arts' continued to stick to the Renaissance themes of Man and the visible world. This situation changed radically towards the end of the century. We find formal interrelationships and connections developing. Suddenly, painters, sculptors and architects discovered that they could all draw from one large common stock of form. Until then they had only been able to manoeuvre on the territory allotted to each by academic art teaching. Now a new freedom of formal expression began, and introduced the chapter of history on which the twentieth century is based.

It is easy to trace the symptoms of this development. Architecture was beginning to produce its own sculptural and painterly elements instead of borrowing them from the 'fine arts'; in so doing it took up again the teachings of the gospel preached by Webb's Red House in the middle of the century. The 'fine arts' were moving away from representation of the human figure and the external world and developing more and more in directions indicated by the formal nature of the materials which they used, towards a vocabulary which made possible in architecture a dialogue in ornamental, decorative or technical terms. For the first time since the end of the Baroque period, the arts abandoned their separate existences and looked again for a common territory, where the boundaries between art forms were no longer valid. The new ideal, similar to that of many centuries before, was the mixture of all forms of creativity to produce the often-invoked 'total art'.

This process, the breaking down of barriers, and overlapping of different art forms, is one of the most important characteristics of twentieth century art and architecture. But in order to understand the extent to which this movement started at the turn of the century, one should not look at the period only from the point of view of 'total art'.

Some of the idioms which the twentieth century owes to this period have already been mentioned above: open, irregular ground-plans (Wright, Willitts house, 1902); asymmetry developed into 'disturbed' form (Mackintosh, Glasgow School of Art, 1897–99; Horta, Maison du Peuple, 1896–99); 'amoebic' building (Gaudí, Casa Batlló, 1905–07); loose arrangements of right-angled spaces (Hoffmann, Palais Stoclet, begun 1905). These and other achievements are not only in the forefront of creative architecture in our century, but anticipate many of the structural features which extend through all branches of art. The extreme formal developments and discoveries of the last years before the first world war – the Cubist montages of Braque and Picasso, the sculptures and other constructions made by Picasso, Archipenko, and Boccioni out of different materials, and the last factory by Walter Gropius and Adolf Meyer (Plate 43) – are all foreshadowed in *fin de siècle* architecture, a fact to which far too little attention has been paid.

When, around 1911, the cubists started to use pieces of newspapers, wallpaper, and other three dimensional objects in their pictures, they turned homogeneous surfaces into heterogeneous ones. This resulted in a pattern of contrasts. Abstract graphic elements (lines and colours) co-existed with fragments of 'actual reality', and the picture surrendered its privacy and opened up and communicated with the non-artistic, profane, real world. The poet Apollinaire wrote in 1913: 'one can paint with anything one wants to; with pipes, stamps, postcards, playing cards, rags, newsprint, wallpaper . . .', and a year before this, Boccioni had called for an 'environmental sculpture' (which would contain 'the architectural elements of the sculptural environment'), and claimed that 'one could use as many as twenty different materials in one work in order to attain real creative emotion'. He included glass, wood, cardboard, iron, cement, horse-hair, leather, cloth, mirror-glass, electric light, etc. His own sculptures (some of which have not survived), the 'sculpto-peintures' of Archipenko, and Picasso's constructions are examples of these theories in practice.

This 'multi-materialism' mixes different levels of reality together. One looks at the abstract geometrical pattern of lines in a cubist still life, and suddenly one notices that a foreign body such as a newspaper cutting has been introduced. The same effect is given by the transparent structure of the Fagus Factory (Plate 43). The multi-storied glass surfaces combine to make a unit criss-crossed with a regular pattern of upright and horizontal lines. The straightforward arrangement of surfaces makes it possible to see directly into the inside of the building, where the work is done. Profane reality is suddenly revealed like a 'foreign body' in the middle of the system of co-ordinates formed by the windows. Chaotic and continuously changing 'reality', represented by everyday production work, merges into the strict, repetitive pattern of the exterior, and anyone looking at the building sees both at the same time.

There is another cubist characteristic which can be seen in the Fagus Factory, the 'interconnecting formal complex' stretching over different parts of the building. Thus, the multi-storied glass walls 'interconnect' the open rooms and the horizontal lines of the floors which split them up. But these floors are not separate in the way that mass is from space (as, for instance, are the upright columns) but participate in the floating vertical surfaces of the glass. In this way the horizontal planes become weightless and unobtrusive, and the glass surface seems to be homogeneous. Just as, in architecture, we find this interconnecting formal complex stretching over the boundaries between functions, in contemporary cubist painting this same type of formal complex can extend across different objects. Juan Gris' *Still-Life with Guitar* (1915, Rijksmuseum Kroeller-Mueller, Otterloo) demonstrates this clearly. The upright sheet of music in the centre is part of an irregular pentagon, the upper part of which fits the slope of the guitar. This pentagon participates in both the sheet of music and the instrument, and constitutes an interconnecting surface complex, a form which – in the same way as the glass wall – is greater than the sum of its parts. Similarly – to give only one of many possible examples – the upright slab of the balcony of the Schröder house (Plate 49) interconnects the two storeys of the house while emphasizing their autonomy by refusing to take account of the horizontal floor-divisions.

These structural textures have become part of the formal vernacular of two- as well as three-dimensional art. The fact that they first appeared in the work of *fin de siècle* architects should strengthen the thesis which suggests that there is a vocabulary common to building, sculpture and painting. The front elevation of Mackintosh's Art School (Plate 22) is an early example of the close juxtaposition of contrasts. The entrance gives the effect of a bizarre 'foreign body' in the middle of the continuity of the façade, which is given regularity by the big windows. The entrance is composed of various unexpected elements which have been deliberately introduced, amongst which one can see the beginnings of 'interconnecting form'. The lower part of the short tower is not clearly differentiated from the wall mass, producing an 'ambivalent' area which belongs as much to the wall as to the tower. In the Palais Stoclet (Plate 32) the staircase windows which extend across different floor levels are clearly the interconnecting formal complex. And the same applies to the two window-strips in Olbrich's Hochzeitsturm (Plate 36).

We have already mentioned an instance where a detail is inserted in such a way that it disturbs a large formal programme. The balcony of the uppermost staircase window in Horta's Maison du Peuple seems almost to have slipped down. This surprising accent disturbs the horizontal flow of form. The confrontation between regular and irregular form can be regarded as a dialogue between order and anarchy, between determinism and free-will, which heightens the effect of both. In Otto Wagner's Majolica House (Plate 24) the pattern of windows contrasts with the plant-like decoration on the walls. Organic and geometric forms are interblended, and are both seen at the same time.

Wright said 'exterior space will become a natural part of the space inside the building'. In his architecture, exterior space plays the same role as the bits of reality put into their pictures by the cubists, making an artificial complex of lines and coloured areas suddenly 'natural' (that is, more real). We can also regard Adolf Loos' contribution to the intensifying of the experience of interior space – his 'three-dimensional planning' – as interconnecting form; if two rooms at different levels are connected they make a spatial complex whose total value is greater than the sum of its parts.

Wright's interpenetration of interior and exterior space gives rise to interconnecting formal complexes which extend over different levels of reality. This expansion is reminiscent of Boccioni's 'environmental sculpture' and Sant'Elia's vast architectural schemes, which could well be regarded as 'environmental' architecture. Like the cubists and futurists, Sant'Elia was striving to achieve a complex total reality, in which different levels of material and content overlap each other; a 'super-architecture' extending from traffic engineering to monuments. Perret's house in the Rue Franklin (Plate 29) used the technique of 'multi-materiality' before the cubists discovered it. The weight-bearing fabric of the building is visible in its façade, which is, like a cubist montage, heterogeneous. The two outside rows of windows exude elegance; the windows are surrounded by a decorative leaf-motif, which is itself surrounded by flat stone bands. But in the middle of the building the 'elegant' cladding falls away and reveals the naked structure of the weight-bearing fabric. The façade is, as it were, stripped bare and different areas of reality interconnect with each other.

Hevesi's analysis of Guimard's Castel Béranger shows how highly attuned were contemporary sensibilities towards mixing material: 'this house has three different façades, and in between them one can see into two courtyards enclosed by iron railings. The artist has obviously been trying to achieve variety, and doesn't allow the straight lines to become too long; he only emphasizes them every now and again, so that unity is maintained. The whole thing is a series of contrasts, both of form and of colour. The building is essentially honest. The artist does not falsify or mask anything. He even dares to let an overhanging floor rest on the ends of a row of iron joists, which he simply puts into an attractive form and covers with a patina. The arrangement of the building masses gives him an opportunity to use different types of windows and window-bays, as well as gables, terraces and staircases. The inhabitability of the interior is clearly expressed in the exterior and the building materials help give a heightened impression of variety. Lower down on the building there are cyclopean surfaces left quite raw, and higher up there is carefully worked stone mixed with red tiles, making structural necessity into additional decoration' (1899).

These short indications should be sufficient to show that modern architecture not only shares the creative problems of painters and sculptors but also, on occasion, can claim to have dealt with them first. But it should be understood that the relationship between architecture and the fine arts was fundamental, and was not something which only existed in the case of joint projects executed by architects, sculptors and painters together – as for instance in the Art Nouveau movement, the Dutch De Stijl group, Russian Constructivism, and the Bauhaus.

The reasons for this creative exchange are clear. The painter who ceases to be concerned simply with imitating reality is enabled to concentrate on creating self-sufficient form. This in turn tempts him to turn from the two-dimensional picture to the three-dimensional shape; and his painting moves towards sculpture. The sculptor who ceases to be bound only to reproduce the human form (which for centuries had been virtually his only subject) suddenly finds himself in an area bordering on architecture. Apollinaire recognized this when he wrote in 1913, 'as soon as the elements making up a piece of sculpture cease to be justified by being an imitation of nature, this art becomes architecture'; (for this reason the Eiffel Tower is not only a turning point in architectural history, but is also part of the first chapter of the history of modern sculpture). And the architect for whom steel and concrete open up new creative possibilities finds himself suddenly able to compete with the sculptor. The widening horizons of creative artists, the virtually unlimited capacity of modern technology and the cross-fertilization between architects, sculptors and painters, have succeeded in breaking down the barriers which existed from the Renaissance until late into the nineteenth century between different art forms, and has allowed them all to overlap freely.

The exposure of the creative process

The outdated distinction between 'architecture' and 'mere building' is still used by contemporary critics. Frank Lloyd Wright campaigned against the 'meaningless reflecting surfaces' of the 'popular steel-frame box-like building'.

A younger architect, Walter Förderer, recently maintained that artistic architecture and functional architecture were not compatible with each other, implying that both had failed: 'the building which is conceived as a work of art, and which is merely seen as a personal achievement, is seldom relevant to the original objective. The architect's preconceived artistic ideas clash with the real function of the building and may produce an object with an independent sculptural value of its own. Standardized building, on the other hand, can at best have an acceptable, planned aesthetic quality, which can be equally irrelevant to its function. Personal and technical solutions at opposite extremes are both equally irrelevant to the specific objective of the building, and both fail in their objective.'

One hesitates to agree unreservedly with this fierce self-criticism since it expects too much from the architect. Functional buildings, as can be seen, for example, from the architectural history of hospitals, have always tended to conform to the contemporary formal idiom. An architect is in a difficult position, and it is asking too much of him to expect him to produce an original work as a solution to every building task he is given. And, of course, he is not always given clearly defined problems. It is usually the architect who has to define what his client really wants. This leaves considerable room for persuasion. The objective is not fixed, but is what the architect makes it.

Form dictated purely by function remains a dream of the nineteenth-century progressives. Their battle-cry against the superficial architecture of the historicists was 'form follows function'. This phrase of Sullivan's has produced much misunderstanding, since it has been taken in only one sense. It was made into a categorical imperative and distracted attention from the complex variety of the modern architectural idiom. Sullivan himself had more comprehensive views on the nature of modern architecture than would be suggested by this short aphorism. He gave architects the following advice: 'then, too, as your basic thought changes will emerge a philosophy, a poetry, and an art of expression in all things: for you will have learned that a characteristic philosophy, poetry and art of expression are vital to the healthful growth and development of a democratic people!'

Form does, of course, follow function. Alberti knew that and Semper believed that art (and not only the art of building) served only one master – necessity. But fulfilling needs and performing functions is not all that form can achieve. In demonstrating function, it makes its own character clear; it, as it were, reveals itself. In 1851, Semper said of the prefabricated American house, that it was not really a house, but a 'frame for furniture'. This statement was important and paradoxical in that it was precisely out of this sober and reserved approach to form that a new formal self-confidence sprang (assuming of course that this 'frame' is taken as having any formal value at all, and is not rejected as a necessary evil, or as a complete negation of form). Semper's phrase illustrates the range of forms possible in functional structures. It applies equally to office skyscrapers and to single volume buildings. These structures have to allow for virtually any kind of interior. The adaptability of the cellular building is less than that of the hall, but it is more obvious. In the Chicago office tower-blocks the layout of rooms on each floor was left partly to the preference of individual tenants, and Olbrich's Secession could be used as either a single- or a multi-space building. Nowadays, the only fixed divisions in the space inside a cellular tower-block are a few structurally unavoidable elements. The most important thing, however, is that today, as eighty years ago, the movable interior walls are not visible from the outside. This means that function follows form, which is the exact opposite of Sullivan's thesis. The inevitable structural logic of these buildings distinguishes and separates them from the permanent or temporary 'contents' inside them, and it is this separation of form and function which gives the buildings their air of aloof self-confident detachment from their functions. Structural functionalism is not simply the inevitable result of the laws of statics and mechanics, but a synthesis of mathematics and intuition. The Eiffel Tower would have turned out very differently had it been built in the coarse, unostentatious form conceived by Koechlin, its Swiss structural engineer. The scope for developing form between the structural calculation stage and three dimensional reality is very difficult to express in words. Sullivan described it as 'poetry' and 'the art of expression'. Two of Wright's favourite expressions were 'life' and 'creation'.

These qualities become particularly relevant in situations in which there is a temptation to use what Wright called 'negative clichés', such as the curtain wall. The load-bearing skeleton frame of a building can be treated in two ways; either it can be made visible, showing through the exterior wall, as a regular system of co-ordinates, or it can be concealed inside the building. In the latter case, the question arises as to what form the exterior wall should take. Since no technical necessity determines form, the exterior wall is left to the architect's taste. And so it becomes an 'interconnecting form', and has a value of its own, quite independent of the functional structure. In this way, glass curtain walls are put round structures, like transparent screens. This makes the exterior wall homogeneous, but, of course, routine and uniformity becomes a temptation. However, the risk of a cliché is counterbalanced, or at least diminished, by the fact that the glass wall reflects the environment like a mirror and makes it a 'part of the reality' (Bense) of the building, adding to the strict surface pattern the charm of the changing play of forms in the reflections.

The poetry of an apartment tower-block by Mies van der Rohe (Plate 67), a sports stadium by Nervi (Plate 59) or a bridge by Maillart (Plate 60), is not the 'aesthetic bonus' which they provide; it is not, as it were, something over and above the structure, but is to be found in the scope for formal creativity left open by mathematics and necessity to pure intuition. It lies in the ability of a building to reveal its function in terms of form, in the relationship between building elements, and the total functional effect of the whole. Thus building does not appear as a closed structure, or as an incomprehensible 'result' but as a spatial, physical and functional 'event' which becomes a formal event by the revelation of the creative process.

Formal self-confidence is, therefore, not only limited to the 'art' of building, with artistic pretensions over and above the performance of function. It extends (in spite of everything said since Ruskin about the difference between 'architecture' and 'mere building') over the whole range of the medium including standardized building, 'non-architecture' (Förderer), 'artistic' architecture, and 'habitable sculpture'.

This does not, however, mean that we can necessarily group all these together. There is obviously a range of values, although this does not mean that 'respectable' buildings (churches, theatres, etc.) are necessarily superior to 'profane' buildings. Accustomed to see their own ideas about form given priority over functional considerations, architects tend to indulge in arrogantly ostentatious form without dealing adequately with functional problems. Mies van der Rohe's New National Gallery in Berlin, for example, was originally designed as an administrative building for Cuba. Sloppy adaptations of this kind are in the same tradition as the uninspiringly monotonous façades of the classicists criticized by Victor Hugo.

The temptation to level everything is understandable. It is connected with the development of functionally neutral structures, which, as we have seen, are the price we pay for the formal self-confidence without which there would be no architecture. But once a formal system has been perfected, there is a risk that it will degenerate into self-justifying torpidity.

If modern architecture is to be preserved from the aesthetic sclerosis, mannerist luxuriousness, and sluggish self-satisfaction of neo-classicism, it must remain experimental and open to change, continuously reappraising its own vocabulary. The danger lies in the closed system and the narrow platform of respectability, once adopted never changed. It is not extremism or utopianism which lead to conformity, but cautious compromise. Förderer, who recommends that architects should try to achieve an artistic mean between the extremes of 'non-architecture' and 'artistic' architecture (while adapting according to the dignity of the building) hopes to reduce the variety of form, and to diminish the range of expression. But this risks being the road to uniformity, narrow-mindedness, and compromise. It would be more fruitful to revitalize the outposts, to merge the different functions of urban architecture, and to push on with the study of all kinds of formal and urban problems, from functionally neutral structures to artistic 'background architecture' (L. Kahn).

Probably nobody has described better the formal language of modern architecture, with its breadth and richness of spatial and plastic concepts, its dynamism and its vitality, than Friedrich Schinkel. The ideas of this architect, whose eclecticism belongs to the past, but whose structural engineering (e.g. the skeleton structure of the Berlin Building Academy, 1832–35) puts him on the threshold of our own period, foreshadowed what was later to become three-dimensional reality: 'aspiring, sprouting, crystallizing, opening up, thrusting, dividing, joining, driving, hovering, pulling, pressing, bending, bearing, setting, swinging, combining, holding, lying, and resting (the last, being deliberately included in contrast to the others, all of which are connected with movement, should also be regarded as an activity) – these are the life-evoking necessities of architecture.'

Werner Hofmann

Introduction to the plates

The following section attempts to show the development of architecture throughout the world since 1850 by means of 112 colour plates of different buildings. These are of course limited to works which can be taken as representative of significant aspects of the history of architecture. A lot of other important buildings from the same period could equally well have been used but have been omitted because they could not be photographed in colour. For this reason a number of important architects are not represented. This does not reflect on their artistic standing in any way. The nature of this book, which is a record of architecture since 1850 in colour, makes it impossible to include many important buildings which are no longer in existence as a result of war, demolition or having been destroyed in some other way. The history of building in our times has had to be illustrated using only extant buildings in their present form.

The main criterion in choosing plates was the quality of the building. They are arranged in chronological order, taking the year when the building began as the date of the building. They are organized into six sections corresponding with six main periods. It is assumed that the reader is interested in seeing the buildings in their present state, as they actually appear, in colour.

The developments illustrated in this book raise some interesting points. Are we, for instance, not still living in an environment which really began to take shape around 1850? Surely those early railway stations, exhibition halls, libraries, warehouses, market halls, office buildings, railway bridges, tunnels, undergrounds, and blocks of flats were solutions to some of the central problems posed by the industrial society? Another point is the interesting geographical distribution of the buildings illustrated. Great Britain is strongly represented as a result of its lead in the industrial revolution (Barlow, Plate 4; Brodrick, Plate 3; Ellis, Plate 6). Joseph Paxton's Crystal Palace, no longer standing, is widely recognized as being the most important building of the whole epoch, and it guarantees England a leading position in the development of this type of building. At the other extreme, English historicism (Shaw, Plate 7; Webb, Plate 2) also led to revolutionary developments with international ramifications leading eventually to Frank Lloyd Wright's architecture (Plate 38).

France also made important contributions to progress. Henri Labrouste (Plate 1) was an outstanding artistic personality. Italy (Giuseppe Mengoni, Plate 5), Austria (Otto Wagner, Plates 24, 30 and 31) and America are also importantly represented. Russell Sturgis (Plate 8) and Henry Hobson Richardson (Plates 9 and 11) are the great personalities of American historicism, comparable with Shaw and Webb in England. Richardson's buildings sparked off completely new developments in both the U.S.A. and Europe (Townsend, Plate 21; Eliel Saarinen, Plate 39).

The Chicago School broadened the scope of architecture as well as its structural capacity. It was here that Sullivan, stimulated by Richardson's ideas, put up his Auditorium Building (Plate 12). In Chicago, too, Jenney built his skeleton-frame buildings and Burnham and Root put up a large number of offices. These were all signs of a new spirit in architecture.

In America, Sullivan (Plate 26) and Frank Lloyd Wright (Plate 35) developed a kind of organic architecture, comparable with that of the European Art Nouveau movement, and produced, particularly in the work of Frank Lloyd Wright (which spans almost seventy years) some of the greatest buildings in modern architecture. In Europe, from 1890 onwards, Art Nouveau flourished. Its leading practitioners were Horta (Plates 17 and 18) and Van de Velde (Plate 19) in Belgium, Berlage in Holland, Wagner (Plate 24), Hoffmann (Plate 32), Olbrich (Plate 36) and Loos in Austria, Sommaruga (Plate 28) in Italy, and Mackintosh (Plates 22 and 23) and Townsend (Plate 21) in Great Britain.

The genius of this epoch in Europe was Antoni Gaudí (Plates 10, 27, 33 and 34) who erected his incomparable buildings in Spain.

One of the most remarkable features of architecture at this time was its new-found sense of colour (Gaudí, Plate 27; Sullivan, Plate 26; Wagner, Plate 24). Wright (Plate 38), Hoffmann (Plate 32) and Loos (Plate 41) had already left Art Nouveau architecture behind by 1910, and were showing the way towards the 'new practicality'. The outstanding products of this deliberately technically-orientated development were the factories, warehouses and offices which Behrens (Plate 40), Poelzig (Plate 42), Gropius (Plate 43) put up in Germany after 1910. At the opposite extreme was architectural Expressionism, mostly concentrated in Germany and Holland (Plate 46).

In the 1920s, a number of remarkable contributions to the solution of the problems of mass housing and individual residential building came from Dutch developments of Berlage's basic work (Oud, Plate 51; Rietveld, Plate 49). Parallel developments were the houses of Mies van der Rohe in Germany (Plate 54) and Le Corbusier's buildings in France. In Russia there took place a complete re-appraisal of the whole concept of architecture (Plate 55).

In about 1930, the most interesting developments occurred in countries further away from the centre of Europe. New solutions came from England (Lubetkin, Plate 63; Owen Williams, Plate 57), Finland (Aalto, Plate 56), Brazil, Spain (Torroja, Plate 61) and Switzerland (Maillart, Plate 60). Duiker (Plate 58) gave Holland a new importance. And buildings by Matté-Trucco (Plate 45), Giuseppe Terragni (Plate 62) and Pier Luigi Nervi (Plate 59), in the wake of the widely influential theories of Futurism, gave Italy international significance for the first time since the Art Nouveau period. Frank Lloyd Wright, the outstanding genius of the period, continued to make new contributions in the U.S.A. An increasing number of immigrants from all parts of the world began to appear in the U.S.A. as well (Schindler, Plate 52; Neutra, Plate 53; Mies van der Rohe, Plates 66 and 67; Gropius; and Saarinen, Plate 70).

Since 1950, the development of modern architecture has been world wide and important new buildings are now to be found in all parts of the world. But America continues to make a major contribution, producing Mies van der Rohe (the later work) (Plate 75); Gropius; Skidmore, Owings and Merrill (Plate 73); Johnson (Plate 105); Goldberg (Plate 98); Sert (Plate 88); Saarinen (Plate 80) and many others; all, however, overshadowed by the later work of Frank Lloyd Wright (Plate 76). Europe produced the later works of Le Corbusier (Plate 68), Scharoun (Plate 84) and Aalto (Plate 91), as well as the achievements of younger architects such as Enrico Castiglioni (Plate 95); Giancarlo de Carlo (Plate 94); James Stirling and James Gowan (Plate 90); Reima Pietilä (Plate 102); Frei Otto (Plate 108) and Hans Hollein (Plate 99).

Candela in Mexico (Plate 110) and Villaneuva in Venezuela (Plate 78) are the most significant talents in Latin America. In Brazil, Costa, Niemeyer and Reidy have produced daring new buildings. In the works of Studer (Plate 77), Zevaco, Azagury

(Plate 111) and others can be seen the beginnings of an African architecture. Israel has produced some outstanding buildings by Hecker and Neumann (Plates 85 and 86) as well as by foreign architects (Johnson's atomic reactor, Plate 87; Kiesler's Israeli Museum, Plate 103). Other important developments are to be found in Asia, in India, in Pakistan and above all in Japan, which has now become the centre of the most progressive modern architecture, as seen in buildings by architects like Tange (Plates 92, 93 and 112), Kikutake (Plate 96), Ohtani (Plate 97), Kurokawa and Isozaki.

The architecture of the period described in this book, which began in about 1850 in the industrially advanced countries, is so rich, exciting, and alive that it has spread across national boundaries to become a real world culture. And in the post-industrial age, we are rediscovering the significance and value of individual nations and regions as well as people.

In spite of the high quality achieved by many important buildings since 1850, it should be remembered that vital contemporary problems remain unsolved or only partially solved (mass housing, building for leisure, traffic, town planning). There are still problems large enough to keep generations to come fully occupied solving them. Many young architects' projects, as yet unexecuted, attempt to grapple with them, but they do not fall within the scope of this volume, which documents the environment in which we live, and the development of architecture since 1850.

Udo Kultermann

The Plates

Plate 1
Bibliothèque Sainte-Geneviève, Paris (1843–50)
by Henri Labrouste

Architectural development around 1850 was characterized by new building problems produced by the new urban industrial society (market places, exhibition halls, libraries, office buildings, factories, stations, warehouses) and by the use of new industrial building materials (iron, glass) appropriate to these building problems. Outstanding examples of this were to be seen in Great Britain (Paxton, Brunel, Stephenson, Ellis, Brodrick), the U.S.A. (Bogardus, Badger, Eads, Roebling) and France.

The pioneers of the new movement in France include Horeau, Flachat, Baltard, Reynaud and Henri Labrouste, whose work culminated in his two great Paris library buildings, perhaps amongst the greatest works of nineteenth-century architecture – the Bibliothèque Sainte-Geneviève (1843–50) (see plate) and the reading and stockrooms at the Bibliothèque Nationale (1848–58). The building problem here was, for the first time, a library for use by the general public. The problem and the solution in the two buildings were thus revolutionary.

The Sainte-Geneviève library, on the Place du Panthéon, is horizontally composed. The round arches of the façade emphasize the links with tradition, but the techniques used for construction were thoroughly modern. The floors are supported by a concealed iron skeleton, extending from the ground to the roof. The main reading room, with two main aisles, is subdivided by bare iron columns. It is 19,680 square feet, and has 420 seats. The library can hold about 100,000 books. The horizontal division of the façade, by means of a broad cornice, separates the lower floor from the emphasized upper storey, with its large rounded arches and glass windows. The lists of names under the windows are a basically historicist touch.

The strict symmetry of the building is comparatively unobtrusive. The centre is gently stressed by the entrance, which pierces only the lower storey, but central emphasis is not repeated higher up, where the composition is horizontal. The façade of the upper storey, with its repetitive pattern of identical equal-sized forms, may have been symbolic of the new spirit of democratic equality typical of the age. People of all classes were intended to be equally attracted by and into the building, which was not built for the select few, or for one man, but, in theory, for everybody. It was the same ideas which prompted William Morris, who was active in England at the same time, to demand 'art for everyone'.

This library influenced both architects who followed Labrouste (Richardson, Plates 9 and 11, who studied in Paris under one of Henri Labrouste's brothers, the architect Theodore Labrouste), and the new engineer-builders (Plate 16). It is thus a key work in the development of a modern type of architecture – an architecture which was to continue right up to the middle of the twentieth century, varying only in style and structure.

I

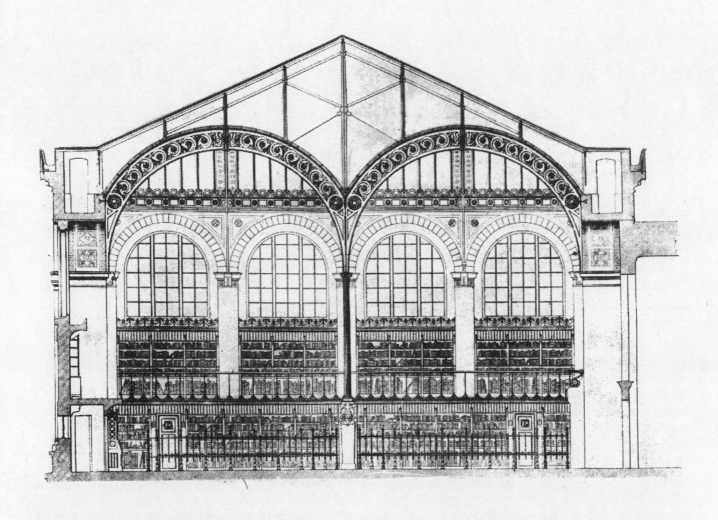

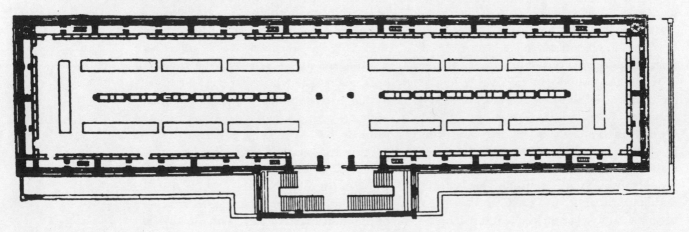

Bibliothèque Sainte-Geneviève, Paris (1843–50) by Henri Labrouste. Plan and section.

Plate 2
Red House, Bexley Heath (1859–60) by Philip
Webb

William Morris was as important as Henri Labrouste (Plate 1) as a founder of modern architecture. Both envisaged a new type of popular architecture based on historical models. At first sight, the house at Bexley Heath looks small and unimpressive. Built by the architect Philip Webb in 1859–60 for Morris, who was his friend, it has become one of the basic buildings of modern architecture. It is nevertheless part of the Neo-Gothic movement, whose proponents sought to revive, in the industrial age, the medieval craftsman's reliability and honesty in his use of materials. But Morris and Webb, unlike the romantic idealist John Ruskin, were very practical. William Morris, who influenced several different areas of culture, wanted to bring the home into line with the new realities of society. He believed that houses should not be status symbols, but simply buildings fitted to the daily needs of the people who lived in them. He refused, however, to come to terms with technology, the synthetic materials, and industrial methods which were being developed so rapidly at the time (Plates 3 and 4).

Webb, who worked with Morris in the studio of G. E. Street, was keen, like Morris, on a new approach to building, and indeed to the whole of culture, based on the craft ideal. He created here a simple brick building, obviously Neo-Gothic in style, but, with its loose arrangement of both plan and structure, well adapted to its function – a principle which subsequently became a central feature of modern architecture.

The two wings join each other at right angles. At the point where they join, there is a staircase giving access to the rooms in both wings. The windows reveal the organization of the rooms inside the building, without any concern for symmetry or pattern.

Between 1860 and 1865, this house was the focus of William Morris' circle. But in 1865 Morris sold it.

The unadorned building has many echoes of traditional architecture. The sub-division of the white framed windows is reminiscent of eighteenth-century English styles, and the sculptural organization of the brick building is similar to the work of William Butterfield.

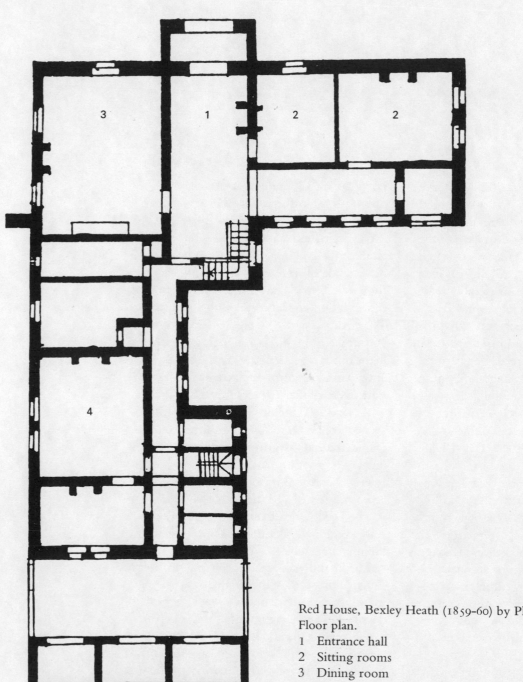

Red House, Bexley Heath (1859-60) by Philip Webb.
Floor plan.
1   Entrance hall
2   Sitting rooms
3   Dining room
4   Kitchen

Plate 3
Corn Exchange, Leeds (1860–63) by Cuthbert
Brodrick

Although William Morris and Philip Webb introduced new attitudes to culture and social responsibility, they were unable to provide any solutions to the problems of the mass society because they failed to come to terms with technology. The solving of these problems was left to architects who were opposed to the movement founded by Morris. The buildings which best fitted the new requirements of the industrial age have only gradually been discovered by historical researchers. The Corn Exchange in Duncan Street, Leeds, is one such building. It is one of the finest works of the architect Cuthbert Brodrick, most of whose buildings are in Leeds, where he also built the Town Hall, an example of late Victorian Classicism (1855–59), the Congregational church (1864–66), Blenheim Baptist church (1863–64), the College of Housecraft in Ilkley (about 1860), the City Baths in Cookridge Street (1882), and various warehouses and office buildings.

The Leeds Corn Exchange is an outstanding early example of the commercial architecture which developed in the middle of the nineteenth century, producing quite new architectural effects. It is an oval building with sandstone façades, and clearly owes a debt to James Bunstone Bunning's Coal Exchange in London. Its exterior makes a powerful impact and has elements which are obviously Neo-Renaissance in style.

The vast interior space (see plate) is even more fascinating and determines the exterior form of the building. The huge oval-domed roof, made of iron, glass and wood, defines the interior space and is the main feature of the exterior appearance of the Exchange. The load is carried by ribs which are semi-elliptical in one direction, and semicircular in the other. Their striking cross-cross pattern anticipates the form of later space-frames. Part of the dome is covered by glass, the rest with wood. There are two rows of round-arched doorways, leading to offices running round the hall at ground and at first-floor level. The rhythm set up at ground level is repeated on the first floor and echoed in the semi-circular ribs of the roof.

The Leeds Corn Exchange is a pioneering early building of the new movement in architecture, and is a proper solution to a technical and economic problem. It is very much in the spirit of the Victorian era, when, in addition to the tendency towards pomp, decoration and exaggeration, there was also a real feeling for honesty of function and materials, clearly seen in the economical Victorian solutions to building problems associated with business and trade.

3

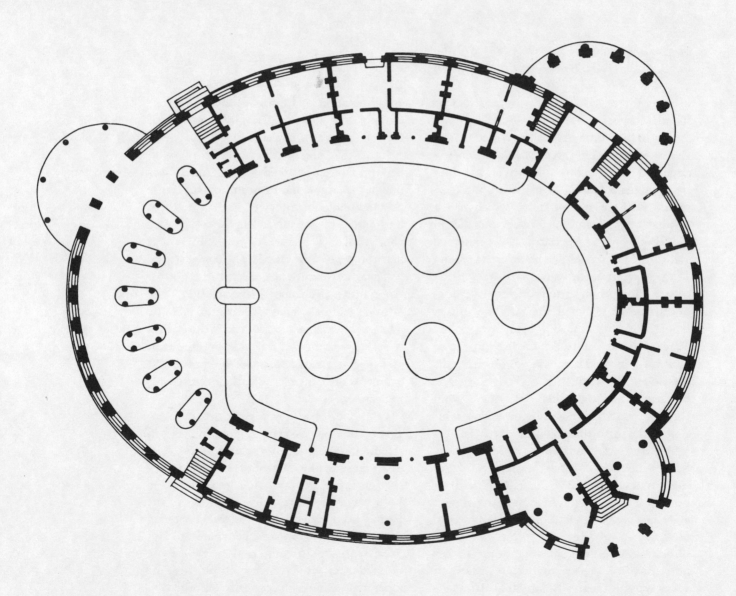

Corn Exchange, Leeds (1860–63) by Cuthbert Brodrick. Plan.

Plate 4
St Pancras Station, London (1863–76) by
G. G. Scott, W. H. Barlow, and R. M. Ordish

In 1865 there was a competition to choose the architect of St Pancras Station, the main station of the Midland Railways, near King's Cross Station, built ten years earlier. As expected, G. G. Scott, who was at that time being given a large number of public contracts, won the competition, which had a limited entry, including Owen Jones, F. P. Cockerell, and E. M. Barry. Scott built the station's Midland Hotel between 1868 and 1874. It contained waiting rooms, ticket offices and administrative offices, as well as hotel rooms. He sited the building just in front of the train shed (begun in 1863 by W. H. Barlow and R. M. Ordish), in strong contrast with it. There was of course a basic difference between the objectives of the hotel and of the train-shed – the one striving for elegance, the other an engineering solution to the problem of roofing over the area where the trains ran in and out of the station. Scott's building, which, unlike the train-shed, is no longer used for its original purpose, was, when it was first built, the biggest and smartest hotel in London, and was in fact one of the earliest multi-functional buildings, although all the rooms in the hotel have now been made into offices. It was a typically revivalist late Victorian Neo-Gothic work, overloaded with heavy forms, a combination of Lombardy and Venetian Gothic, with a touch of English and French Gothic thrown in as well.

In contrast, the building by Barlow, who had previously worked with Brunel, was one of the largest and most important transport buildings of the time – a hall 690 feet long and 245 feet wide, still in use today. The roof is made of glass and iron, clearly and harmoniously combined. The span of the hall was not exceeded until the erection of Contamin's Machine Hall at the Paris World's Fair in 1889, with a span of 376 feet. The roof, which is subdivided by thin bands of light, is supported on wide pointed iron arches. The train-shed is one of the earliest examples of economy nevertheless resulting in beauty.

For a long time it was only Scott's Neo-Gothic building which was admired. Then attention concentrated exclusively on Barlow's engineering. But both were typical of their age, and quality could be achieved in both ways. In several other buildings of the period both styles are so closely combined that they cannot properly be separated. But in St Pancras Station in London, we can see the extent to which the two could become separated, almost dialectically opposed to each other.

4

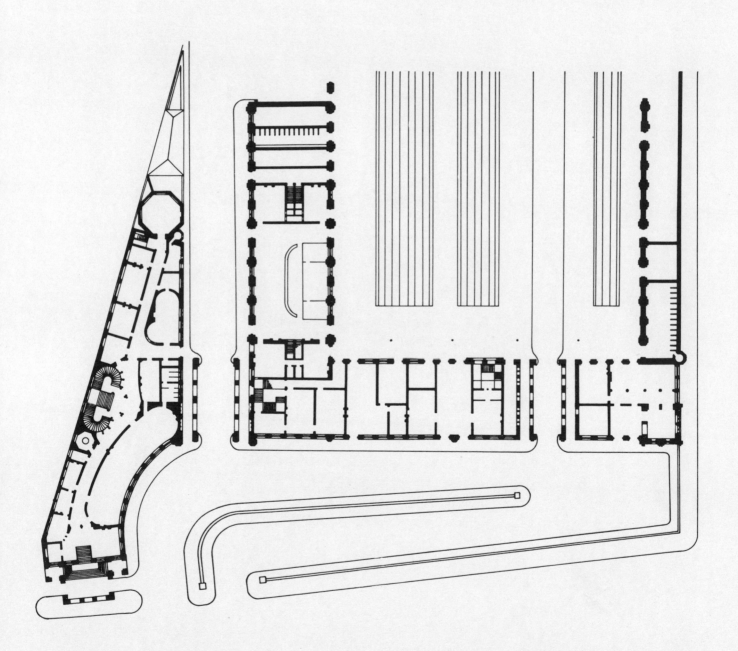

St Pancras Station, London (1863–76) by G. G. Scott, W. H. Barlow and R. M. Ordish. Ground plan.

St Pancras Station, London (1863–76) by G. G. Scott, W. H. Barlow and R. M. Ordish.
Front of Station and Hotel, from an engraving.

Plate 5 (page 61)
Galleria Vittorio Emmanuele II, Milan (1865–67) by Giuseppe Mengoni

One of the building problems which arose repeatedly around the middle of the nineteenth century was that of the arcade made up of a number of shops. As part of the process of urbanization of large cities, efforts were made to group shops, offices, restaurants and streets into a unit. The first Burlington Arcade in London (1815–19), the covered Galerie d'Orléans in the Palais Royale in Paris by Percier and Fontaine (1829–31), greenhouses in large botanical gardens, exhibition halls such as Paxton's Crystal Palace in London (1851), early warehouses, and shopping arcades in major cities are all examples of this trend. It is an aspect of architecture which has recently been receiving renewed attention with the modern interest in overall environmental planning.

After 1900, arcades of this kind were built in several European centres (Brussels, Genoa, Turin, Leningrad, Moscow and Naples). The Galleria Vittorio Emmanuele II in Milan by Giuseppe Mengoni is one of the most beautiful and famous of these arcades, and runs between the Piazza del Duomo and the Piazza della Scala. Mengoni's design dates back to 1861. The building was dedicated to the Italian king's efforts towards unification, and was named after him. Mengoni beat Camillo Boito in the design competition for the building; Boito subsequently criticized Mengoni's design fiercely.

The influence of England, then much more developed industrially, was considerable; the building was financed by English money, certain parts of it (the iron and glass) were imported from England, and the construction was actually executed by an English firm, which was advised by, among others, Matthew Digby Wyatt. The design is clearly influenced by, for instance, the Crystal Palace and London stations. The arcade consists of two streets, which cross each other, covered by a barrel-vaulted glass roof. At the point where the two 'aisles' cross, an interior square is created, crowned by a glass dome 164 feet high and 120 feet in diameter, and decorated with paintings and sculpture. The main gallery, which is 640 feet long altogether, links the cathedral and the opera house, two central features of Milan, creating an enclosed space between two open areas. Here urban life could develop, and the 'Salotto di Milano' became one of the town's focal points socially. Mengoni's original plans were even more ambitious, and included covering the west side of the Piazza della Scala with glass arcades as well.

The main work on the Gallery lasted from 1865 to 1867. On 15 September 1867 the building was ceremoniously opened in the presence of the king. But it was not until 1877 that the decoration of the interior with painting and sculpture was completed. In the same year, Mengoni, who was only forty-eight, fell from a scaffolding inside the arcade and was killed. His fame at the time was considerable and the news of his death was reported throughout Europe. His obituary appeared in the third issue of the *American Architect* in 1878. In 1911 Franz Kafka praised the arcade, which had been increasingly forgotten: 'It has virtually no superfluous decoration. One's gaze can sweep along its whole length without interruption, and this, as well as its height, makes it seem short, while in no way detracting from it. The arcade makes a cross through which air can flow freely.' In 1912 Carlo Carrà also rediscovered this great nineteenth-century work. In 1943 it was heavily damaged by bombing, and reconstruction work was completed in 1949.

This important Milan building is typical of the 'Umberto I style', which, as the name suggests, is associated with the restoration of the monarchy in Italy. Parallel movements took place in other countries such as France, Austria, Germany and Belgium. They were attempts to revive links with previous centuries in both architectural and political terms. This can be seen in the way the characteristics of classical buildings (e.g. triumphal arches, and market places such as the Forum of Trajan) were introduced into contemporary buildings such as exhibition and market halls. It is therefore typical that Mengoni should have built the walls of his arcade in a historical style while using modern glass and iron techniques for the roof. This is therefore symbolic architecture, which combines the two elements superbly. Also, for the first time, account is taken of the relationship between the building and its urban environment.

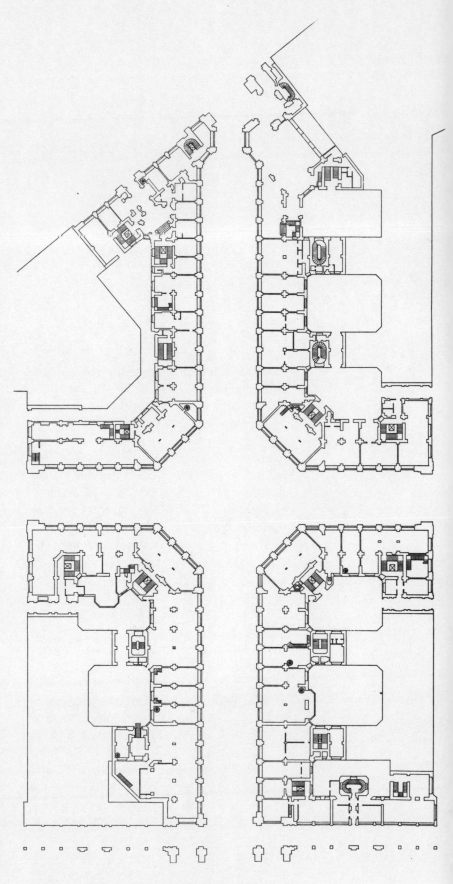

Galleria Vittorio Emmanuele II, Milan (1865–67) by Giuseppe Mengoni. Ground plan.

5

Galleria Vittorio Emmanuele II, Milan (1865-67) by Giuseppe Mengoni.
Elevation of the triumphal arch on the Piazza del Duomo.

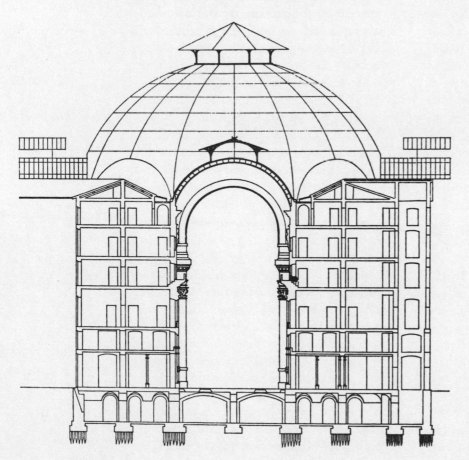

Section.

Plate 6
Oriel Chambers, Liverpool (1864–65)
by Peter Ellis

Major nineteenth-century buildings are still being discovered. The work of the English architect Peter Ellis, for example, was barely known until the appearance of an article by G. Woodward in the *Architectural Review*, 119 (1956). Ellis lived and worked in Liverpool between 1804 and 1884. The development of industry in England during this time made fresh thinking imperative, and produced a large number of creative architects.

Oriel Chambers at 14 Water Street, Liverpool, was commissioned in 1863 by the Revd. Thomas Anderson as a replacement for Covent Garden Chambers, which were destroyed by fire. The building is an early example of the type of commercial architecture which is usually thought to have begun around the end of the century in Chicago, and which is normally associated with the steel skeleton technique. The epoch-making importance of this building has only recently been recognized. Ellis anticipated the Chicago style with his use of cast iron columns and beams in this four-storey building, and in the extent to which he managed to construct the exterior walls of glass. He had not, however, developed a proper skeleton system. The bottom and the top floors of the building are lower than the intervening three storeys, from each of which projects a row of oriel windows (hence the name of the building). On the gable are the initials T.A. (Thomas Anderson), his motto 'Stand Sure', and the date (1864).

Peter Ellis had an office of his own in this building. The whole mass is held together by upright half columns, almost like buttresses, which taper to a point above the top of the building. The symmetry of the building is softened by the raised entrance extending to the first floor, and the octangular fan light above it, which corresponds to the octagon in the gable.

It is a building which clearly has fundamental affinities with contemporary Neo-Gothic, in spite of its large protruding windows designed to admit the maximum amount of light into the interior (an idea which W. L. Jenney, in particular, adopted in his Chicago skyscrapers). But his contemporaries did not understand Peter Ellis, who put up a second building at 16 Cook Street. In the issue of *The Builder* dated 22 June 1866 there was an article in which Oriel Chambers, which had just been completed, was sharply criticized.

The building is a masterpiece of early commercial architecture. In the middle of the nineteenth century, business buildings became recognized as a new and leading form of architectural development. The importance of the work of Peter Ellis, which may have been seen by Louis Sullivan when he travelled to Paris via Liverpool, lies in the fact that he took account of the requirements of the work which would be done inside the building (by providing a glass façade), and still managed to produce a solution which is both formally and stylistically convincing. The building combines the new requirements of commerce with the traditional requirements of style. It is a starting point for modern architecture because its proportions are ideal, even by traditional standards, and it performed the functions required of it at the time superbly.

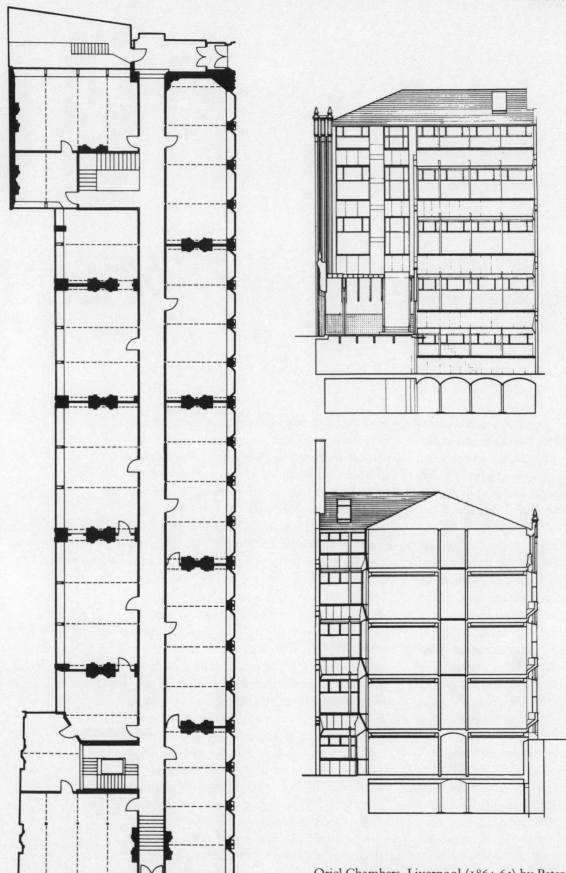

Oriel Chambers, Liverpool (1864–65) by Peter Ellis.
Plan and elevations.

Plate 7
Old Swan House, London (1876) by Richard Norman Shaw

Richard Norman Shaw was one of the best reputed architects of his time. He was much travelled and read, and helped shape the late Victorian era in England. Many of his buildings helped to establish simplicity and honesty in the use of materials as new objectives, as demanded by his fellow student William Morris (Plate 2), with whom he worked in the Studio of George Edmund Street. Shaw's architectural style depends on simple forms and clear arrangement, and is generally called 'Queen Anne'. He executed many buildings including churches, administrative buildings and New Scotland Yard in London (1887–90). He is particularly famous for a series of residential houses which are designed to fit into a row of houses on a street.

The Old Swan House, dating back to 1876, is probably the most important of these. The character of the building is given largely by the main material used, brick. The three storeys, symmetrical within themselves, are clearly distinguished from each other and differently composed. The ground floor has a few narrow windows of different widths. The first floor is emphasized by three wide bow-windows. The second floor has seven mannerist, narrow, gothicizing windows, the width of which echoes the pattern of the ground floor. The third storey also has seven windows, two narrower ones on the sides and five in the middle. The three gabled windows in the roof form the upper edge of the composition. Note the way these windows extend round the corner. This is a motif which was to attract attention thirty years later in Olbrich's Hochzeitsturm in Darmstadt, 1907 (Plate 36).

Shaw placed particular emphasis on the organization of the rooms inside, which were partly decorated by the firm of Morris and Co. The clear, simple, carefully thought-out and dignified composition of the building demonstrates the revival of interest, in Shaw's time, in eighteenth-century bourgeois architecture. But it also forms a starting point for twentieth-century residential architecture. In this building, with its obviously eclectic style, models from the past are so harmoniously and artistically incorporated that architects like Mackmurdo, Voysey, Ashbee, Mackintosh (Plates 22 and 23) and even Wright were influenced by it.

Shaw also took part in the planning of Bedford Garden City (1878).

7

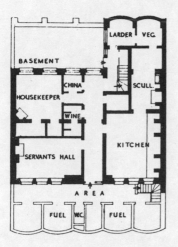

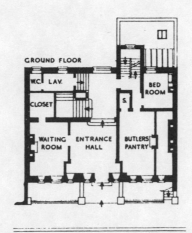

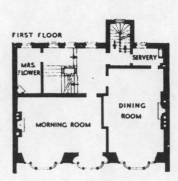

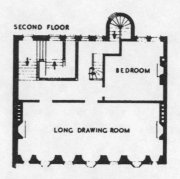

Floor plans.

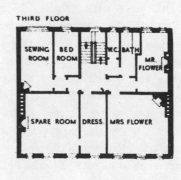

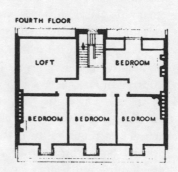

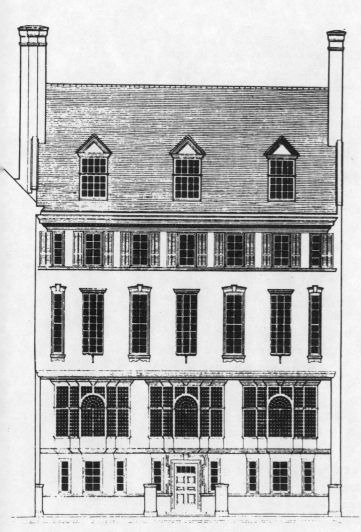

Old Swan House, London (1876) by Richard Norman Shaw.
Elevation.

Plate 8
Farnam Hall, Yale University, New Haven,
Connecticut (1869–70) by Russell Sturgis

The radical attitudes of the 1850s were succeeded in the 1870s by an architecture which still had historicist tendencies but emphasized monumentality more strongly than before. Revival of tradition was central to new requirements produced by the mass society. In an age which tended towards superlatives, expansion and power, we also find an emphasis on social responsibility (William Morris), on the connection between culture and morality (Tolstoy), and a sceptical approach to history (Nietzsche).

In the U.S.A. it was mainly in university architecture that historical models were used. The search for tradition and new roots was expressed by borrowing historical motifs from European architecture, while a revival of tradition occurred in Europe too.

Farnam Hall at Yale University in New Haven by Russell Sturgis (who was educated in Germany) is a remarkably mature example of basically Neo-Gothic university architecture. Its dignity and beauty derives from its simplicity and solidity, making it comparable with Webb's buildings (Plate 2). Richardson (Plates 9 and 11) later developed these historicist ideas and made them into a key element in modern architecture.

Farnam Hall looks closed, old and dignified, like a castle. It has long façades, rhythmically interrupted by projecting semi-circular towers. Brown brick and green copper roof contrast with each other. Above the semi-basement there are three main storeys, separated from each other by horizontal cornices. These contrast with the upward thrust of the pointed-arched windows and the pointed tops of the projecting stair-towers. On each section of the façade there are three broad pointed-arched windows on each of the first two storeys, and above each, on the third storey, there are two narrower windows with rounded tops. The stair-towers are flanked on each storey by narrow windows, half as large as those on the third storey. The attic windows continue the rhythm. The round elements of building break up the horizontal flow of the façades by their form as well as by the two windows set into each between the second and the third storeys.

In spite of using historical styles, Russell Sturgis, who later built Durfee Hall and Battell Chapel (1876) at Yale, has managed here to create a consistent, logical building of high quality, typical of the period.

8

Farnam Hall, Yale University, New Haven, Connecticut (1869-70) by Russell Sturgis. Elevation.

Plate 9
Crane Library, Quincy, Massachusetts (1880–
83) by Henry Hobson Richardson

Just as Webb (Plate 2) and Shaw (Plate 7) laid the basis for English historicist architecture, Henry Hobson Richardson, only a few years younger, influenced a whole generation with his work which, although also historicist, had a uniquely American independent style. His buildings are not only the starting point for the brilliant achievements of modern American architecture, but also exercised considerable influence on European architecture (Townsend, Plate 21; Saarinen, Plate 39). Richardson's historicism, his deliberate references to Spanish and French romanesque, and the creative power of his adaptations, created a bridge between tradition and the new building problems. His work, which uses only traditional building materials, was one of the origins of modern architecture. Sullivan's admiration for Richardson was expressed both in words and in the design of his Auditorium Building (Plate 12) in Chicago, which is heavily influenced by Richardson's Marshall Field Department Store.

Richardson designed a large number of buildings, including warehouses, churches, hospitals, universities, private houses, police stations, railway stations and bridges. But the building which recurs most frequently in his work is the library, and it is here that his development can be traced with the

most value. His most convincing libraries are in Woburn, North Easton, Burlington, Malden and Quincy, near Boston (see plate). Richardson was commissioned to design this small building in 1880. The rooms inside it are arranged asymmetrically, and the large entrance portal is pushed over to the right, with a rounded projecting staircase tower next to it, both under one gable. The entrance portal, over which the date of building is inscribed, is Syrian in style, and it is fairly clear that Richardson's knowledge of Syrian architecture was derived from the second volume of C. J. M. Vogué's *Syrie Centrale* (2 vols., Paris 1865 and 1877) which appeared in 1877. To the left of the entrance there are four pairs of windows just below the roof, divided by pillars, while to the right the windows are sub-divided into rectangles, with eight squares above and four rectangles below. There is a similar arrangement of windows on the end wall, though here the division is into twelve squares and six taller rectangles. The symmetry is broken by the two upper gable windows, which are slightly out of line with each other, as well as with the larger windows underneath them. The massiveness of the whole is emphasized by the big roof with its characteristic narrow 'eyelid dormers' and the use of Milford granite for the rest of the building.

9

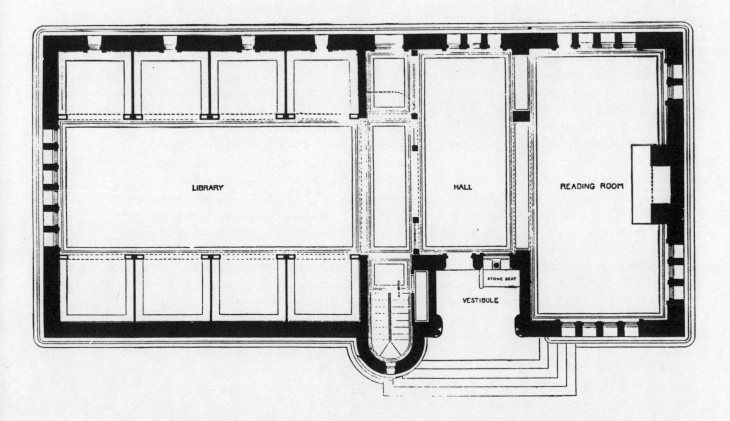

LIBRARY

HALL

READING ROOM

STONE SEAT

VESTIBULE

Crane Library, Quincy, Massachusetts (1880-83) by Henry Hobson Richardson. Plan.

Plate 10
Church of the Sagrada Familia, Barcelona
(1884–1926) by Antoni Gaudí

Antoni Gaudí was probably the most important European architect of the period around 1900. His work marks a transition from historicism to a new style of architecture. Gaudí made this transition despite continuing to use traditional building materials. He worked on several buildings in Barcelona (Plates 27, 33 and 34), but his greatest effort went into the building – which remained incomplete on his death – of the Church of the Sagrada Familia, which has become the symbol of Barcelona. It has often been suggested that this work be continued. The fact that this unique nineteenth-century religious building monument remains unfinished is symptomatic of the change of emphasis in building problems which has resulted from the growth of mass society since 1900.

Gaudí took over work on the church in 1884, and from then on applied himself to it with desperate intensity. The church had actually been started in 1875, and its form based on a Neo-Gothic design by Vilar de Pilar in 1882. The Joseph Chapel in the Crypt, designed by Gaudí in 1884, was available for use in 1885. The work continued without interruption from 1887 until 1893. In 1891–1903 the portal and existing parts of the transept of the Birth of Christ were built. In the following years up to Gaudí's death, the towers on this transept were constructed.

Although these represent only a small part of the original plan, they have become a dominant symbol for the whole town. Most of the rest of the plans survive.

The superb fragment of the Sagrada Familia demonstrates the inevitable failure of an attempt to build a cathedral with traditional techniques and materials at a time when more attention was being paid to other building problems, demanding new techniques and materials (Plates 13 and 16).

The Sagrada Familia was originally intended by the architect to be more than merely a church for a small community. It was to have been the centre of a complete environment, including schools and workshops, in which community life would be completely reorganized. Gaudí spent the last years of his life very near the church, in a little room where he lived and worked. Here he experimented with weights on wires in order to calculate the strength of his arches, made casts of living people and animals, and produced designs for mosaics and paintings. Gaudí, the artist, in co-operation with his architects and workers, opened up a new world of creative possibilities. He had a vision of a new art, and of a modern religion nourished by the great traditions of the past.

But he was almost alone in this world of his, and he was bound to fail.

10

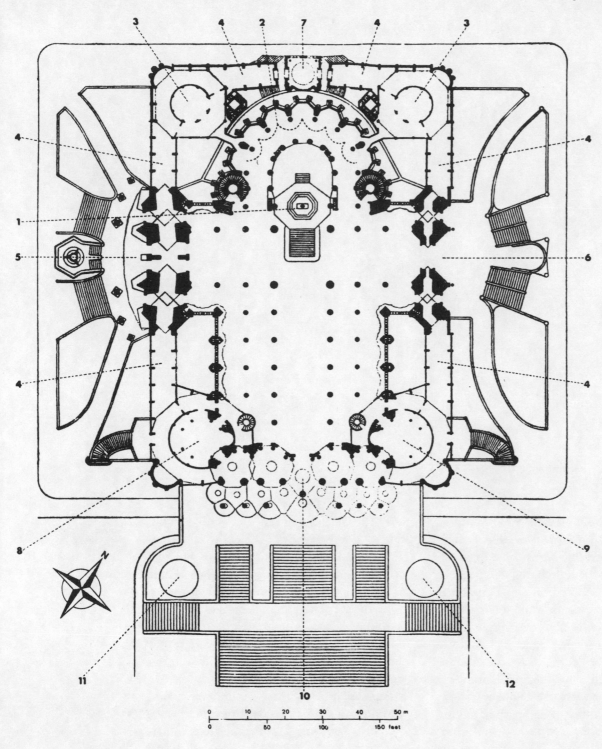

Church of the Sagrada Familia,
Barcelona (1884-1926)
by Antoni Gaudí. Plan.

1 High altar
2 Chapels of St Joseph
3 Sacristy
4 Cloister
5 Façade of the Passion
6 Façade of the Nativity
7 Chapel of the Assumption

8 Baptistery
9 Chapel of Penitence and confessional
10 Glory façade
11 Purification by water:
    fountain with a jet 20 metres high
12 Purification by fire:
    giant triple candelabrum

Plate 11
John J. Glessner house, Chicago (1885–86) by
Henry Hobson Richardson

Apart from the Marshall Field building, which was so important to the Chicago School, Richardson's most mature work was his last, a private house which he never lived to see completed. In this building he achieved what was, at the time, a remarkably disciplined structure for a single-family house. The house is L-shaped, and stands on a corner site at 1800 South Prairie Avenue. With an annexed wing, containing stables, it encloses a large courtyard. The living rooms open onto this quieter side of the building. Bedrooms, dressing rooms and the library face onto the street. The five-cornered window bay of the dining room projects into the courtyard. The stable wing, the kitchen, the servants' rooms, the washroom, etc. adjoin the dining room. The large door into the courtyard in the entrance wing on South Prairie Avenue is set to the left (visible on the left edge of the plate). The symmetry which appears in the photograph is in fact disturbed by the entrance, and makes this building a precursor of the deliberately disturbed symmetry of Art Nouveau. The two simple chimneys are, however, placed quite symmetrically on this wing. The round arch over the entrance portal, typical of Richardson, is here merely indicated.

The arrangement of the windows on the upper storey corresponds to the interior functions of the building. The way that materials are handled – on the street side, granite, on the court side, brick, both used equally well – is a 'protomodern' characteristic of the building. Frank Lloyd Wright was later to develop this idea (Plate 38), with his new, dynamic unfixed concept of space which was to become typical of twentieth-century architecture. The imperceptible outward slope of the façade on the ground floor (visible in the gutter on the right) foreshadows the masterly use of this motif in the Monadnock block (Plate 14).

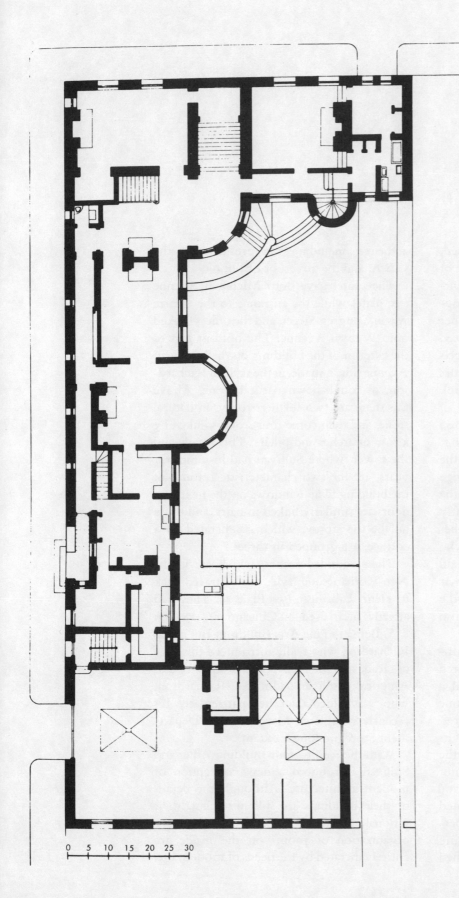

0 5 10 15 20 25 30

John J. Glessner house,
Chicago (1885-86)
by Henry Hobson Richardson.
Plan, main floor.

Plate 12
Auditorium Building, Chicago (1886–89) by
Dankmar Adler and Louis H. Sullivan

So far as modern architecture is concerned, it is in Chicago that the greatest number of significant buildings can be seen, representing a continuous and unbroken development. Chicago grew faster than any other city in the nineteenth century, and produced a large number of important architects whose work during the eighties and nineties is usually known as the Chicago School. Louis Sullivan was the most important of these, and the greatest building in Chicago of the period is the Auditorium Building, designed by him. This now contains the Roosevelt University. T. E. Tallmadge called it 'our Palazzo Vecchio'. It is one of the most important building complexes of early American architecture, and it marks the beginning of the career of Louis Sullivan, who at this stage was still working in successful partnership with his older partner, Dankmar Adler. Frank Lloyd Wright, who joined the firm of Adler and Sullivan in 1887, also worked on the Auditorium Building.

The building problem involved was important and unusual – what was required was a large office building, a hotel and a theatre, combined. This was therefore one of the first multi-functional cultural centres. In the middle was the theatre with its enormous auditorium, from which the building took its name, although it was not visible on the outside. It had 6,000 seats, and was famous for its acoustics. It was opened on 9 December 1889 with a special performance (including Adeline Patti singing 'Home, Sweet Home') for a distinguished audience, including the president of the U.S.A. and the governor of Illinois.

The Hotel gave onto Michigan Avenue (see plate) while the entrance to the theatre was in Congress Street, and the offices looked onto Wabash Avenue. The bottom part of the exterior of the building, on the Michigan Avenue side, is made, in the style of Richardson, of rough-hewn natural stone. Above this there are two further storeys in natural stone, and then come four storeys linked by a row of arches and pillars. This arcade and the tower, where Sullivan had his office for years, are the two characteristic features of the building. The windows on the next two floors are similarly linked in pairs, and those on the top storey, which is separated by a cornice, are grouped in threes.

These rounded arches, which are in the Neo-Romanesque style, can be traced back to Henri Labrouste (see Plate 1). They had already been used in Chicago in 1884 on S. S. Beman's Fine Arts Building. But it was Richardson who really introduced this type of façade and the Neo-Romanesque style to America. Sullivan admired Richardson, who was older than he, particularly his recently completed Marshall Field Department Store (no longer extant).

With the Auditorium Building Adler and Sullivan introduced a new conception of modern architecture. Although the details of their buildings are still historicist, their rational functionalism and revolutionary organization of rooms on the inside are entirely dictated by the needs of modern life.

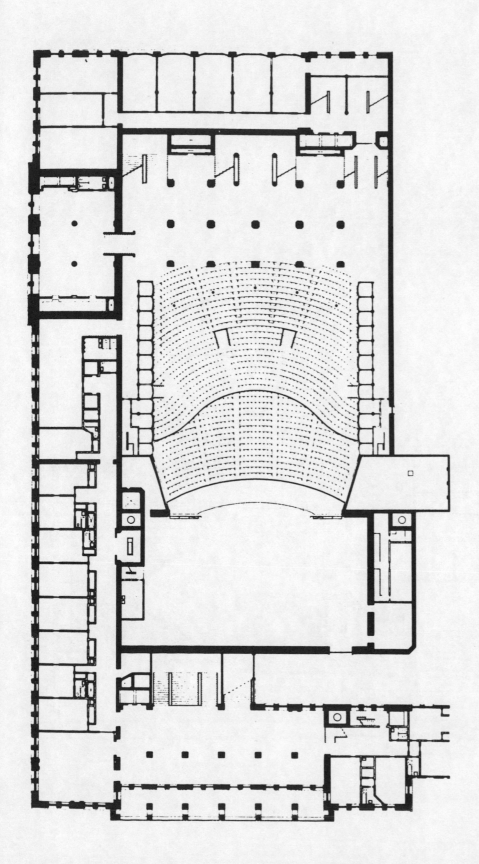

Auditorium Building, Chicago
(1886-89) by Dankmar Adler and
Louis H. Sullivan.
Plan, second floor.

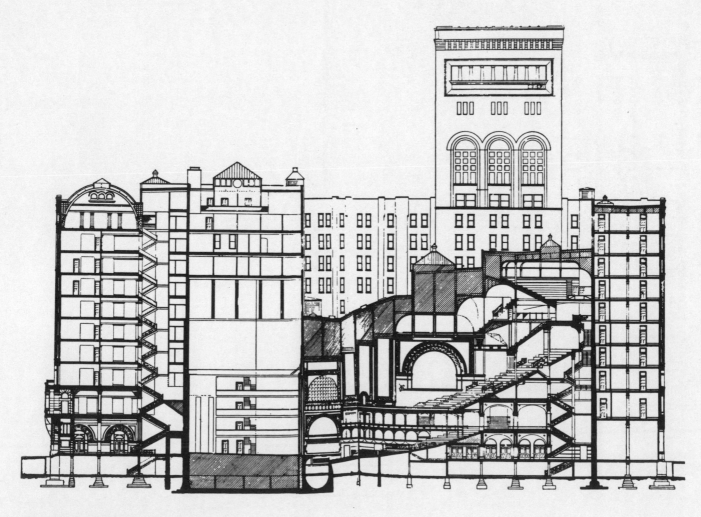

Auditorium Building, Chicago (1886–89)
by Dankmar Adler and Louis H. Sullivan.
Longitudinal section.

Plate 13 (page 95)
Leiter Building II, Chicago (1889) by William
Le Baron Jenney

In 1871 the centre of Chicago was virtually burnt to the ground. The reconstruction of this area gave several important architects the opportunity to use new techniques in maximizing the usage of the limited space available in 'the Loop' which is the central area of Chicago, bounded by a loop of the Chicago River.

In 1879, William Le Baron Jenney, six years older than Richardson, and educated, like him, in Paris, though not at the Ecole des Beaux Arts but as an engineer at the Ecole Polytechnique, built the first Leiter Building, using pure skeleton building techniques, with cast iron columns as supports. He finally proved the practicability of this new technique with which architects had been experimenting since the middle of the nineteenth century. Between 1883 and 1885 his Home Insurance Building, held by Sigfried Giedion to have been the first real skyscraper, was built. It was demolished in 1929. In 1889, he built the enormous second Leiter Building which is still used as a store by Sears Roebuck. The eight-storey building extends right across the block between State, Wabash and Congress Streets.

It can be compared with Richardson's earlier Marshall Field building, only a few blocks to the north, and with Adler and Sullivan's Auditorium Building (Plate 12). In comparison, both buildings look old-fashioned and their affinities with the Palazzo Pitti stand out. Jenney virtually disregarded problems of form and concentrated on function; it is as though the form was merely the result of functional requirements and structural techniques. The proportions of the building are not in fact simply chance-effects, and Jenney's buildings are still basically historicist and traditional, as is demonstrated by the barely noticeable three-storey pillars, and their capitals. On the inside, the high-ceilinged rooms are subdivided by thin supporting pillars.

With his revolutionary skeleton building techniques, Jenney influenced the whole Chicago School. Most of the next generation of Chicago architects passed through his office, and he directly influenced Louis H. Sullivan, Daniel Burnham, John Wellborn Root, Martin Roche and William Holabird. He can reasonably be regarded as the father of the Chicago School.

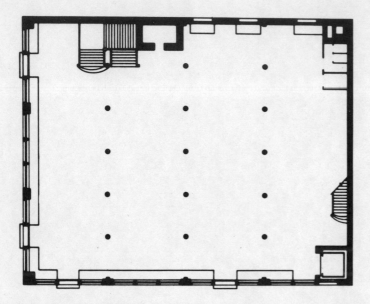

First floor.

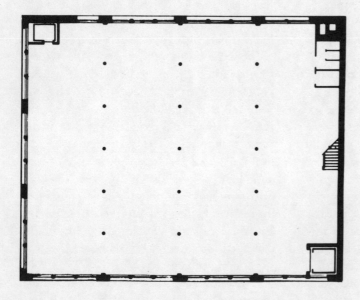

Fifth floor.

0 5 10 15 20 25 30 35 40

Leiter Building I, Chicago (1879) by William Le Baron Jenney. Plans.

13

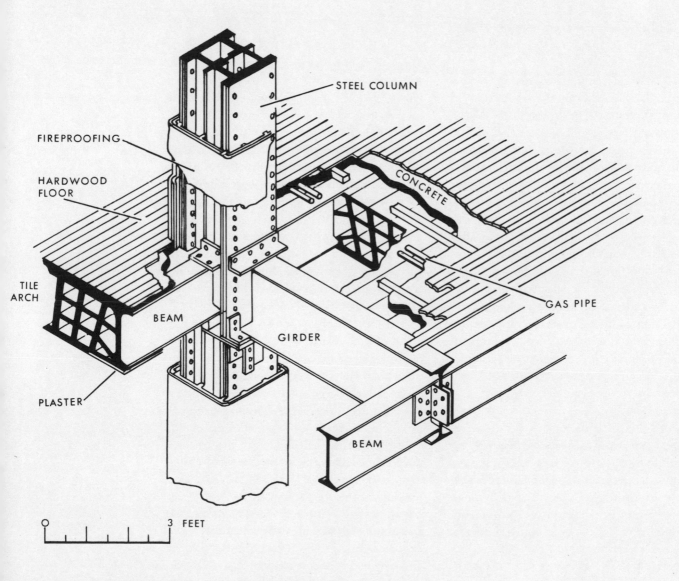

STEEL COLUMN

FIREPROOFING

HARDWOOD
FLOOR

CONCRETE

TILE
ARCH

BEAM

GAS PIPE

GIRDER

PLASTER

BEAM

0   3 FEET

Fair Store, Chicago (1890–91) by William Le Baron Jenney.

Detail showing typical column and beam joint.

Plate 14
Monadnock Building, Chicago (1891) by Daniel
Burnham and John Wellborn Root

It was a new technique, skeleton building, which really characterized the revolution in high-rise building in Chicago after 1871. The works of Jenney (Plate 13) and Adler and Sullivan (Plate 12) set the pattern. John Wellborn Root, who had worked in Jenney's office, played a significant role in the development of skeleton building.

His masterpiece, finished only after his death, was the Reliance Building. He also designed an equally important building using the traditional structural technique of load bearing walls – the Monadnock Block (originally called the Monadnock and Kearsarge Building). It is situated on the corner of Jackson and South Dearborn Streets, and is an office block with sixteen storeys, made of brick. The first designs and discussions with the client, Peter and Shepard Brooks, took place in 1885.

Building the foundations of the massive walls in the comparatively soft earth of Chicago, basically unsuited to heavy buildings, was a considerable achievement. The architects made the walls curve slightly outwards at ground floor level, as Richardson had done in the Glessner House (Plate 11) and as is now fashionable again with quite different materials. The roof also projects, rather like an Egyptian pylon. The sculptural form of the building, its moulded foot, roof and corners, and its sensitively formed light-catching bow windows, are features which give it its special quality. The total lack of ornament allows the superb arrangement and sculptural composition of the building to stand out. The design and lack of ornament are undoubtedly the responsibility of John Wellborn Root, although there was a rumour in Chicago that an unknown designer in his office had worked out the plans in his absence. Root is supposed to have agreed not to use any decoration after initially having some doubts. This building, which was no doubt excessively expensive because of the thickness of the masonry walls on the lower storeys, marks the end of the phase of architecture based on the principle of the load bearing wall. It does nevertheless express certain future trends; it is an imaginatively executed building, and a complete solution of the building problem involved. It is still used as an office block.

The sculptural emphasis on the ground floor is not continued in the annexed building (on the left of the plate) which was added to the south, on Van Buren Street, by Holabird and Roche in 1893, using the skeleton technique, in co-operation with the engineer Corydin T. Purdy. These architects also made the roof cornice project even more. This annexe virtually doubles the size of the building, and disturbs the original proportions of Burnham and Root's building.

14

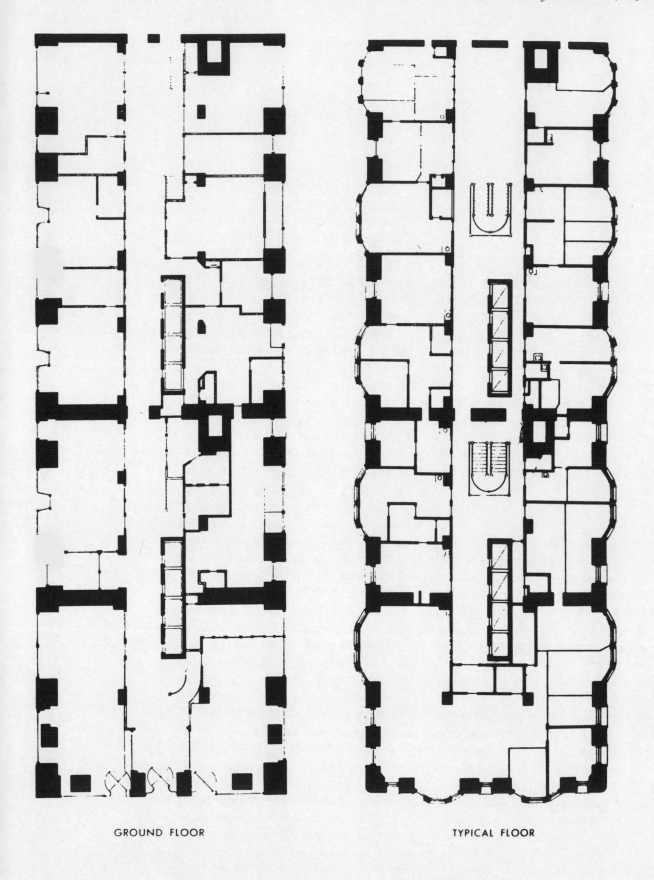

GROUND FLOOR   TYPICAL FLOOR

Monadnock Building, Chicago (1891) by Daniel Burnham and John Wellborn Root. Plans.

Plate 15
Bridge over the Firth of Forth, Edinburgh (1881–
89) by Benjamin Baker and John Fowler

Ever since the construction of the railways, communications buildings, such as bridges, canals and tunnels, have formed a very important part of modern architecture, and some of them can be taken as representative of their age. The Forth Bridge is one of the most powerful of the surviving monuments of this time.

The daring suggestion of bridging the Firth of Forth, and thus connecting Edinburgh with the north of Scotland, was first made in 1818. The bridge was to begin at Queensferry, and to have a span of up to 2,000 feet. This plan was, however, never executed. In 1860, another bridge was planned over the Firth of Forth, this time south of South Queensferry. But it was not until 1873 that this suggestion was taken seriously, and a Forth Bridge Company started. Another plan was put forward by Sir Thomas Bouch for a suspension bridge with two spans, each of 1,580 feet. After the disaster, on 29 December 1879, at the Tay Bridge, one of the most famous early works by Sir Thomas Bouch, in which 75 people were killed, the building over the Firth of Forth was immediately stopped. The job was transferred to two other engineers, Benjamin Baker and John Fowler. In 1881, their plan for a cantilever bridge was adopted. The contract was signed in 1882, and the work began in 1883. About 4,600 workers were employed on building the bridge. There were 57 major accidents and 106 minor casualties. The enormous bridge was finished in 1889, the same year as the Eiffel Tower. It is over one and a half miles long and its greatest unsupported span is 1,710 feet. Part of the bridge rests on the island of Inchgarvie. The supports carry a total of 50,958 tons of steel.

After the Tay Bridge disaster, safety was made one of the most important features of the bridge, as the enormous steel tubes made by Siemens (which had to be repainted every three years) demonstrate. The bridge has no cladding or historicist details. Its builders' prime concern was to secure it against the force of the wind, and make it stable enough for mass transport. The total cost of the bridge was, not surprisingly, high – £3,600,000. Two trains can still cross the bridge at top speed at the same time, which is most unusual for a bridge of this age.

The bridge was dedicated on 8 March 1890 by the Prince of Wales, later King Edward VII. William Morris called it the 'height of ugliness'. But a contemporary expert, Mehrtens, who was present at the opening ceremony, recognized the genius of the two constructors. He pointed out that the bridge was not only a remarkable technical achievement, but also one of the first great constructions to prove that a steel structure, too, could have a beauty of its own.

Konrad Wachsmann has recognized the bridge's spatial-structural system and the way it differs from the more two-dimensional system used in the Crystal Palace. The Forth Bridge introduced a new phase of industrial building technology and is one of the most powerful buildings of the period. The cast iron parts of the northern bridge were replaced by steel in 1946 and 1947.

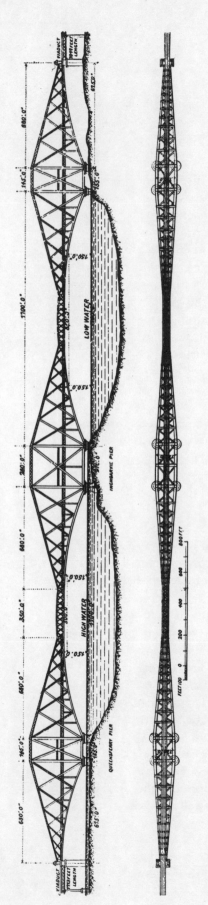

15

Bridge over the Firth of Forth, Edinburgh (1881–89)
by Benjamin Baker and John Fowler.

Plan and elevation.

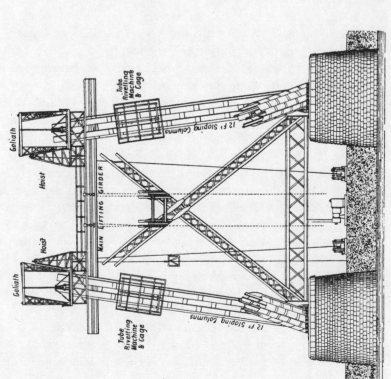

Diagram showing construction of one of the towers.

Plate 16
Eiffel Tower, Paris (1887–89)
by Gustave Eiffel

During the preparations for the 1889 World Fair in France in commemoration of the centenary of the French Revolution, several suggestions were made for a suitable memorial of this event, including, for instance, a giant guillotine. Eventually the project put forward by the great bridge and hall constructor, Gustave Eiffel, was adopted. The young man had in fact already worked as the assistant of J. B. Krantz on previous Paris world fairs (e.g. 1867). He was, however, destined to achieve his greatest fame as a constructor in 1889.

The 990 feet tall tower, which was believed at the time to be impossible to build, was designed by Eiffel with the assistance of the Swiss constructor, M. Koechlin (who has recently been claimed by the Swiss to have been the real designer of the building), the Frenchman Naugier, and the architect E. Sauvestre. Eiffel, with his experience of building bridges in several European countries, and his tenacity in pursuing this project, proved that his design could be executed, although a contemporary mathematician calculated that it would collapse once it reached a height of 750 feet. On 28 January 1887 work was begun on laying the foundations of the tower, divided for reasons of safety into four independent masonry bases, followed by the assembly of the individual parts of the tower, all separately produced in the factory (including 15,000 iron pieces, and 2,500,000 joints, with a total weight of 7,000 tons). By March 1888, the tower had reached the height of the restaurant. By May the second platform was reached, and by December the top was virtually completed. The whole tower took $21\frac{1}{2}$ months to assemble. On 31 March 1889, it was completely finished, and was ceremoniously dedicated at the Fair's opening.

When it was first opened, the lift was not yet ready and Eiffel was the first man to climb its 1,710 steps. A twenty-one gun salute was fired from the first storey, provoking Huysmans to remark that here was a 'steeple of Notre Dame of the Hard Heart, a steeple without a bell, but with a cannon to announce the beginning and the end of office hours, summoning the faithful to the Mass of Finance, the Vespers of Speculation, with a cannon saluting the liturgical feasts of Capital with its gunpowder salvoes'. Public opinion was not nearly as enthusiastic about the building as its constructor, and there was a violent controversy about the destruction of the Paris skyline. Several artists protested passionately about the tower, including the architect, Garnier, the composer Gounod, and the writers Maupassant, Verlaine and Huysmans.

Nevertheless, the Eiffel Tower has gone down in history as a new idea in building – the first real example of the frame building technique which makes no distinction between interior and exterior. The extreme possibilities of new material were demonstrated, and new dimensions were opened up for building in the future – dimensions which have only really been exploited during the twentieth century. The ornaments on this historicist tower were mostly removed in 1937. Attempts have been made since then to claim this as an anti-historicist building contrasting with the trends of its era.

The Eiffel Tower, like the new building techniques used by architects working at the same time in Chicago (Plates 12–14) and the structure used in the Forth Bridge, is an example of the new technological architecture, always striving for superlatives and for achievements demanding the most modern techniques.

16

Eiffel Tower, Paris (1887-89) by Gustave Eiffel.
Elevation.

Plate 17

Tassel house, 6 Rue Paul-Emile Janson, Brussels (1892–93) by Victor Horta

As in the U.S.A., European architects concentrated increasingly on solving problems thrown up by the new growth of towns, making use of the new synthetic industrial building materials, iron and glass. Skeleton building and historicism were combined, using the elemental and organic forms typical of this period. The organic architecture foreseen by Louis Sullivan and exemplified in the early works of Wright was merely a local variation of the revolutionary European movement known as Art Nouveau, which began mainly in Belgium.

The house built for the engineer Tassel, in what was previously the Rue de Turin, Brussels, is famous as the first example of this style. For the first time all the architectural features of Art Nouveau were combined in one building. The house is one of a row, and at first sight it is not markedly different from the buildings on either side of it. On closer inspection, however, it is precisely this lack of ostentation in its design which allows its quality to be clearly seen. Each of its three storeys has a large glass window in the middle, where the main rooms are. These windows are wider on the higher storeys. The rooms on either side, however, have windows which get narrower towards the top of the building, becoming narrow slits on the third storey, contrasting with the three broad central windows, and the balcony in front of them. The façade, as in the Solvay house (Plate 18), is completely symmetrical, and slightly curved and broken up into open areas by iron elements. The central part of the façade projects forward, in the manner of the Rococo revival which was at its peak a few decades earlier. The same style can also be seen in the earlier works of Gaudí. Horta put into practice the theories of Viollet-le-Duc, who had earlier advocated the use of iron as a structural element in architecture. Ever since Horta and Sullivan used it so brilliantly, iron has ceased to belong merely to the vocabulary of the engineer, and has become a legitimate architectural means of expression.

The reserved exterior of the house hardly suggests the unusual arrangement of the rooms inside. The main feature is a large two-storey hall on the ground floor giving access to all other rooms. The design of the interior is based on combining space and surface ornamentation into an overall linear composition. Everything is subordinated to the rhythm of the sweeping, curved line, always turning in unexpected directions. This is well demonstrated in the often illustrated staircase, with its narrow iron column extended by its linear plant ornamentation into the surrounding space. The column is thus both functional and ornamental.

The original furniture, which was matched to each room, is no longer preserved. In 1958, the building was partially altered, and the entrance hall renovated. But Horta's synthesis between space and linear elements of composition, colour and spatial dynamic, can still be appreciated, and it is this which makes this house one of the key buildings of Art Nouveau architecture.

17

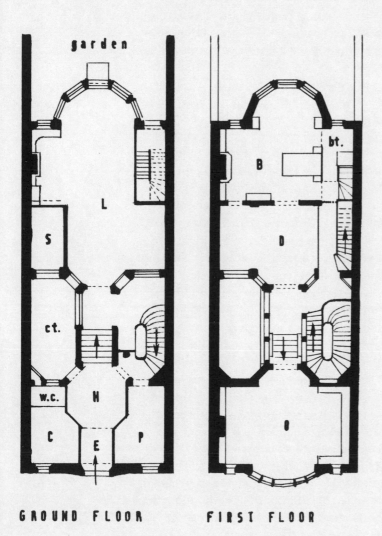

GROUND FLOOR   FIRST FLOOR

← 23 ft. →

Tassel house, 6 Rue Paul-Emile Janson,
Brussels (1892-93).
by Victor Horta.
Plans, ground floor and first floor.
L Living room
H Hall
C Cloakroom
P Porter
D Dressing room
S Scullery
ct. Courtyard
D Entrance
B Bedroom
O Office

Plate 18
Solvay house, Brussels (1895–1900)
by Victor Horta

The Solvay house in Brussels is a much admired masterpiece of Art Nouveau architecture. Like the earlier Tassel house in the former Rue de Turin (Plate 17) the building illustrates the greatness of its architect, Victor Horta. Unlike the Tassel house, it is still preserved in its original condition. Ernest Solvay, like Alphonse Stoclet (cf. Plate 32) was a late nineteenth-century industrialist who became a patron of architecture. Works commissioned by him from Horta include a memorial in 1894, the Solvay laboratories in 1896, and a Pavilion in Brussels in 1901. The luxurious house in the Avenue Louise is in the same category as other important rich bourgeois single family houses of the period (Plates 23 and 32).

Horta was commissioned to do this building in 1893. The work began in 1895, and was completed in 1900. It is situated in one of the great avenues of Brussels, in which other important contemporary buildings can also be found. It has a strictly symmetrical façade. The entrance portal is on the left side. The second and first floors are visually combined by the forward swing of the façade on both sides, and the metal columns (visible on the upper left of the illustration) extending across both floors and dividing the two window-bays. The clearly proportioned stone façade, with its large glass windows, is enlivened by the filigree-like iron ornamentation on the balconies beneath the windows and on the first floor between the window-bays. The plant-like curves of the ornamentation of the window-bays on the third floor and of the balconies,

and the projecting and receding forms of the façade are reminiscent of Rococo.

The curvilinear forms of the exterior are repeated in the interior. The rooms are subdivided by ornamental iron work similar to that on the façade. The metal is openly displayed, but ornamented, and is an integral part of the curved spatiality of the total composition of the house, so much so that it seems cast in one mould. The doors, furniture, lamps and other interior items all contribute to the rhythm of the interior.

The main rooms of this five-storey house are on the first floor, just as they were in Frank Lloyd Wright's Robie house (Plate 38), which was built about a decade later. These rooms include a music salon, a billiard room and a dining room. This last leads onto an open terrace and the garden. On the second floor are the more private rooms, including the library, bedrooms and bathroom. The third floor is for children, the completely separate roof floor for servants.

The intelligent and economical use of space, and the way that it is left open or closed according to functional requirements, demonstrates the genius of Horta, and is reminiscent of the economy of some Rococo building forms – albeit under quite different conditions. In both, ornament and structure are inseparably combined. The building, an organic whole, reflects the social, economic, structural and aesthetic characteristics of its time. It set a new trend in architecture, although the private single-family house was a type of building which received less and less attention from architects as time went on.

18

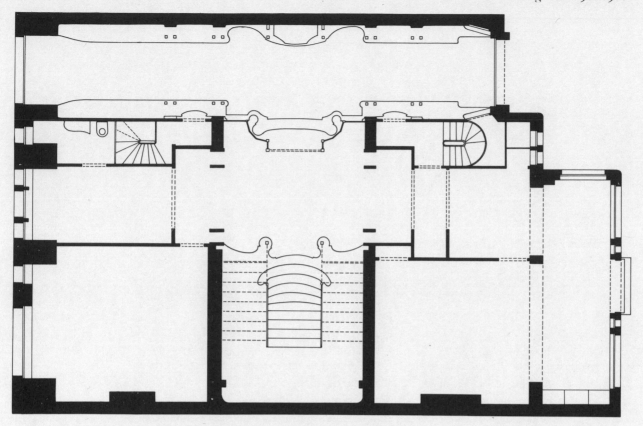

Ground plan.

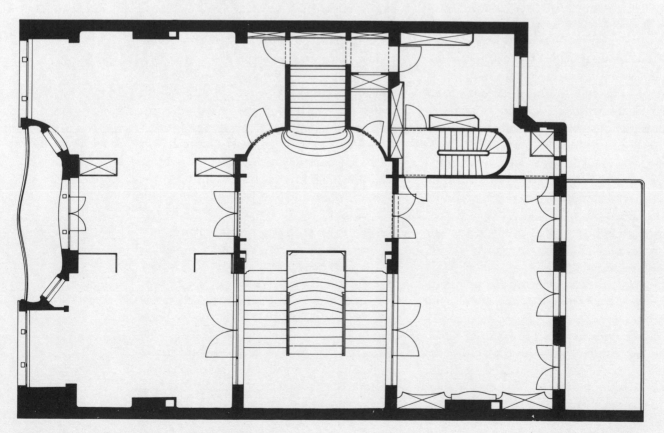

Solvay house, Brussels (1895–1900) by Victor Horta.

First floor plan.

Plate 19
Bloemenwerf house, Uccle near Brussels (1895–96) by Henry Van de Velde

In the last decade of the nineteenth century, Henry Van de Velde wrote, 'most people accept the formal world in which they live, just like the dog accepts his kennel, the horse his stable and the cow its stall'. He advocated general reform on the lines of William Morris' arts and crafts movement. In Belgium, as in Great Britain earlier, it was the feeling that life and living were becoming false that generated these new ideas, which Van de Velde considered 'common sense'. Like the Bauhaus in Weimar (Plate 50), Van de Velde thought that he had discovered the key to architecture, the ultimate style. As Morris, who commissioned a house from Philip Webb (Plate 2), Van de Velde, both painter and theorist, commissioned a building in line with his own ideas. He has described this house in great detail in his autobiography. The Bloemenwerf house can be seen today to have been very much a product of its time, and, like Horta's sophisticated houses, it can be regarded as one of the first examples of Art Nouveau in architecture. It is interesting that the non-architect Van de Velde used concepts which other architects at the time were trying to discard: the symmetrical façade, the gable and the mansard roof. The symmetry of the entrance façade is in fact imperceptibly disrupted by the window to the lower right, and the large main windows, which are now similar, were originally different. There is also a window bay projecting from the adjoining side façade which breaks the symmetry. The

lions beside the entrance were added at a later date.

It is the design of the interior that is the most novel feature. The room is clearly defined as a functional area for family life. The central feature of this house, as in Horta's Tassel house, is a two-storey hall, giving on to all the rooms on both the ground and first floor. The numerous acute and obtuse angles of the plan betray the amateur in Van de Velde. He said himself, 'when I decided to produce plans for our house, I had no idea of architecture whatsoever. I was completely self taught'. Nevertheless, he did subsequently produce some remarkably mature buildings (Hagen, Cologne, Weimar).

In comparison with the contemporary works of Victor Horta in the same town, which Giedion regarded as less progressive than the Bloemenwerf house, and in comparison with earlier single-family houses by Wright in Chicago, the naïve originality of this building has the same charm and conviction as the pictures of Henri Rousseau.

The whole of the interior was designed by Van de Velde, whose 'common sense form' was applied to everything, including furniture, wallpaper, carpets, cutlery, plates, book binding, fashion etc. As it stands today, the green paint on the wooden parts of the gables emphasizes the horizontality of the house. Originally, only the slightly projecting narrower boards were painted, emphasizing the verticals more strongly and giving the building a contemporary appearance.

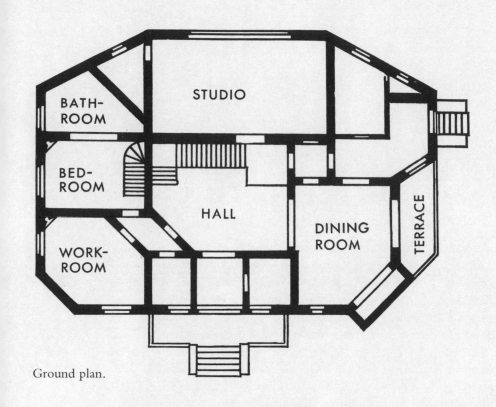

Ground plan.

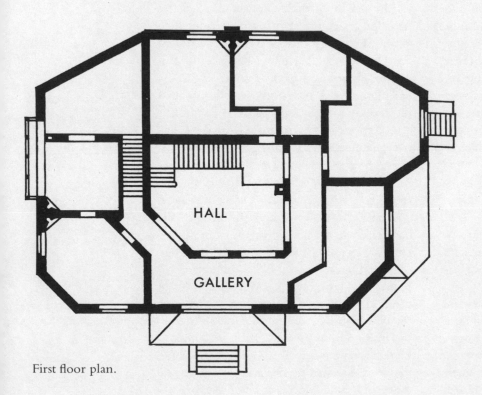

First floor plan.

Bloemenwerf house, Uccle near Brussels (1895–96) by Henry Van de Velde.

Plate 20
*Exchange, Amsterdam (1897–1903) by Hendrik
Petrus Berlage*

Hendrik Petrus Berlage's chief work illustrates the state of architecture in Holland at the turn of the century, as Horta's buildings (Plate 17 and 18), Sullivan's Carson Pirie and Scott Department Store (Plate 26) and Mackintosh's Glasgow Art School (Plate 22) illustrate Belgian, American and Scottish architecture of the same period. The Amsterdam Exchange is now considered one of the outstanding works of Dutch architecture. The old stock exchange, built in the middle of the nineteenth century, was burnt down. A competition was announced for a new building in 1897. It was entered by, amongst others, Otto Wagner. It was won by the Dutch architect, Berlage. Berlage had been educated in Zurich in the tradition of Semper, and had then taught for a while at Frankfurt-am-Main. He was regarded as the successor of the great master of Dutch historicism, Petrus Josephus Hubertus Cuijpers. He built the new Exchange between 1898 and 1903.

The designs for the Exchange went through several stages during 1897. In them one can trace the way the structure of the building was progressively simplified, and the historicist detail reduced further and further. In the first design there are still clear echoes of Romanesque building forms, reminiscent of the cathedrals in Mainz and Worms. The main entrance is vaulted like a choir, and the crowning tower is in a North Italian Gothic style. It is an eclectic design, like those of Berlage's predecessor, Cuijpers. But the second design is more abstract, disciplined and severe, though it incorporates a number of historicist religious forms. The third design is much closer to the final building. Horizontals and verticals are balanced, the basic cubic form becomes more evident, and religious motifs are replaced by secular ones. But even this design, like the building, still has several historicist elements, although they are subordinated to an overriding discipline which emphasizes the simple, comprehensible building masses and the unadorned brick walls. In fact, Berlage retained a good deal of ornamentation, such as the capitals, window surrounds, decorated portals and sculptural building forms. But he also demonstrated in practice what he had always maintained in his writings, that undecorated brick walls can be beautiful.

The metal roof structure of the great hall (see plate) combines iron, glass and brick in one superb engineering ensemble, showing that Berlage fully understood the techniques requisite for his materials. One of the most interesting features of the building is its fitness for its urban environment. Its rectangular tower is a dominant feature of the town. On the Damrak side, the arrangement of windows, symmetrical about the centre of the building, sets a rhythmical pattern for the whole street.

This is an important piece of modern Dutch architecture. It is one of Berlage's major achievements, and a source of several different trends in Holland (De Stijl, Amsterdam School, Dudok). Even so great an architect as Mies van der Rohe (Plate 54) has Hendrik Petrus Berlage to thank for several important influences.

20

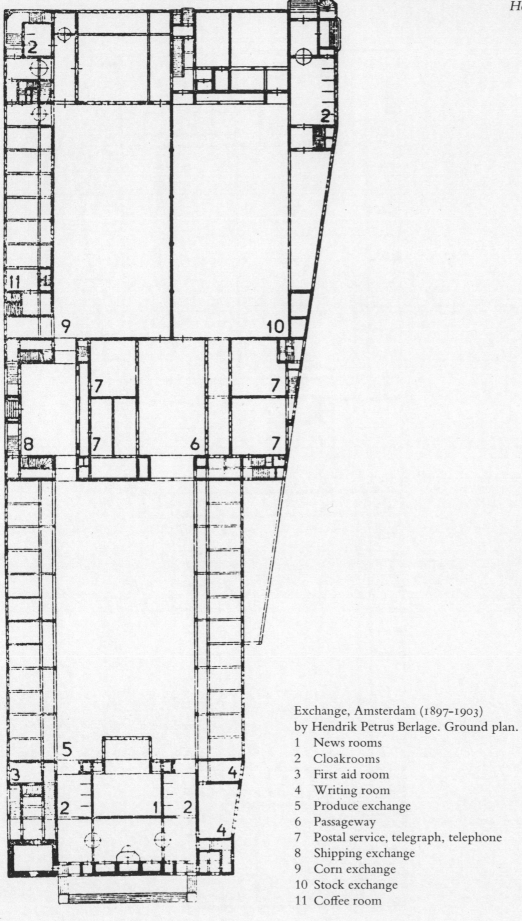

Exchange, Amsterdam (1897–1903)
by Hendrik Petrus Berlage. Ground plan.
1 News rooms
2 Cloakrooms
3 First aid room
4 Writing room
5 Produce exchange
6 Passageway
7 Postal service, telegraph, telephone
8 Shipping exchange
9 Corn exchange
10 Stock exchange
11 Coffee room

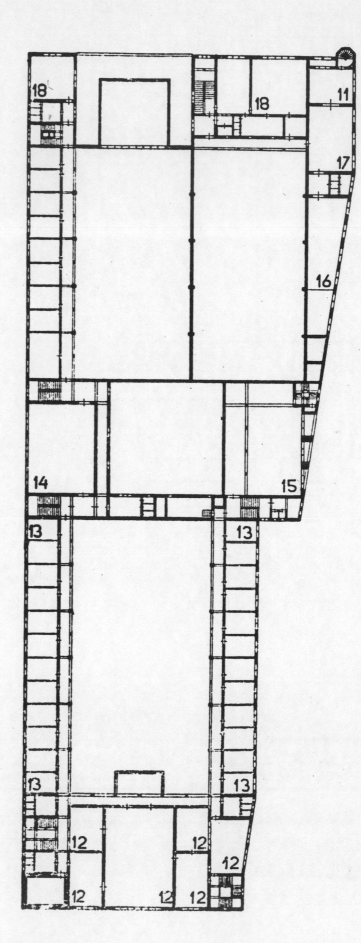

Exchange, Amsterdam (1897–1903)
by Hendrik Petrus Berlage. First floor plan.
11 Coffee room
12 Chamber of commerce
13 Offices
14 Auction room
15 Meeting room
16 Reading room
17 Billiard room
18 Management

Plate 21 (page 129)
Whitechapel Art Gallery, London (1897–99)
by C. Harrison Townsend

As with Sullivan, Mackintosh, Olbrich and other contemporary architects, one of Townsend's most important buildings is for public art exhibitions. It is the Whitechapel Art Gallery in London, which still serves its original function. Other buildings by Townsend, such as the Horniman Museum in London (1900–02) can also be put into the same category.

Whitechapel Art Gallery is one of the few examples of English Art Nouveau architecture which is comparable with the equivalent type of building on the continent. Like most of these, it depends not so much on right angles and flat planes as on curves and moulded forms. The building also has similarities with American architecture, and can perhaps be regarded as one of the first examples of American influence in European architecture. The major influence is the American Henry Hobson Richardson. Points of similarity are, for instance, the large arch over the entrance, a motif previously used by Townsend in his Bishopsgate Institute (1892–94), and the frieze over the row of windows, reminiscent of Richardson's Trinity Church in Boston. Townsend

himself influenced Austrian architecture, as, for instance, in Joseph Maria Olbrich's Vienna Secession building, which had a similar function (Plate 25), and also had plant ornamentation laid on its surface. These ornamental reliefs are similar to Louis Sullivan's organic designs (Plate 26).

The impact of the Whitechapel Art Gallery comes above all from its massively emphatic street façade, with the recessed entrance portal on one side and its round arch reminiscent of Richardson's Romanesque. Most of the lower part of the building has inevitably to be closed, but a row of rectangular windows with a 1 - 6 - 1 rhythm is let into the wall halfway up. The end windows, set apart from the others, are in line with the emphatic corner towers, which accentuate the top of the façade, in contrast to the receding middle section. The two windows here were in fact cut in later. Originally, all the middle row of windows were criss-crossed with metal, but the two end windows are now plain.

Townsend's building is a closed structure defined more by volume than by linear forms.

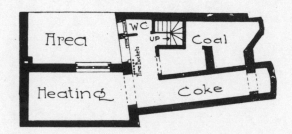

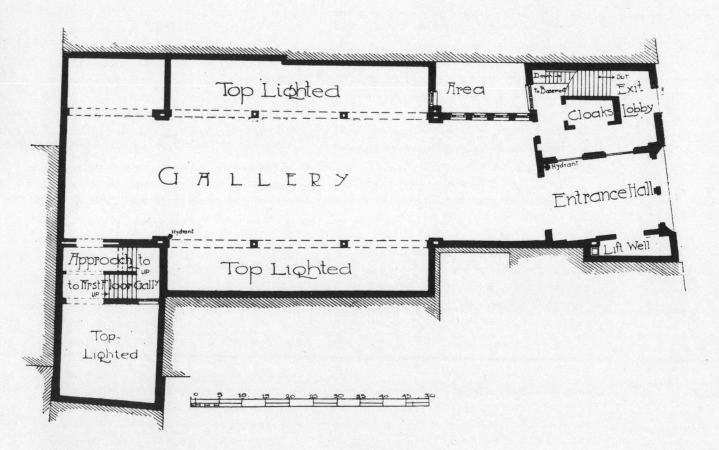

Whitechapel Art Gallery, London (1897-99) by C. Harrison Townsend.
Ground and basement plans.

21

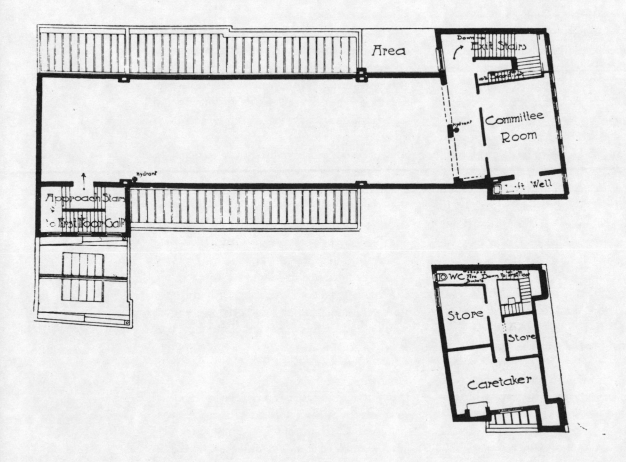

Whitechapel Art Gallery, London (1897–99) by C. Harrison Townsend.
Plans, first floor and second floor.

Plate 22
Art School, Glasgow (1897–99, 1907–09) by
Charles Rennie Mackintosh

In 1897, the young Scots architect, Charles Rennie Mackintosh, who had been working for eight years as a draughtsman in the office of the architects Honeyman and Keppie, received his first major commission as an independent architect. This was for the building of the Art School in Glasgow, for which he won the competition.

This building, the first section of which was completed in 1899, became the sensation of Europe, and had a tremendous influence on continental architecture. As early as 1904, Hermann Muthesius had recognized Mackintosh as one of the outstanding architects in Britain, if not in the whole world. Like Wright (Plates 35 and 38), Horta (Plates 17 and 18), Gaudí (Plates 33 and 34), Loos (Plates 37 and 41) and Berlage (Plate 20), Mackintosh was one of the key architects working at the turn of the century.

The Glasgow Art School is his best building. It is spread out along the length of a backward-sloping site. On the street side are large drawing studios, excellently lit by the enormous front windows. At the back of the building are the teachers' rooms, offices, and other rooms. The left wing contains an assembly hall, the right a library, added in 1907–09.

It is the front façade that is regarded as most typical of Mackintosh's work. The entrance is emphasized by deliberate asymmetry. The big studio windows are on both sides, four to the right, three to the left.

Balance is restored by the tower and the windows just beside the entrance. The two outside windows on the right have only four panes in contrast to the five pane widths of the four remaining windows on either side of the entrance.

The stone wall and iron railings along the street unite the two parts of the building in a symmetrical rhythm, producing the 'disturbed symmetry' typical of Art Nouveau, and seen in buildings by Horta (Plates 17 and 18), Sommaruga (Plate 28) and Hoffmann (Plate 32).

A balance is achieved between stone, glass and metal. Everything fits into Mackintosh's overall composition, which emphasizes mass and clearly-defined volume. The stone provides the volume, the glass the rhythmical surfaces and the iron the linear connection between the two.

The importance of Mackintosh's building lies in the way he has solved a comparatively new building problem with the techniques available at the time, nonetheless respecting local Scots tradition. This principle was to become very important in the new architecture.

A new universality can be seen in the equal emphasis of interior and exterior and in carefully planned interiors, including furniture, carpets, and crockery. Mackintosh's achievement amounts to one of the major artistic events of the period around 1900. It was a level he never reached again.

22

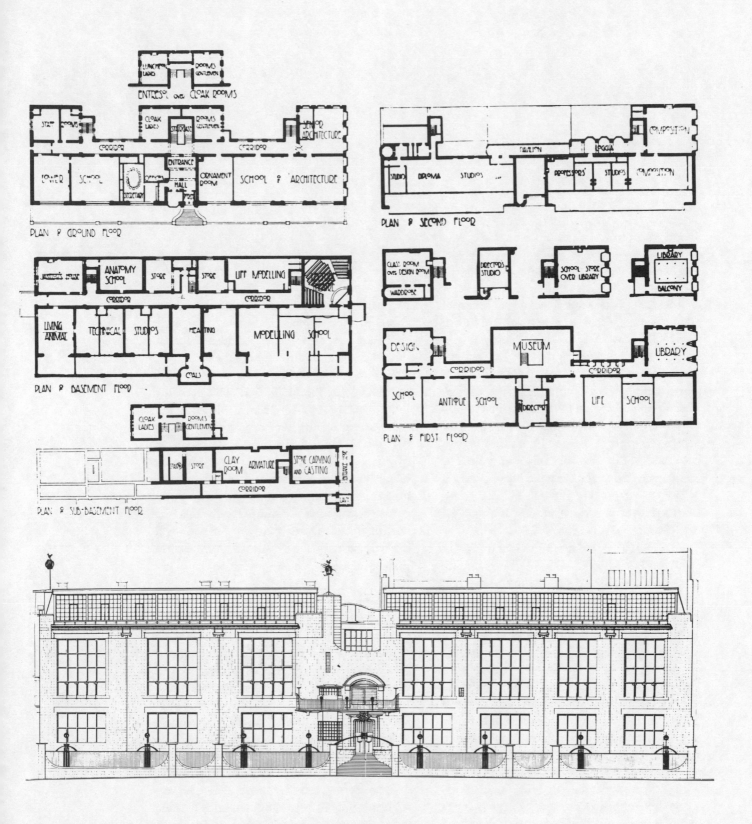

Art School, Glasgow (1897-99, 1907-09) by Charles Rennie Mackintosh.
Floor plans and elevation.

Plate 23
Windy Hill House, Kilmacolm near Glasgow
(1899–1901) by Charles Rennie Mackintosh

In the few years during which he received commissions, Charles Rennie Mackintosh built Glasgow Art School (Plate 22) and some large country houses. Amongst the latter, Windy Hill House in Kilmacolm is outstanding, and is similar in many ways to the more ambitious Hill House in Helensburgh (1902–03) which was built a few years later. Mackintosh designed both the exterior and the interior of this luxurious house. The same was done by Frank Lloyd Wright (Plate 38), Josef Hoffmann (Plate 32) and Victor Horta (Plates 17 and 18) at about the same time.

The client for the Kilmacolm house, William Davidson, had the building sited on a steep hill with a commanding view over the valley. The house has childrens' rooms, a living room and a dining room on the ground floor. To the north, round the bend of the L-shaped ground-plan, there is a kitchen, a pantry, and a wash-room. Thus there is a clear division between living and service areas. On the first floor, there are seven bedrooms, five in a row to the south, two to the north, with windows which face east.

The material used by Mackintosh was local sandstone clad with traditional silver-grey finishing material. With its steeply pitched roofs, its smooth walls and the windows cut simply into the walls, Windy Hill is only slightly different from the tradi-tional Scottish farm house. Both fit harmoni-ously into the sloping landscape, expressing the character of the countryside clearly and functionally in architectural terms.

But the free composition of the plan, together with the integrated design of the whole of the interior, from the drawing room fireplace to the beds, lamps, wall ornaments, built-in furniture and the garden furniture, make this a superbly composed ensemble, with a charm and significance of its own. The south façade, with its regular rows of windows, is quite flat, while the north entrance façade (see plate) has several different surfaces and a number of differently shaped windows which loosen the composi-tion.

A typical Mackintosh touch is the semi-circular staircase unit on the north-west corner of the house, with its verticals emphasized by the vertically elongated windows. The contrast of uprights and horizontals, relieved by semicircular and steeply sloping forms, the smooth wall sur-faces and the smoothly undulating rough stone wall on the street, and the play of light on the stereometric projecting and receding cubes are characteristic features of this type of architecture, at once simple and highly sophisticated. The building had considerable influence on continental architecture, par-ticularly on Olbrich and Hoffmann in Vienna.

23

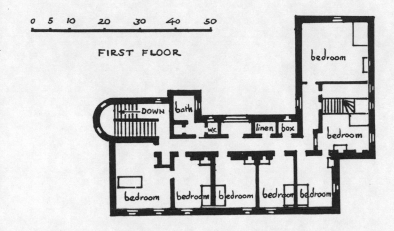

FIRST FLOOR

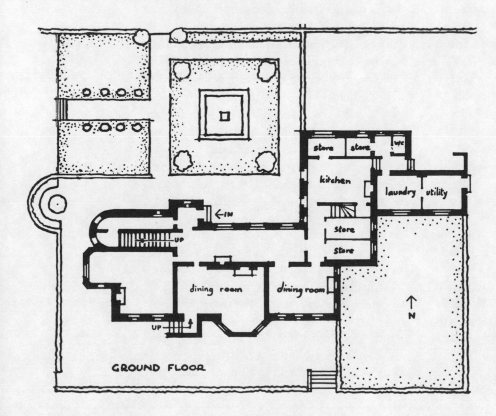

GROUND FLOOR

Windy Hill House, Kilmacolm
near Glasgow (1899–1901)
by Charles Rennie Mackintosh.
Plans, ground floor and first floor.

Plate 24
Majolica House, Vienna (1898–99)
by Otto Wagner

Otto Wagner built the house at 40 Linke Wienzeile in 1898–99, the same year as the house next door, No. 38. The house takes its name from the coloured tiles which protect it from weathering. It is a six-storey house, with nine regular window openings, flanked by recessed bays at the ends. The building is connected to the adjacent No. 38 by a balcony. The symmetrical design and the sculptural and painted decoration of the building is reminiscent of Louis Sullivan's work in the U.S.A. (Plate 26).

The framed structure of the building is covered with an extremely delicate pattern of colours and forms. The majolica slabs (for which Otto Wagner had partly to pay himself) are arranged in a subtly balanced pattern of forms and colours (pink, mauve and turquoise) which, like the filigree bronze-coloured balcony railings and metal supports, breaks away from, and yet emphasizes, the severe symmetry of the house. It is difficult today to recognize in this house the 'wild secessionism' which made Wagner's biographer, Josef August Lux, classify it as a 'foreign body' in Wagner's work.

Wagner has done more than provide the minimum functional building. The Majolica House is a complete technical solution of the building problem of a city apartment block, complemented by a complete artistic solution as well. The external skin of the building not only provides a solution to the problem of weathering – still a difficult problem today – but an outstanding example of Art Nouveau decoration. The exceptionally beautiful staircase is similarly decorated.

In the violent dispute concerning polychrome colouring and the monochrome of traditional architecture raging in architectural circles since the time of Hittorf, Labrouste and Semper, Wagner was a passionate advocate of the former. Although the Majolica House is perhaps the most outstandingly beautiful example of this, Wagner's other buildings (Plates 30 and 31) also demonstrate the importance he attached to colour in architecture.

24

Majolica House, Vienna (1898-99) by Otto Wagner.
Preliminary drawing of front elevation.

Plate 25
Secession Gallery, Vienna (1898-99) by
Joseph Maria Olbrich

A short time after Townsend's Whitechapel Art Gallery in London (Plate 21), the design for which had already been published in the magazine *The Studio* in 1895, an important exhibition building was erected in Vienna. Despite English influences, it was an individualistic building, with a place of its own among the significant buildings of the turn of the century.

A movement called the 'Sezession' (Secession) was founded in 1897 as a protest against the conventional artistic establishment. This movement was to have its own building, and it is creditable that its execution was entrusted to a pupil of Otto Wagner, the thirty-year-old Joseph Maria Olbrich. It was Olbrich's first building. Previously he had travelled in Italy and worked in Wagner's office on the Vienna tram system. His first independent work, as with Mackintosh, had world-wide influence and brought him further important commissions, such as the invitation from Ernst Ludwig von Hessen in Darmstadt to found an artists' colony and permanent exhibition of architecture (Plate 36). The Vienna Secession building is basically rectangular. The two symmetrical blocks of the entrance façade, with their large unadorned wall surfaces, are joined by a cross piece above the recessed entrance, on which is inscribed the motto, 'Der Zeit ihre Kunst, der Kunst ihre Freiheit' ('Each age has its art, and each art its freedom'). Behind this rises a three-quarter-spherical dome of cut away metal, set amidst four tapering Egyptian-type towers. It is this dome which gives the building its characteristic appearance from a distance. It is a symbol of the integration of nature and art, as epitomized in the phrase 'Ver Sacrum'. The simple arrangement of symmetrically composed cubes ranks this building with works by Mackintosh and Wright, even though the comparison with these two architects emphasizes the extent to which Olbrich was still under the influence of Wagner at the time. Although he uses the basic geometrical forms, rectangles, cubes and spheres, extremely well, they are not used with complete geometric purity, but in imitation of historical prototypes. The exhibition rooms inside are superbly lit by glass roofs.

Adolf Loos, who had already seen the new American architecture, rejected this building completely. Nevertheless Olbrich's work was seen by its contemporaries as a European equivalent to the work of Frank Lloyd Wright. The charm of this sensitively proportioned building, based on cubic form, lies in the interplay of decorated and undecorated elements, and the way it is crowned by its floral sphere. The ornamental accents on particular parts of the building (Gustav Klimt designed the bronze doors) are intended to give symbolic architectural expression to the contents of the building.

25

DER·ZEIT·IHRE·KVNST
DER·KVNST·IHRE·FREIHEIT

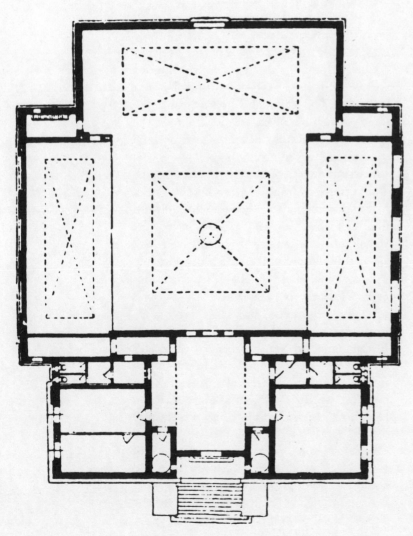

Secession Gallery, Vienna (1898–99)
by Joseph Maria Olbrich. Plan.

Plate 26
Carson, Pirie and Scott Department Store,
Chicago (1899–1901, 1903–04)
by Louis H. Sullivan

Sullivan and Dankmar Adler had completed the Auditorium Building in 1889, a cultural centre for the rapidly growing new city of Chicago. Sullivan also built some high-rise buildings in Buffalo and St Louis which represented a new approach to the large office block. After the Chicago World's Fair in 1893, and the financial crisis which followed it, Sullivan's partnership with Dankmar Adler broke up, and from 1895 onwards he was on his own. From then on, he was given very few commissions, and in 1924 he died in great poverty. One commission he got during this period, however, resulted in his most important building, the Carson, Pirie and Scott Department Store (the building originally carried the name of Schlesinger and Meyer and was given its present name in 1904). It is still a very impressive building, and continues to perform the function for which the architect originally designed it.

It is situated on one of the main crossroads in Chicago, only a few yards from the Reliance building by Burnham and Root, and Sullivan's own Auditorium Building. The site was chosen by the client for its suitability as a store. The corner site is very cleverly used by making the corner of the building round and placing the main entrance there. This round part, with its strong vertical accents, is clearly distinguished from the two wings, and forms a kind of tower, as requested by the client. The building was originally intended to have nine storeys and three wings.

The ground floor had to be surrounded with shop windows and, with the mezzanine floor, it forms a base for the building above, with ornamental bronze designed mostly by George G. Elmslie, who was working in Sullivan's office at the time. The original plan envisaged six more storeys, all with the same beautiful three-part Chicago windows, made possible by the skeleton technique. Sullivan also designed the interior rooms, which are subdivided only by slim supports. The original furniture and the lamps, which can be seen in, for instance, the Men's Bar, which is still used for its original purpose, show the unmistakable touch of a superb designer. The top storey was originally recessed by Sullivan, and kept rather lower than the other storeys, which meant that it formed an end treatment to the remaining functional storeys and base, and all combined into a single composition. This original organic character has since been disturbed. In 1906, while Sullivan was still alive, Burnham and Co. were commissioned to extend the building with five further units on State Street, in Sullivan's style. They also extended the building upwards, and the top storey was brought back into line with the remaining storeys. For a long time, the altered building, which now seems slightly mechanical and stereotyped, was considered, from the purist point of view, as 'more modern'. Between 1960 and 1961, a further extension to the south wing was added on the State Street side by the firm of Holabird and Roche.

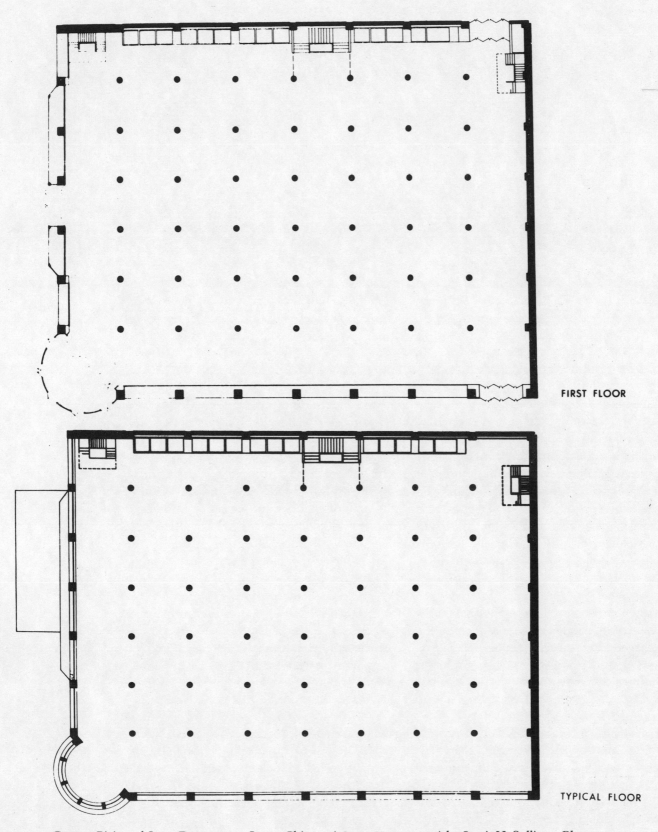

FIRST FLOOR

TYPICAL FLOOR

Carson, Pirie and Scott Department Store, Chicago (1899-1901, 1903-04) by Louis H. Sullivan. Plans.

Plate 27
Güell Park, Barcelona (1900–14)
by Antoni Gaudí

The original plan for this site, the Muntanya Pelada, as drawn up by Gaudí and his long-time patron, the industrialist Eusebio Güell, envisaged a residential estate of about nine and a half acres with a shopping centre and an open air theatre. This fascinating project, which could have been one of the major architectural achievements of the early twentieth century, was never executed. Work on it was stopped in 1914, and what remains is an incomplete example of Art Nouveau environmental planning similar to what architects were trying to achieve in other parts of the world (cf. the English Garden Cities, Olbrich's Mathildenhöhe in Darmstadt, and Wright's Chicago housing projects). But Gaudí achieves something splendid here. The way he combines art, nature, building, garden and the view over the town right up to the sea is quite new.

The wild trees and plants in the area were left largely undisturbed. Rather than try to fight against their nature, the architect attempted to 'extend' them, to adapt his building to them, and to give them support where he felt it necessary.

Even though the estates could not be executed as originally planned, there remains today the public park. On the sloping site are extensive gardens, arcades, winding paths, flights of stairs, terraces, tunnels, gates, statues, fountains, benches and pavilions, and a splendid view over Barcelona and Gaudí's unfinished Sagrada Familia church (in the middle background of the plate), right up to the sea. In the centre of the park, there is a large artificial terrace supported on a colonnade. This was originally intended to be a place of assembly and open air theatre for the planned workers' estate. Along the edge of the terrace there is a curving bench decorated with pieces of coloured ceramic by Gaudí and Josep Jujol. The form of the bench is not only decorative but also allows for either informal groupings or privacy for people sitting down. The brilliant colourfulness of the ceramic pattern, composed entirely of pieces of rubbish, has an imaginative power, which, albeit much later, provoked a new appraisal of the role of colour in architecture and the art of landscaping. North African influences can be clearly seen.

Here Gaudí acted as planner, architect, painter, sculptor, landscape artist and entrepreneur, thus more than fulfilling Ruskin's requirement that an architect be a painter and a sculptor as well. It is unfair to dismiss Gaudí's work, as was done for a long time, as the product of undisciplined imagination and over-indulgence. On the contrary, everything is part of a total concept. Gaudí was a constructor and environmental planner, who saw Gothic, Classical and Oriental styles merging into one, who wanted to produce order out of multiplicity, and who opened up a new world of experience.

27

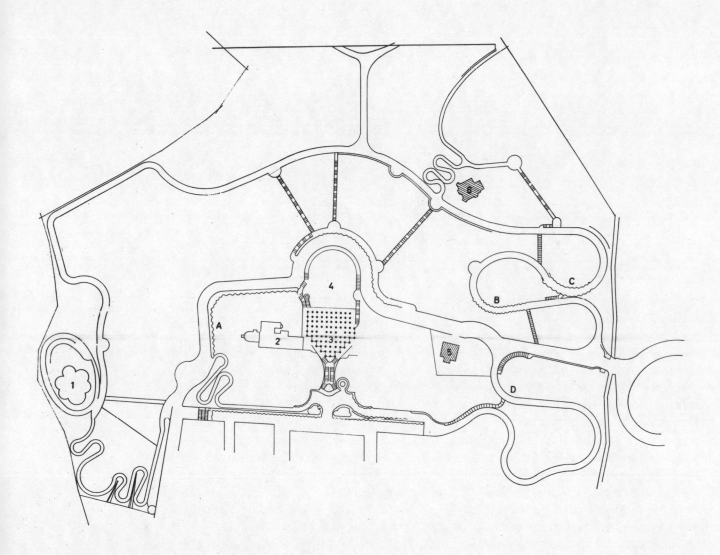

Güell Park, Barcelona (1900–14) by Antoni Gaudí. Plan.

1 Hillock with Calvary group originally intended for the chapel
2 Former house of the Güell family
3 Hall with pseudo-Doric columns, intended as a market for the projected colony
4 Main square
5 Chalet belonging to Gaudí
6 Chalet belonging to Dr Trias
A Portico adjacent to the Güell house, with promenade above
B Portico with three rows of columns and promenade above
C Portico with three rows of columns spaced alternately, and promenade above
D Portico with double row of columns spaced alternately, and promenade above

Plate 28
Palazzo Castiglioni, Milan (1901–03) by
Giuseppe Sommaruga

Giuseppe Sommaruga was a pupil of Boito, Beltrami and Wagner and a contemporary of the Art Nouveau architects who were working in other parts of Europe at that time. He was deeply interested in the developing of a new kind of architecture. He was chosen to build the Italian Pavilion for the St Louis World's Fair in 1904. For this he designed a historicist building, typical of its time, with some Art Nouveau elements. In the Palazzino Comi in Milan, a later building, the influence of Frank Lloyd Wright can be clearly seen. His most important building, the Palazzo Castiglioni, exemplifies the northern Italian version of the transitional style between historicism and Art Nouveau.

The apparent symmetry of the three-storey building is emphasized by the entrance, which extends up to the level of the first floor, but is disturbed by the difference between the right and the left wings. The right wing, with the three pillar loggia motif repeated on the third storey, the entrance on the ground floor, and the balcony on the second floor, outweighs the abbreviated left wing. Both wings are, however, the same height, which gives them some connection. A carefully thought-out system of open and closed cubes gives the exterior the requisite plasticity. The horizontal roof form is symmetrically punctuated by three pairs of quadrangles. The structure is based on the new techniques introduced by Hennebique, using concrete floors.

The special charm of the building lies in its clear and easily comprehensible form covered with rich sculptural ornamentation fitted carefully into the composition of the building. Two monumental figures by Ernesto Bazzaro which originally stood at either side of the entrance were replaced shortly after the completion of the building by the more modest figures which are still there. The rear of the building is less sculptural than the street façade, and involves the use of more iron and glass.

28

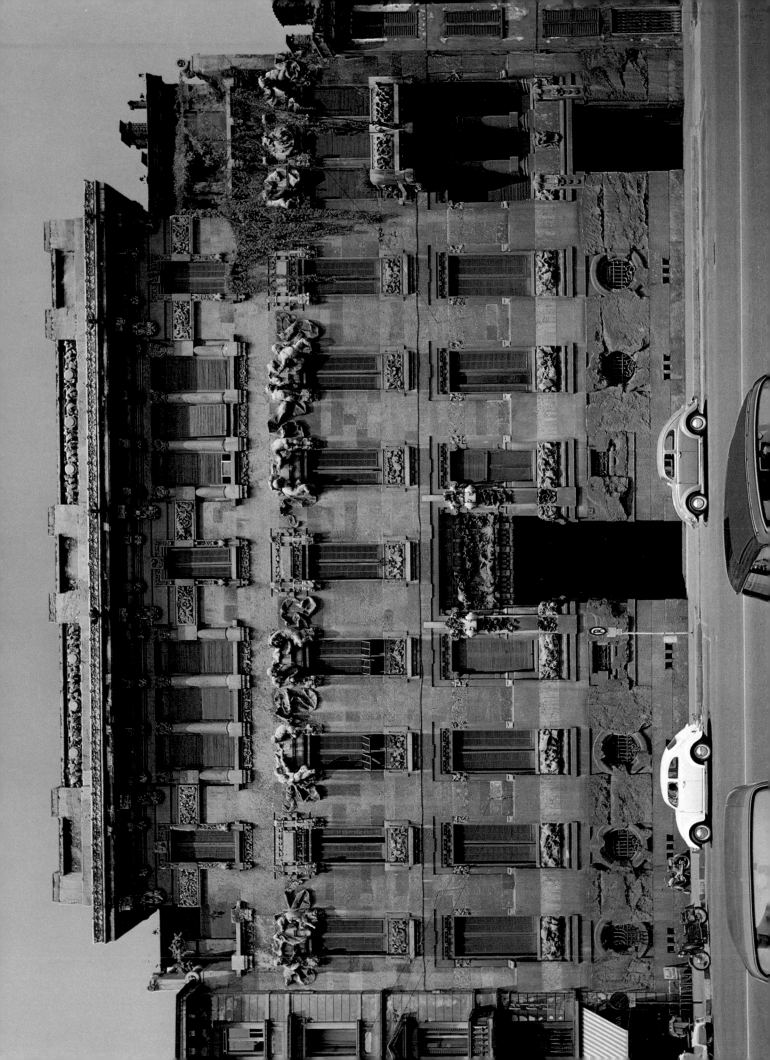

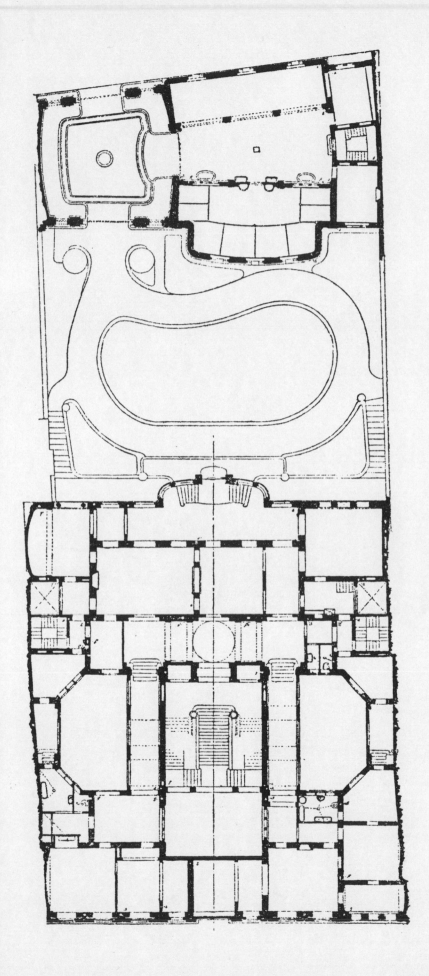

Palazzo Castiglioni, Milan (1901-03)
by Giuseppe Sommaruga. Plan.

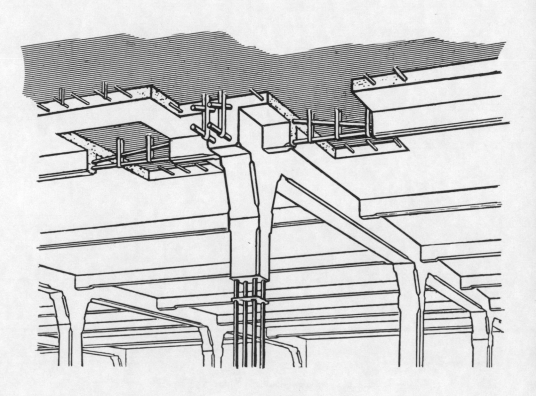

Diagram showing structural techniques developed by
François Hennebique (1842-1921)

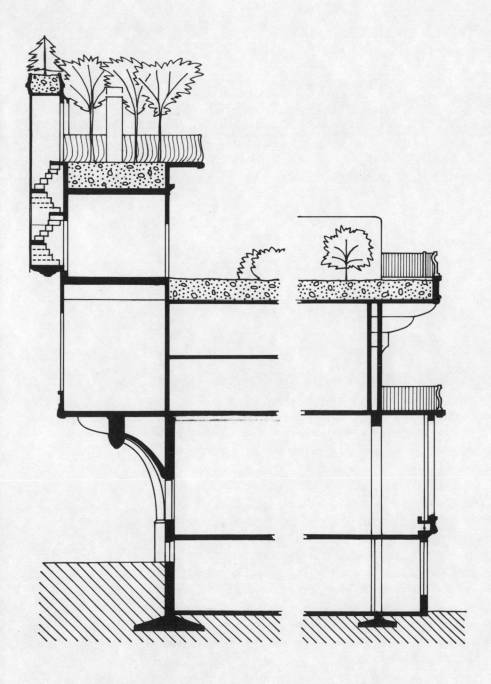

Villa at Bourg-la-Reine (1904) by François Hennebique.
Use of reinforced concrete made possible his exploitation of
the cantilever.

Plate 29
House at 25 bis Rue Franklin, Paris (1902–03)
by Auguste Perret

In his work, based on the experience gained by the engineers Hennebique, Freyssinet and Coignet, Perret achieved a substantial advance in the use of concrete. Just as Sullivan found an architectural expression for the steel skeleton (Plate 26), Perret found an expression for reinforced concrete. Next to Frank Lloyd Wright (Plate 35), who was working in America at the same time, Perret was one of the most important architects to make use of this new material. Both men evolved new structual laws which greatly influenced twentieth-century architecture.

One of the buildings that came to play a most important part in this development was the house in the Rue Franklin, built by Perret in 1902–03 and in which he had his offices for many years. The house was re-markable for the way in which the architect used the reinforced concrete skeleton for the framework, the floors and the walls. By this means he achieved a hitherto unknown free-dom of planning, as well as being able to fill in the outer walls very largely with glass. Perret's skill and the possibilities of the material were put to the test by the project-ing vertical blocks of the façade, which were not supported by the wall at the bottom, but were carried on recessed pillars. Also im-important is the fact that the reinforced concrete skeleton was no longer concealed but expressed, giving evidence of the actual structure of the house.'The house is lighter at the bottom . . .', wrote Sigfried Giedion, adding that the banks had refused a mortgage for the house on the grounds that it looked unsafe, as though it might collapse at any moment.

The façade is no longer treated as the surface of a cube, being an open form so constructed as to create an organic whole with the skeleton.

29

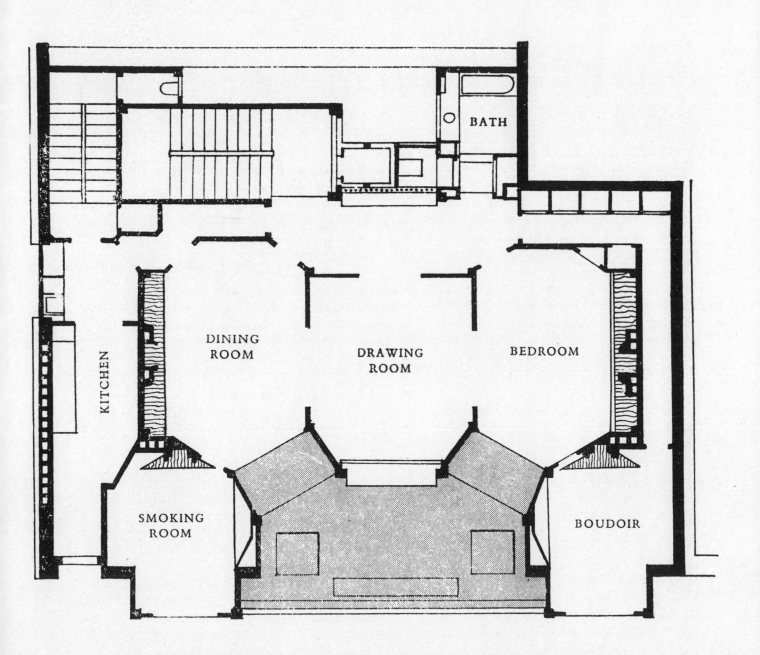

BATH

KITCHEN

DINING ROOM

DRAWING ROOM

BEDROOM

SMOKING ROOM

BOUDOIR

House at 25 bis Rue Franklin, Paris (1902–03) by Auguste Perret. Plan.

Plate 30
Church on the Steinhof, Vienna (1903–07) by
Otto Wagner

Otto Wagner's Steinhof church, Vienna, Antoni Gaudí's Church of the Sagrada Familia in Barcelona (Plate 10) and Frank Lloyd Wright's Unity Church in Oak Park (Plate 35) are the three most important early twentieth-century religious buildings. All three architects tried, in their own way, to produce churches adapted to contemporary life. The Steinhof church is the dominant feature in the complex of buildings which make up the Lower Austria Lunatic Asylum in south Vienna. The base of the building is made of irregular stones, above which the walls are clad with white slabs. The roof has a high dome. The plan is composed of two rectangles and these intersect, thus forming a cross-shape.

The large crossing underneath the dome dominates the form of the interior. The church therefore is almost symmetrical about one central point. The entrance is emphasized by pillars and a large arched window. The four bronze angels, by Otmar Schimkowitz, standing above the entrance on pillars, repeat the motif of the bronze figures on the two small towers on the entrance side of the building. The dome, higher on the outside than on the inside, and its cubic base recalls Palladio, as Wagner's biographer, Josef August Lux, has pointed out. The lateral thrust is taken up by an iron ring, which means that no buttresses are needed. Although limited to the materials available at the time, Wagner has here achieved his objective, '. . . a church for the people of today'.

The light, marble-clad interior, arranged around the altar and chancel, corresponds to the clearly composed exterior. The Viennese artists Schimkowitz, Moser, Eder and Luksch co-operated on the decoration of the building. Byzantine ornamentation fits into the geometrical pattern.

The ground-plan, as in all of Wagner's religious buildings, is reminiscent of Fischer von Erlach. The architect may also have seen K. F. Schinkel's Nicholas church in Potsdam, which this church resembles in many ways. So this unusual and long misunderstood building is in fact part of a continuing European architectural tradition. Its influence can be traced in Antonio Sant'Elia's brilliant designs, in Eliel Saarinen's Finnish buildings, and in Edwin Lutyens' design for Liverpool Cathedral.

As with most of Wagner's buildings, it was violently attacked when first built. Protests were made, particularly by the religious establishment, against the attempt to adapt a House of God to modern life. Hans Tietze claimed that it was, '. . . a church for irreligious people'. Josef August Lux, however, considered it friendly and full of character, and the Archbishop of Vienna, on the occasion of the dedication of the picture behind the main altar, called it a 'genuinely holy place'. The building is still considered controversial.

30

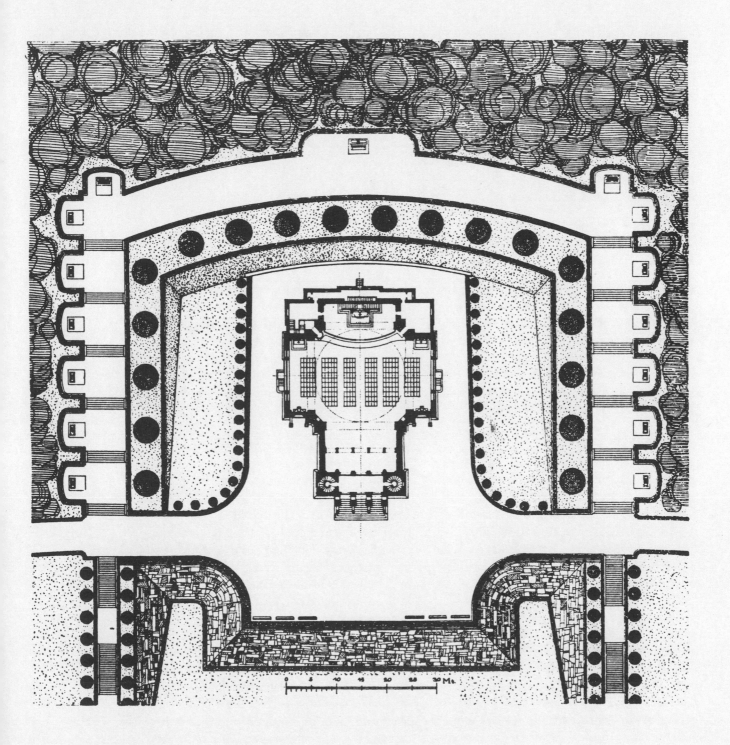

Church on the Steinhof, Vienna (1903–07) by Otto Wagner. Plan.

Plate 31
Austrian Post Office Savings building, Vienna
(1904–06, 1910–12) by Otto Wagner

The Vienna Post office Savings building by Otto Wagner is a key work in the development of twentieth-century architecture. Wagner entered the competition for this building in 1903. Even though he did not comply with the conditions, putting all the counters in one room, he won first prize and was awarded the commission. He put the counters in the courtyard of the building under one huge glass roof.

The massive six-storey structure, with its enormous ornamental roof decorations, was built from 1904-06. Situated in Georg Koch Square, the building is one of the few modern buildings to fit entirely successfully into its environment. Between 1910 and 1912, a special room for dealings in securities was added.

The exterior skin of the building is made weather resistant, on the street side, by the use of granite facing on the base and white Sterzing marble slabs above. On the courtyard side it is faced entirely with ceramic slabs, which are held in place with aluminium bolts arranged in a geometric pattern–a kind of functional ornament. The strict symmetry of the entrance façade is emphasized by the central element and balcony in front of the governor's room and by the letters beneath the roof works.

The glass covered hall (see plate) had a clarity and lightness not previously achieved and is still impressive today. This functional, light building was built long before the arrival of 'rational architecture'. It was a strong influence on the younger generation of architects at that time. The glass ceiling was originally intended to be suspended on wire cables beneath an outer glass roof. In the end it was fixed directly underneath the outer glass roof, separated by an iron load bearing structure. The hall has warm-air heating, and a special heater between the ceiling and the roof keeps the roof free of snow, ensuring that the interior is always well lit. The floor is made of glass bricks arranged in a geometric pattern, thus letting light into the basement as well.

The Post Office Savings building in Vienna was built with the most modern building materials of the time. All the ceilings in the rest of the building, for instance, are made of reinforced concrete, while the front roof supports, bolts, railings, warm-air fans and the supports on the inside, are made of aluminium or are aluminium-clad.

31

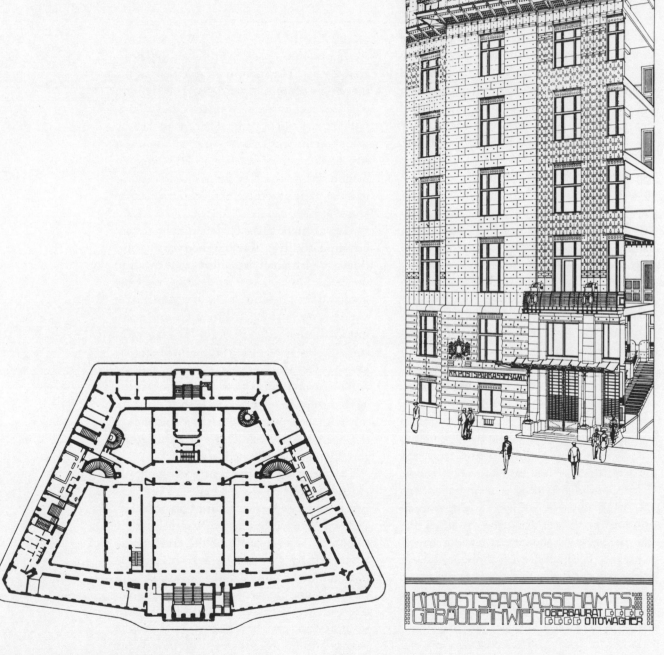

Austrian Post Office Savings building,
Vienna (1904–06, 1910–12) by Otto Wagner.
Plan and sectional drawing.

Plate 32
Palais Stoclet, Brussels (1905–11)
by Josef Hoffmann

During an extended stay in Vienna, Alphonse and Suzanne Stoclet became admirers of the young architect Josef Hoffmann after seeing his Moll house. Previously, Hoffmann had executed only a few minor buildings. In 1905 the Stoclets commissioned him to build them a house – a place which was to become one of the intellectual centres of Europe.

The building is situated at 281 Avenue Tervueren, in Woluwe St Pierre, an elegant suburb of Brussels. It is one of the most expensive products of the cult of luxury and good living at the turn of the century. It is partly two-, partly three-storeyed, based on a square module and on the colours black and white. The main façade has a hidden symmetry, concealed by the tower which narrows in steps towards the top, and by the annexes. The vertical glass band of the staircase window on the street façade leads visually up to the tower. The strict rectangularity of the building is relieved by the semicircular projections of the bow window next to the main entrance, and of the eastern end of the garden façade, and by the shallow recess in the façade which seems, from the garden, to draw one into the main room. Corresponding to these curving elements are, on the exterior, the large square framed window in the terrace wing between the staircase window and entrance to the courtyard, and the small flower-dome on the top of the tower, rather like the massive metal dome of the Vienna Secession building (Plate 25). The curved motif is repeated in the barrel-like casetting on the ceiling of the hall.

With its low, roofed entrance on the street façade (see plate), its monumental entrance pavilion, the terrace next to the staircase, the recessed 'bridge' over the entrance to the courtyard, the tower and the terraces to the east, the building seems to reach out into space in vertical and horizontal steps. The main material used on the outside is white marble slabs. The framing of all edges, corners, windows and doors, with gilt ornamental metal friezes, makes the walls seem like mere surfaces without any load bearing functions. This effect is heightened by the way the windows appear to have been superimposed on the structure afterwards.

The ground floor is defined, as in the house in the Rue Emile Janson by Horta (Plate 17), by a hall extending right through the house, onto a terrace leading into the garden. The ground floor also contains a dining room, a study, a drawing room and a music room, with a stage. To the west stretches the servants' wing, containing the kitchen, servants' quarters, garages and the entrance to the courtyard. It also shelters the garden from the wind. On the first floor are nurseries, bedrooms and bathrooms, and on the second, two childrens' rooms, guest rooms and servants' quarters.

The large hall in the centre of the house extends up to first-floor level. This idea was first introduced by Horta and Van de Velde, and was later adopted by Wright and Le Corbusier. The severity of the architecture is relieved by roof garden terraces, garden passages, and railings, and is overlaid with plastic decoration by Hans Metzner, filigree-like iron work round the balconies on the second floor on the garden side and the passage round the tower, and floral Art Nouveau metal railings running round the street and the east front of the building. On the inside, works by Gustav Klimt and

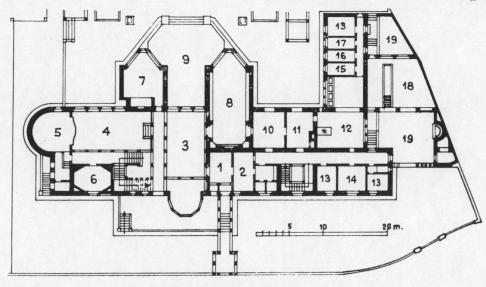

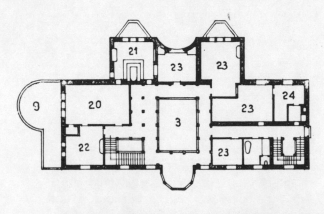

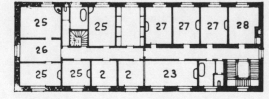

Palais Stoclet, Brussels (1905-11)
by Josef Hoffmann.
Floor plans.
1 Entrance
2 Cloakroom
3 Hall
4 Music room
5 Platform
6 Saloon
7 Smoking room
8 Dining room
9 Terrace
10 Breakfast room
11 Pantry
12 Kitchen
13 Servants' quarters
14 Servants' dining room
15 Coal storage
16 Food storage
17 Cold storage
18 Garage
19 Courtyard
20 Bedroom
21 Bathroom
22 Toilets
23 Nursery
24 Nurse's room
25 Servants' bedroom
26 Dressing room
27 Guest room
28 Workroom

George Minne, and the important Stoclet collection, are fitted as integral parts into the design.

During the process of building, Hoffmann altered his original designs considerably, working in close and friendly co-operation with his clients. The Palais Stoclet, which has undergone only minor alterations since it was built (the old copper roof was replaced, the drive into the courtyard slightly widened, and a few technical improvements made inside), is a splendid architectural expression of the last phase of bourgeois stylish life in the grand manner.

Plate 33
Casa Mila, Barcelona (1905–10) by Antoni Gaudí

The apartment building first became a significant problem towards the end of the eighteenth century. Theophil von Hansen's Heinrichshof in Vienna was one of the pioneering buildings of this type. The concentration of large numbers of people in towns demanded a new approach to the organization of mass residence. Gaudí, in his Casa Mila, has provided one of the few convincing solutions.

This apartment block, like almost all Gaudí's buildings, is incomplete. But even today it makes a lively impact. It is called 'La Pedrera' ('the stone quarry') because its shape is reminiscent of natural forms. The curved contours of the five horizontally ranged storeys are a motif unique in modern architecture. The building was originally intended to form the base for an enormous statue of the Virgin de la Gracia, but this was never completed because of the political disturbances in 1909. The strange demonic chimney forms on the roof were originally intended to form a religious bestiary. Without the central sculpture they are virtually meaningless. This has naturally led to a lot of misunderstanding.

The building stands at the corner of the Paseo de Gracia. It is composed of an emphatic base, five upper storeys (all with different floor plans) and a roof area. The roof apartments have recently been installed by the architect Barba Corsini. The apparent irregularity of the building turns out, on closer inspection, to be an artistically organized, basically symmetrical system. Outside the traffic runs along the Paseo de Gracia, inside there are two main courts, of different size, with curiously shaped wrought iron gates and stairs.

The whole of the exterior is roughened by hammer. This gives an even light-catching surface (*cf*. Plate 89) interrupted only by the iron railings on the balconies, produced in co-operation with Josep Jujol. Overall, the stone looks like reinforced concrete.

Shortly after the completion of the building in 1914, the poet Francesco Pujols wrote that only 'Wind, Sun and Rain, wrested by prayer and imprecation from the heavens, and forming stone as dictated by the laws of time, could be compared with the stone masons roughening the stone as directed by Gaudí'.

33

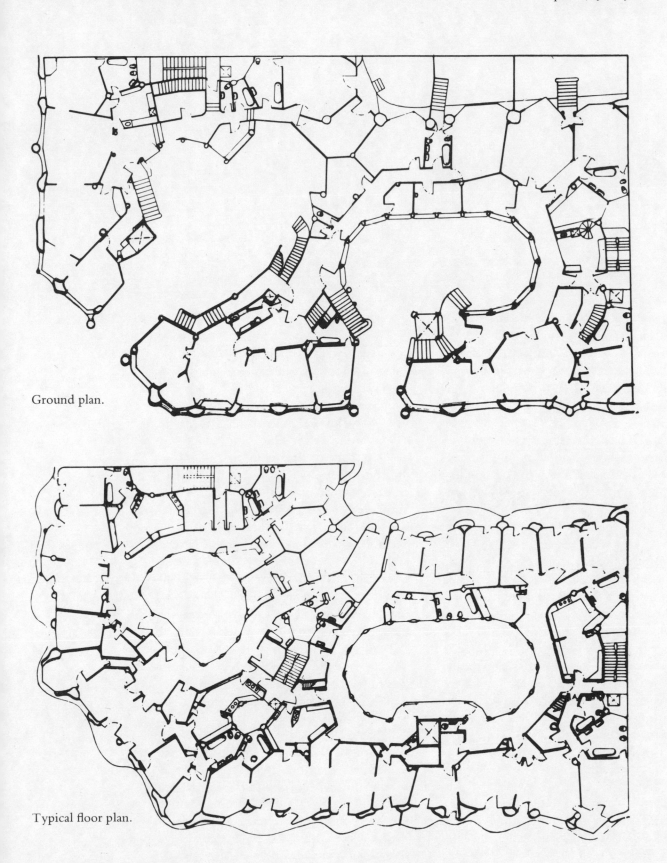

Ground plan.

Typical floor plan.

Casa Mila, Barcelona (1905-10) by Antoni Gaudí.

Plate 34
Chapel of the Güell Colony, Santa Coloma
near Barcelona (1908–13) by Antoni Gaudí

Gaudí executed several projects besides his great uncompleted church of the Sagrada Familia in Barcelona (Plate 10). In 1898 he was commissioned to build a small chapel for the Güell Colony, a workers' estate near Barcelona. Gaudí used this as an opportunity to experiment. For the first ten years he produced drawings and theory. The building work was not begun until 1908, and progressed so slowly that by 1915, when it was finally stopped, only the crypt and the entrance were completed. In 1913, Gaudí handed over the job to his pupil Francisco Berenguer. In 1915, the parts of the building which had been completed were dedicated.

This incomplete building is one of the most interesting of Gaudí's works. The vaults, bricked and ornamented with pieces of coloured tile, were not mathematically calculated, but were based on trial-and-error experiments using weights on strings. The supporting columns are set at various angles following the line of the arches. This allows them to take up both the vertical and horizontal thrusts, without buttresses. The whole seems almost to have grown rather than to have been built. Some of the pillars are made of a single stone, some of brick, some covered with a stone mosaic. They are as similar to, and as different from, each other as the pine trees in the surrounding wood.

In Santa Coloma, Gaudí used only simple materials, even rubbish, available in the neighbourhood. Columns and arches are decorated with broken tiles. The irregular windows are all different in form, colour and size – like flowers. In front of them are filigree iron railings which are in fact parts of some dismantled spinning machines from the nearby Güell cotton mill. Gaudí's creative use of materials produces a new awareness of surface values – a fact which was only recognized some time after his death. Regularly and irregularly laid bricks, raw and smoothed stone and glazed tiles are all intermixed in this building. Every window and every pillar in this brilliant fragment has its own shape. Gaudí also designed the seating in the interior himself.

There is a drawing in which Gaudí shows how he envisaged the church complete. It was to have had an overall sculptural form with towers similar to the towers of the Sagrada Familia in Barcelona.

In Santa Coloma hyperbolic paraboloids, curved walls, and sloping pillars are all used to achieve maximum strength. The experience acquired in this building was to help Gaudí in the execution of his huge Temple for the Poor in Barcelona. Although his daring ideas could not be executed with traditional materials, these experiments are forerunners of later structures, in completely different materials (Plate 61).

34

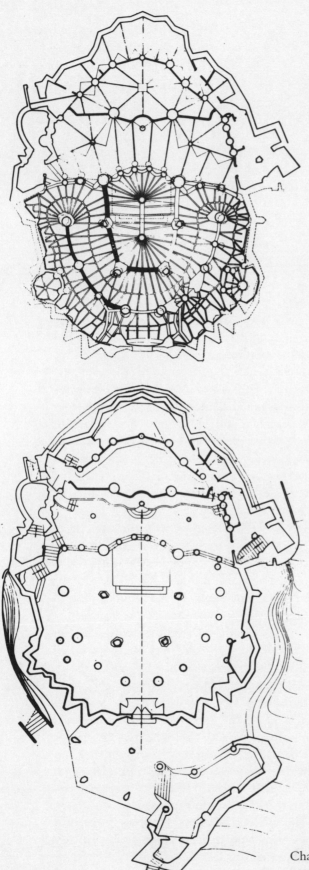

Chapel of the Güell Colony, Santa Coloma
near Barcelona (1908-13) by Antoni Gaudí. Plans.

Plate 35
Unity Church in Oak Park, Chicago (1906–07)
by Frank Lloyd Wright

Frank Lloyd Wright is the most important architect since 1850. He was originally influenced by the Chicago School and the work of his teacher, Louis Sullivan (Plates 12 and 26), by whom he was introduced to the concept of organic architecture.

One of his most important buildings, showing his transition from Art Nouveau towards a rational, technical approach determined by the nature of materials, is the Unity Church in Oak Park, Chicago (see also the Robie house in Chicago, Plate 38). In this church, as in contemporary buildings by Gaudí (Plates 10 and 34) and Wagner (Plate 30), we see a new approach to church architecture which takes no traditional forms for granted. The building is based on a square module, and the material used is concrete.

This was 'poured and tamped in forms in situ', as claimed in the description of the building published in 1906, obviously written by Wright himself. Form and materials complement each other superbly. Wright demonstrated the potential here of the new building material concrete.

The whole complex consists of an auditorium on Lake Street (Unity Temple), and a parish house (Unity House) on Kenilworth Street (linked to the back of the temple). The two parts of the building are connected by an entrance building with a rectangular plan and vestibule. Together they make up the shape of a cross. In its arrangement of space, the building is heavy and monumental; in its simplicity it is classical. It was something quite new, and was remarkably cheap: Wright had only $40,000 to spend.

On the inside of the upper storey of the building there is a discipline of form and decoration which was at the time new to Wright. The basic module is again the square, with a Greek cross inside it. The carefully planned relationship of cubic and linear elements, modified by differences in height, is repeated in the interlocking of flat surfaces and rectangular linear decoration which define the space. The lighting is almost entirely from above, which gives the required religious effect as well as being most practical. The lamps extend the cubic, rectangular composition right into the interior space. This idea foreshadows spatial concepts used in the Midway Garden Restaurant and was subsequently very influential in Europe (De Stijl, Bauhaus, Le Corbusier).

This period of Wright's architecture, in which the influence of Art Nouveau is still clearly to be seen, can also be connected with the cubist movement. Like the cubists in Europe, Wright was showing the way to a new treatment of space in art. Another point of similarity with the cubists is the colour scheme, strictly limited to brown, red and white, which is an important part of the total effect of the room. The cubists were restricting their colours, to brown, black and grey. The forms in the glass windows in the roof are very similar to the forms subsequently employed by Piet Mondrian, although he used very different colours.

35

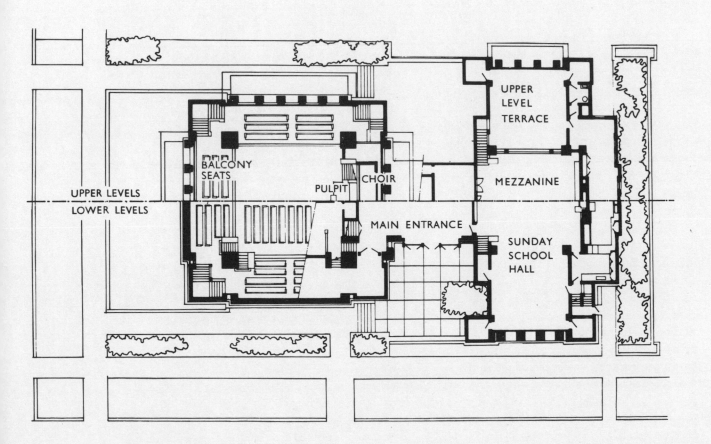

Unity Church in Oak Park, Chicago (1906–07) by Frank Lloyd Wright. Plan.

Plate 36
Hochzeitsturm (Wedding Tower) on the
Mathildenhöhe, Darmstadt (1907) by Joseph
Maria Olbrich

After attracting a lot of attention with his building for the Vienna Secession (Plate 25), Olbrich was invited by the Grand Duke Ernst Ludwig to Darmstadt, to take charge of one of the great exhibitions of modern architecture, entitled 'Ein Dokument Deutscher Kunst' ('A Document of German Art'), and begin building the artists' colony on the Mathildenhöhe (the heights of Mathilda).

Although he also brought in Peter Behrens to work with him, Olbrich executed most of the buildings himself, including the Christiansen, Habich, Deiters, Keller and Glückert houses. He also designed the gardens, the main entrance to the artists' colony, the huge Ernst Ludwig House, his own private house, the orchestra stand, and the Pavilion of the Arts. He planned the whole settlement, which makes this one of the very few early examples of Art Nouveau town planning. He also built, in other parts of Darmstadt, the Ganss house (1902), the Prediger house (1904), various tombs and fountains, and the railway station (1907).

The Hochzeitsturm on the Mathildenhöhe, was completed in 1907 and is the greatest of Olbrich's Darmstadt buildings. It crowns the whole environmental complex. With its arch-shaped roof, the tower is reminiscent of Hanseatic brick buildings, and is a dominant feature of the town, of the kind demanded ten years later by Bruno Taut for his 'expressionist' towns. The tower was built to celebrate the wedding of the Grand Duke and is a symbolic accent in an area full of symbols of Life and Marriage. Architecture, garden, design, sculpture and poetry all combine in this thematically planned work of art.

The simple arrangement of the windows, asymmetrically composed, in horizontal bands, and running round the corner of the tower – a motif used by Shaw forty years earlier in the Old Swan House in London (Plate 7) – influenced later architects. Together the Hochzeitsturm and Palace of Free Arts (also built in 1907) form a spatially related group of buildings and represent a new approach to town planning.

36

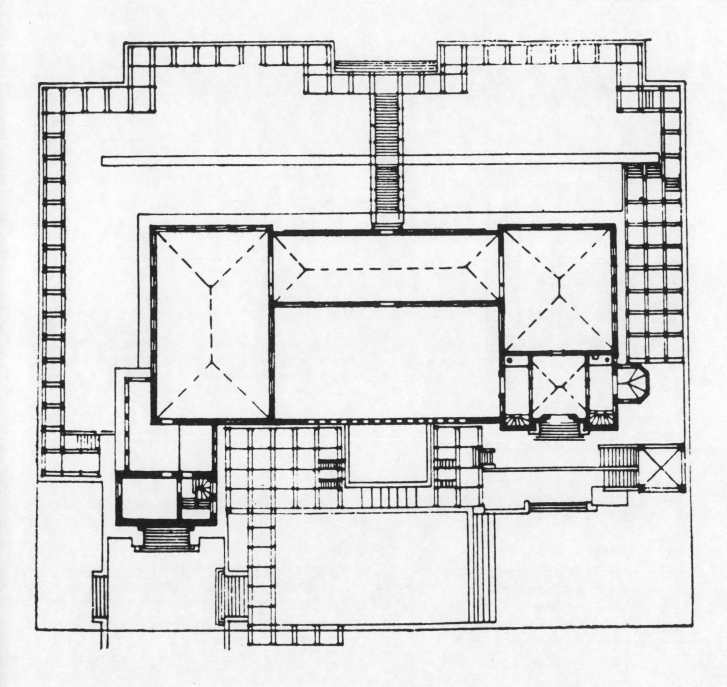

Hochzeitsturm (Wedding Tower) and Exhibition buildings on the Mathildenhöhe, Darmstadt (1907) by Joseph Maria Olbrich. Plan.

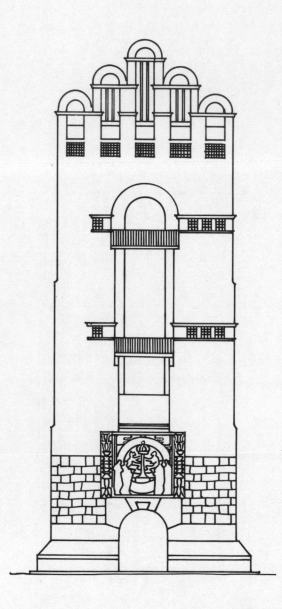

Preliminary design for the Hochzeitsturm.

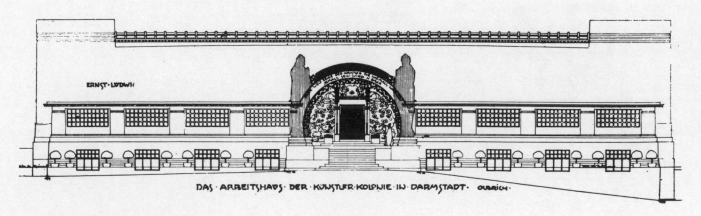

Ernst Ludwig house, Mathildenhöhe Settlement, Darmstadt (1899)
by Joseph Maria Olbrich. Front elevation.

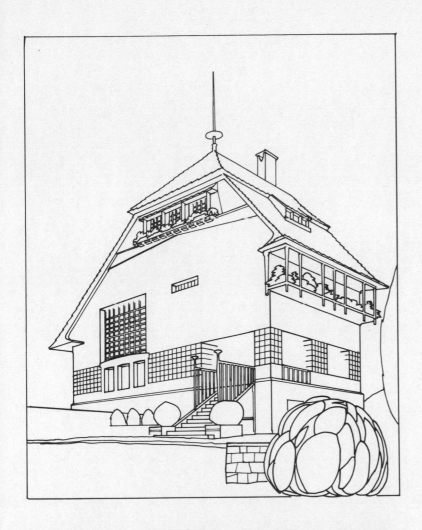

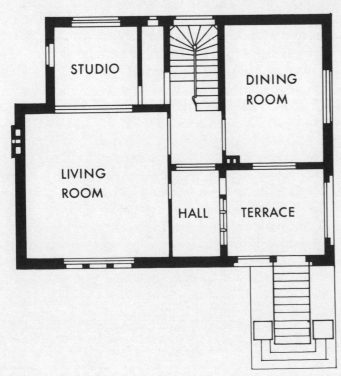

Olbrich house, Mathildenhöhe
Settlement, Darmstadt (1900)
by Joseph Maria Olbrich. Drawing and plan.

Plate 37
*American Bar (previously Kärntnerbar), Vienna
(1907) by Adolf Loos*

Before executing his very few commissions for new buildings (Plate 41) Adolf Loos had designed some interiors in which his tremendous architectural ability was demonstrated in microcosm. One of the best of these interiors is the bar in the Kärntner Passage in Vienna, recently restored. Exterior and interior were originally designed as one inseparable unit. Both windows were framed on the outside with Skyros marble cladding and the façade was developed symmetrically around the central entrance door. Even the name of the bar, picked out in broken glass, fitted into the overall design.

Unlike the exterior, which is now altered, the interior can be seen in its original form. The dimensions of the very small space ($11 \times 23 \times 11$ feet) were completely changed by interior effects. To the left of the entrance, the bar stretches along the entire length of the room. The wall behind it, like all the other walls in the room, is extended visually by mirrors. The ceiling extends the space upwards with its coffered forms. Opposite the bar are two seating-bays, with tables. The expensive furnishing materials are delicately matched, and were all chosen to heighten the effect of quality and spaciousness. The floor is made of black and white tiles, the walls are covered with dark mahogany, the seats are upholstered in black leather and the ceiling is covered with a yellowish brown marble. All lighting is indirect, with the tables lit inside. A door between the seating-bays leads to the cloakroom in the basement, where mirrors set at an angle extend the room.

The atmosphere in this little bar is cosily exclusive. As usual, Loos combined distinction and comfort. Loos changed the whole nature of the room by means of illusion, and in so doing created a spatial harmony whose impact cannot be missed by anyone who enters the bar.

37

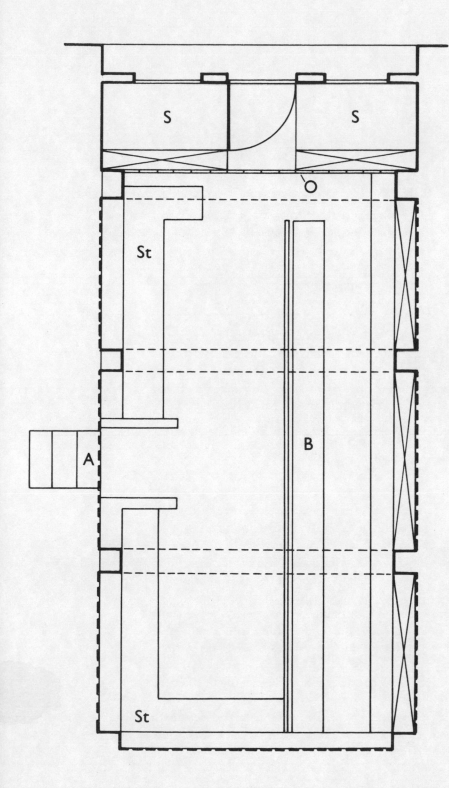

American Bar (previously Kärntnerbar),
Vienna (1907) by Adolf Loos.
Plan.
A Stairway down to cloakroom
B Bar
O Panel of translucent onyx squares
   above inside of entrance
S Storage
St Seating
   Thick dotted lines for mirrors.

Plate 38
Robie house, Chicago (1909)
by Frank Lloyd Wright

The house built for Frederick C. Robie, which now forms part of the University of Chicago, is the peak of Frank Lloyd Wright's prairie architecture. It was built to run alongside a street on a narrow site in the south of Chicago, at that time a fairly sparsely populated area. The building has all the characteristic features of Wright's new architecture. The house develops outwards from a central point, the chimney, in cubic layers arranged in such a way as to draw exterior space into the house. The living area is raised above the ground level. When the house was first built this room afforded a much more extensive view than is now possible. The living area merges with the dining area. Wright's concept of flowing space, developed before 1900, can be seen in this central part of the house, particularly in the masterly handling of the window wall, whose wooden cladding seems to merge into the roof and the built-in furniture.

Wright had repeatedly declared, quoting Lao Tse, that the reality of a house was not the four walls and the roof, but the space which they enclosed. Originally, the floor in front of the chimney sloped slightly downwards and there was a seat on the north side with a view onto the regular row of windows, which gave this side of the room the appearance of an ornamentally pierced wall. On the ground floor there are billiards, play-rooms, guest rooms, a kitchen, and rooms for servants, on an axis parallel to that of the living area. The bedroom, with its own balcony, like all the other rooms, is on the smaller third storey.

There is a superb balance between the horizontal brick surfaces edged with concrete and the horizontal, slightly sloping, roofs, held together by the verticals of the chimney. Admirers of this house have often compared it with a ship, and soon after being completed, it was nicknamed the 'battle ship'. The different horizontal levels are like decks, the balconies like bridges, the chimney a mast.

The garage, which has since been altered, was originally designed as an integral part of the building. The subordination of the whole building to an overriding integral design is reminiscent of the structuring of space by means of surface and lines which was at that time being achieved by the cubists in Europe. This building is perhaps the purest expression of the architecture of the 'machine age' which Wright wrote about. It is the best illustration of pre-First-World-War American architecture in the context of international architectural developments. For the first time an American architect had developed a classic expression of modern architecture, fit to be placed alongside the great buildings of previous centuries.

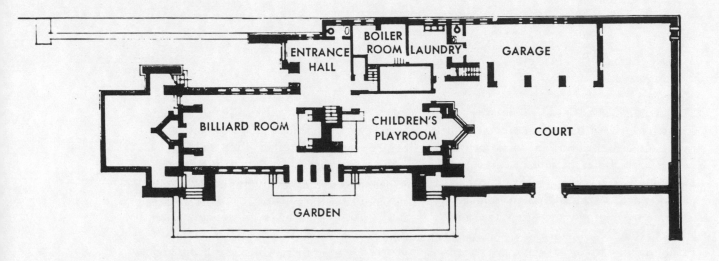

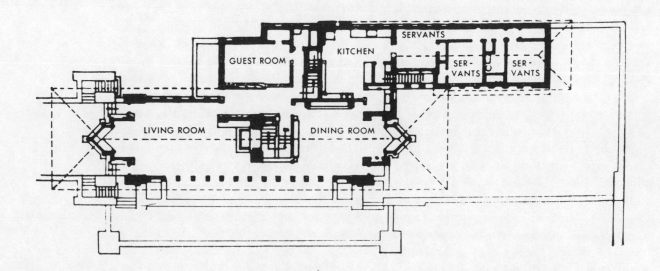

Robie house, Chicago (1909) by Frank Lloyd Wright.
Plans, ground floor and first floor.

Plate 39
Railway Station, Helsinki (1910–14)
by Eliel Saarinen

The starting-point of modern Finnish architecture, which has been so important in the twentieth century, was the main railway station in Helsinki by Eliel Saarinen, the solution of a modern building problem. Saarinen had previously built a number of important buildings, including the much admired Finnish Pavilion for the World Exhibition in Paris in 1900 and the National Museum in Helsinki (1901). He had, till then, always worked with Lindgren and Gesellius, who later became his brother-in-law. In 1904, the team won the competition for the design of the railway station for the Finnish capital. But Saarinen revised the plans of the building himself before it was built (1910–14), and the station can be regarded as very largely Saarinen's own work.

The plan is symmetrical with the exception of the tower on the south-east corner. It has three large halls covered with reinforced concrete and glass, and powerful round arches in the entrance portal and in the roof over the platforms. Its forms are predominantly Neo-Romanesque and it is thus closely linked with the works of the American architect H. H. Richardson (Plates 9 and 11). The structural design and the geometric ornamentation of the main entrance make this building a symbol of the break in Finnish architecture from previously predominant local tradition. The vertically composed granite walls and the vaulted copper roofs contrast with each other. The building is symmetrical about the arched main entrance, which is flanked by four monumental sculptures each carrying a lamp; the latter are by Emil Wikström. The arrangement of the interior can be clearly seen on the exterior, a practical development which was then new.

Helsinki station is one of a number of major new railway buildings which were erected in the first decades of the twentieth century, including the new Stuttgart station by Paul Bonatz (1913–27) and Darmstadt station by Joseph Maria Olbrich (1907). But this is the most important building from the period of transition leading towards a new rational architecture, and the first building of its type in Finland. After this Finnish architecture rapidly gained a world wide reputation (Plates 56, 72, and 91).

Eliel Saarinen later became famous for his town hall in Lahti and his prize-winning design for the Chicago Tribune building. After this success, Saarinen went to the U.S.A., where, with his son, Eero Saarinen, he had a tremendous influence over the new generation of architects. Important buildings by his son (Plates 70 and 80) brought modern Finnish architecture fame and recognition throughout the world.

39

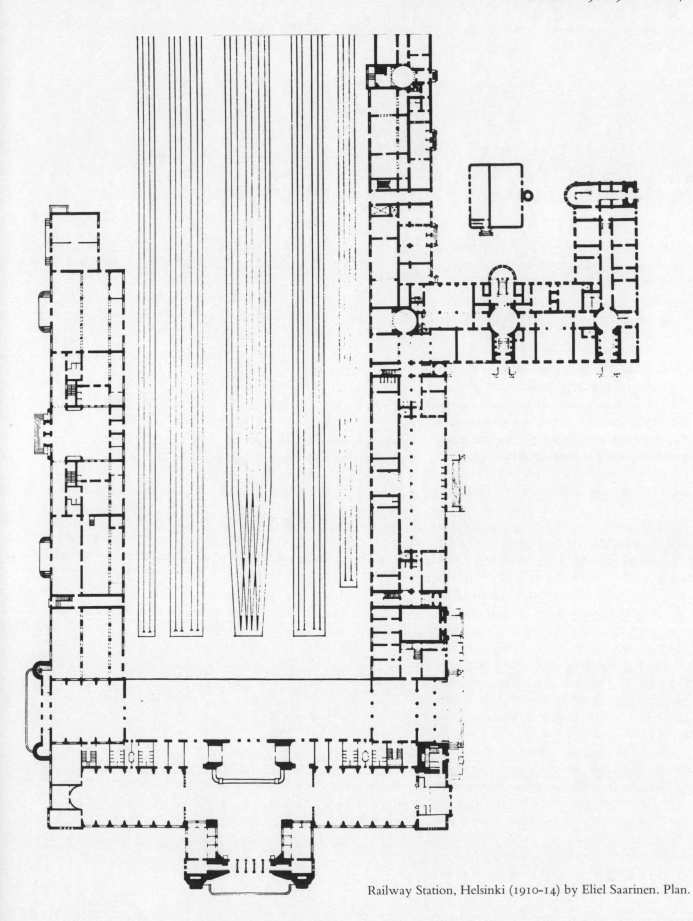

Railway Station, Helsinki (1910–14) by Eliel Saarinen. Plan.

Plate 40
AEG Turbine Factory, Berlin (1909)
by Peter Behrens

Walter Gropius, a pupil of Peter Behrens, recognizing the importance of the AEG Turbine Factory, compared it to Contamin and Dutert's great Machine Hall at the 1889 Paris Exhibition. Although the dimensions of the two buildings are quite different – the Machine Hall had a free span of 345 feet – they do have a certain similarity in that both structures rest on the articulated supports. Walter Gropius wrote, in 1911, 'this building is the only example, so far, of an individualistic artistic treatment of a modern engineering structure with modern building materials (iron and steel). It is a monumental building in the best sense of the word making a mockery of the idea that iron and steel are characterless materials.' Gropius himself was later to develop the tradition of industrial architecture initiated here (Plate 43).

Practicality and monumentality are indeed powerfully united in this building. Iron and glass are combined. The iron supports taper towards the base, as in Contamin's Machine Hall. The glass surfaces of the exterior walls slope slightly inwards. A new plasticity was achieved with new, synthetic materials previously regarded as un-architectural. As soon as it was completed, the factory was as strongly criticized as praised. Ludwig Hilberseimer attacked the huge, superfluous corner pylons. Admirers praised the uncompromising use of iron and steel.

Richard Hamann, the art historian, has described this early example of German industrial building: 'In this factory', he writes, 'construction takes place inside constructive art and rational creation is united with rational production.'

40

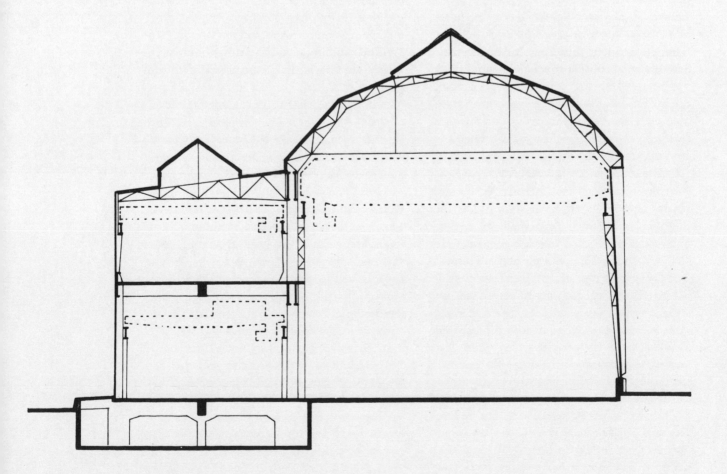

AEG Turbine Factory, Berlin (1909) by Peter Behrens. Section.

Plate 41
Store on the Michaelerplatz, Vienna (1910–11)
by Adolf Loos

Adolf Loos was already over forty when, after having worked on several smaller commissions (Plate 37), he was finally given an opportunity to design a major urban building. The Goldman and Salatsch Building on the Michaelerplatz stands in a dominant position between two streets, the Herrengasse and the Kohlmarkt, leading into a square. It is near the Classical façade of St Michael's church and opposite the neo-Baroque façade of the Hofburg (designed by Semper and von Hasenauer, begun 1881).

The building had almost no decoration on it. This so disturbed the contemporary Viennese that building work had to be stopped for a time, and the architect became seriously ill. On close inspection the building can be seen to be most carefully composed. The domestic and commercial sectors are clearly separated from each other by the use of different materials and types of façade, above and below. The two lower storeys are clad with Cippolino marble from Euboea. The four residential storeys above are simply plastered. The regularly distributed windows were originally cut straight into the walls without any decoration. This was considered so intolerable by people at the time that various suggestions were made for altering the façade, and in the end totally inappropriate flower boxes were added.

The two lower storeys facing the square were originally left virtually open by Loos, thus seeming to bring the square into the building. The shop windows, like the flower boxes, are a subsequent addition. This was one of the first porch façades. The passer-by could look at the window displays at leisure before actually going into the shop. The ground floor containing the shops extends into the storey above, with a mezzanine floor above it, originally containing the dressing and cutting rooms of the firm Goldman and Salatsch. The visually arresting columns which support the mezzanine storey stand on a step which compensates the difference in levels between Herrengasse and Kohlmarkt (about one and a half feet).

The corners of the building on the side facing the square project forward almost imperceptibly, making the façade appear to close off the square. The slight angle in the wall can be seen on the two horizontal cornices running across the façade, on the marble cladding of the ground floor, on the plastered middle section and on the completely undecorated copper covered roof. This was a compositional technique previously formulated by Louis Sullivan (Plate 12), both in theory and practice, in his approach to the high-rise office block. The large projecting section of the Herrengasse façade, made necessary by the projecting corners, is balanced by making the last vertical row of windows project also.

This building, brilliant in its structure, its use of materials and the way it fits, unostentatious and yet dominant, into the environment, is the only major commission which Adolf Loos managed to execute. His remaining plans, with the exception of a few pioneering single family residences and small interior decoration jobs, never got beyond the drawing board.

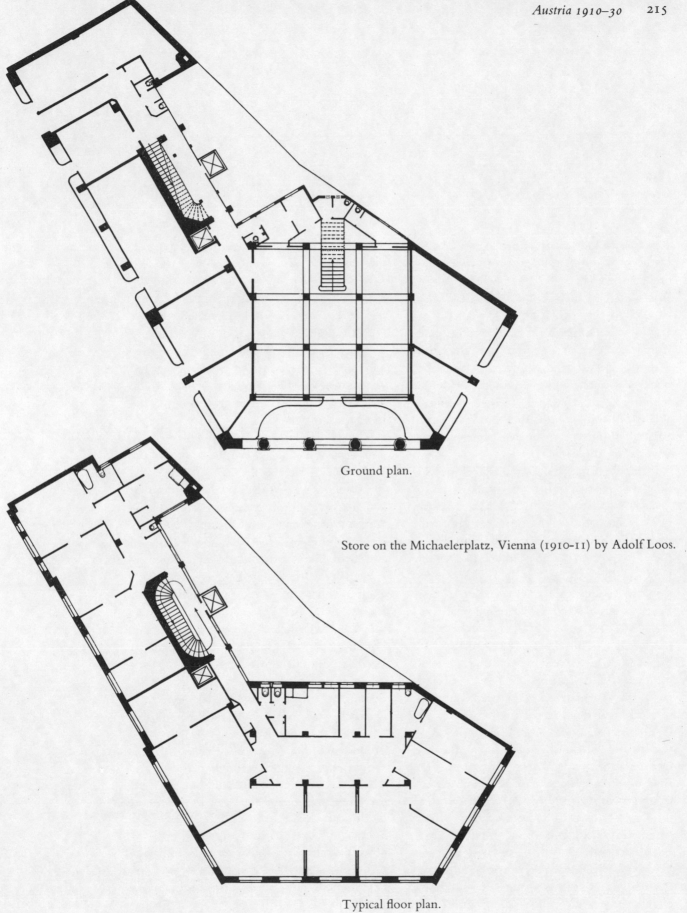

Ground plan.

Store on the Michaelerplatz, Vienna (1910–11) by Adolf Loos.

Typical floor plan.

Plate 42
Commercial building, Breslau (1911)
by Hans Poelzig

This is one of the earliest European solutions of the problem of the administrative office block. It was built before the First World War and can therefore be regarded as a parallel to the earlier office towers in the U.S.A. (Plates 12 and 14). The predominant technique used in America was the steel skeleton. In Europe it was the new synthetic material concrete which was used in skeleton building (Plates 29 and 60). This building is also comparable with the Goldman and Salatsch Building on the Michaelerplatz in Vienna by Adolf Loos (Plate 41).

Hans Poelzig's work and development ran parallel to that of Peter Behrens (Plates 40 and 47). Between them they laid the foundations of modern German architecture. This subsequently developed in two main directions: the rationalism of architects like Walter Gropius (Plates 43 and 50) and the expressionism of Erich Mendelsohn (Plate 46). Poelzig was Director of the Breslau Academy from 1903 to 1916 and had a very wide knowledge of all types of architecture. In his work he gave valid expression to several different stylistic concepts. He also managed to use the new material, reinforced concrete, in a way that fitted its nature.

In this office building in Breslau, he took full advantage of the potential of the reinforced concrete skeleton structure. The four upper storeys are horizontally composed by means of concrete bands underneath the windows (where the names of firms were originally fixed) and ornamental railings. Each floor projects a little beyond the one below it. This involved the use of concrete beams and supports inside the building, enabling the walls to be filled in with large glass surfaces. The windows are very broad, like windows in Chicago (*cf.* Plate 26), and subdivided into three parts. These, and the massive tapering columns, give the building its characteristic rhythm. The fourth storey recedes slightly, leaving room for a balcony enclosed by an ornamental balustrade corresponding to the concrete bands below the other storeys. The triple rhythm of the windows is repeated, though smaller, in the low attic storey.

The corner site of the building is fully exploited by Poelzig. The relationship of the building complex to the street corner, and the receding top storey, are both points of similarity with the original form of Sullivan's Carson, Pirie and Scott Store (Plate 26).

Theodor Heuss, Poelzig's biographer, said of this building, '. . . there is something inhibited in the functional connection between column and beam by means of consoles and the massive bases of the heavy rectangular pillars.' Nevertheless, he singles out this building, one of the first office blocks in Europe to use the new techniques, as a work of 'pioneering daring'. Other buildings designed at this time by Poelzig include a chemical factory in Luban near Posen (1911–12), a water tower in Posen (1911), a group of residential buildings in Breslau (1910–21), and exhibition buildings in Breslau (1913). The Breslau Commercial building is more consistent and logical than any of these, and is also more important. It still makes a lively and individualistic impact. It is given a sculptural quality by its imperceptibly projecting storeys, its contrasting system of tapering vertical supports, its recessed upper storey, and its shell-like vaulted roof.

42

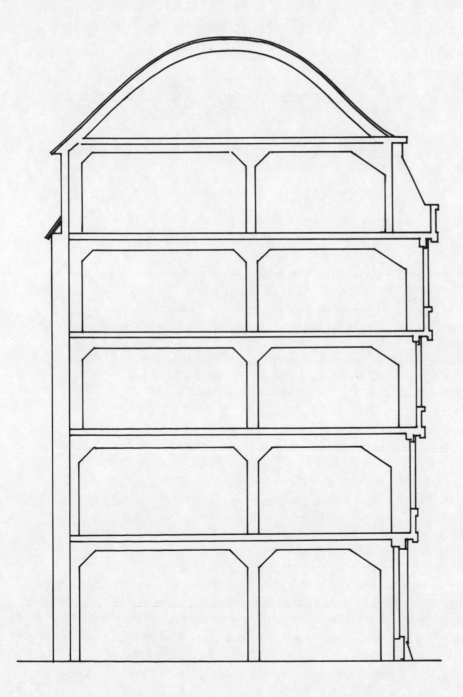

Commercial building, Breslau (1911) by Hans Poelzig. Section.

Plate 43
Fagus Shoe-last Factory, Alfeld an der Leine
(1911–13) by Walter Gropius

On 29 January 1911, Walter Gropius gave a lecture in the Folkwang Museum in Hagen entitled, 'Monumental art and industrial building'. In this lecture he explained his own approach to a modern industrial architecture, comparing it with examples of the theories and buildings of his teacher, Peter Behrens, and showing his own designs for a shoe-last factory to be built near Hanover.

This building, one of the epoch-making works of modern architecture, was constructed in co-operation with Adolf Meyer in 1913. Nikolaus Pevsner has called it the beginning of twentieth-century architecture. It is distinguished from Peter Behrens' industrial buildings chiefly by the direct way it deals with the technical process of production, dispensing with expressive elements (Plate 40). Gropius designed the entire building, down to the minutest detail, after a thorough analysis of the work which was to be done in it.

The young architect, who until then had not built anything independently, offered his services to his clients in a letter, in which he said, 'May I submit my services as an architect for the splendid new factory which you intend to build. I am thoroughly acquainted with all the problems of this type of building, having worked under Professor Peter Behrens on the new factory buildings for AEG. I can offer you an artistic and practical design' (7 December 1910). As a result, Gropius was given an opportunity to demonstrate the objectives of modern architure, and he announced its programme in this building long before founding the Bauhaus. Its basic principles were total functionalism, absence of ornamentation, straightforward and honest use of modern materials, and rejection of symbolism.

The characteristic feature of this simply composed three-storey building is its glass façade (see plate). Narrow strips of yellow brick form the base and the top of the building, and the nine verticals which subdivide the glass walls, make, as it were, a framework for the steel-mounted glass. It was the first time that a factory had been built with non-load-bearing walls – a feature clearly demonstrated by the absence of supports at the corners of the building. This is the first application of the curtain wall technique, later to become so widespread. The glass walls, extending round the corners of the factory, and the muted colours of the materials, give the building a transparency which suits its function. In spite of being built more than half a century ago, it looks like a modern building, even today.

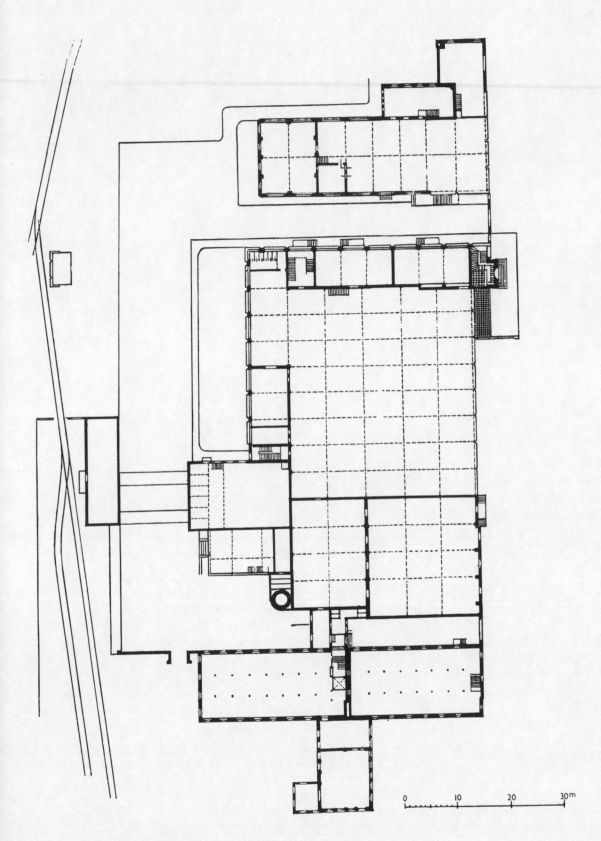

Fagus Shoe-last Factory, Alfeld an der Leine (1911–13)
by Walter Gropius. Plan.

Plate 44
Dodge house, Los Angeles (1915–16)
by Irving Gill

This building, commissioned in 1914 by Walter Luther Dodge, was completed in 1916. It was designed by Irving Gill and stood at 950 North King's Road, Los Angeles. It is one of the many houses built for families of big bankers, landowners and industrialists in the first two decades of the twentieth century, and as such can be classed with the Solvay house by Horta (Plate 18), Windy Hill by Mackintosh (Plate 23) and the Palais Stoclet by Hoffmann (Plate 32).

It is a key building in the development of architecture on the West Coast of America (and is a seldom-recognized parallel to the achievements of Hoffmann in Brussels (Plate 32) and Adolf Loos in Vienna a few years earlier). This tradition was later continued by the architect R. M. Schindler (Plate 52) who emigrated from Austria to the United States of America.

Before this building, Irving Gill had been known mainly for his single-family houses in the Bay Region Style. He had tried to give this style a Mexican flavour, suited to Los Angeles. With the Dodge house, he developed a new technique, composing the form of the house out of white cubes arranged loosely on the large site.

The house and its large garden deliberately face away from the street. The large living room on the ground floor gives onto the garden, forming part of the irregular, terrace-like rear elevation of the building. The clear, geometrical, basic forms of the house, the way it is broken up by terraces, roof-gardens and balconies, and the way the windows, gently disturbing the strict form of the building itself, are cut into the walls, are all reminiscent of Loos.

Until recently it was one of the few early examples of this revolutionary technique still extant in its original form, in its original surroundings. The site was, however, valuable for development, and plans were submitted for putting up several apartment blocks on the site. Town planners put forward proposals for preserving the building but it was demolished in 1970.

44

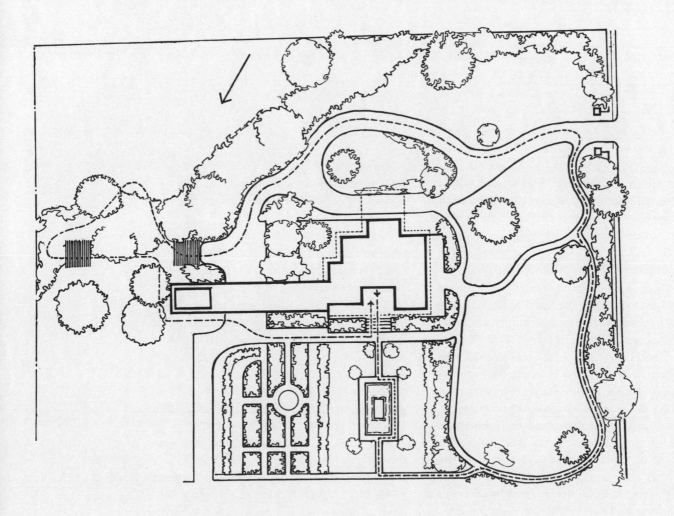

Dodge House, Los Angeles (1915-16) by Irving Gill. Plan.

Plate 45 (page 231)
Fiat Works, with car track, Lingotto near Turin
(1919–23) by Giacomo Matté-Trucco

Futurism in architecture was on the whole limited to manifestos and treatises (although it should be remembered that there was a time when Frank Lloyd Wright was considered a futurist). The real leader of the Italian futurists was Antonio Sant'Elia, who produced a number of designs, but never managed to execute any buildings. The result was that Italian architecture remained on the whole conservative after the First World War, and only a few of its buildings can be counted as having any international significance. One of these is the Fiat works in Turin, an enormous industrial complex typical of the rational trend in architecture at the time. The racing car was the central feature of the lyrical exaggerations of the futurists and here, indeed, it is the car for which this building, determined by clear cut economic and technological requirements, was constructed. Speed and dynamism are no longer merely elements in a utopian futurist theory; here they have become translated into reality.

The roof forms a test track 1,200 yards long and 27 yards wide, reached by a spiral ramp leading up through several floors. Building and road are combined for the first time. This echoes distantly some of the futurists' ideas, but it is so rationalized that little of the pre-war emotional content remains. Morton Shand compared the reinforced concrete system of supports of the storeys with organic forms. It seemed to pre-empt the forms later developed by Pier Luigi Nervi.

It was the use made of the roof that was the real breakthrough. Le Corbusier later used roofs for playgrounds, swimming pools, etc. Using it for testing cars was, however, and remains, unique in modern architecture. The building is still in use.

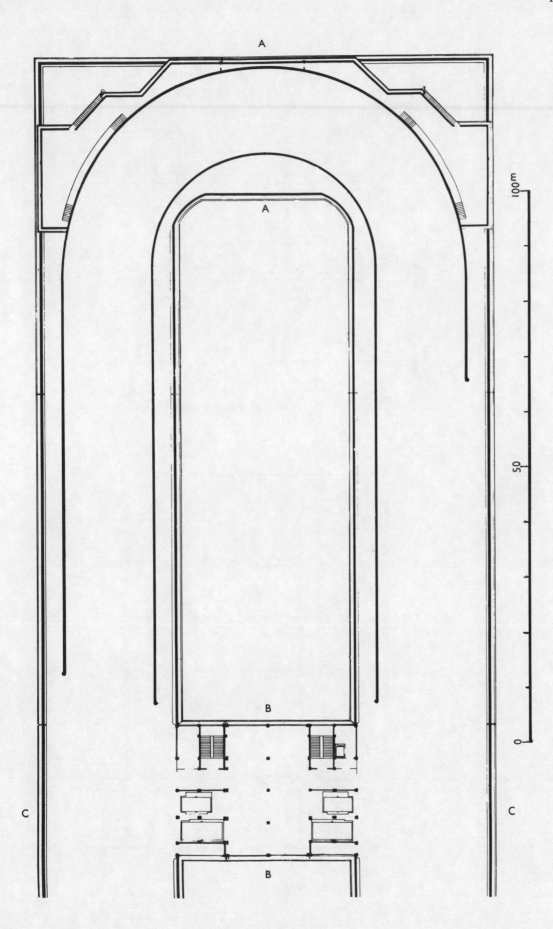

Fiat Works, Lingotto near Turin (1919–23)
by Giacomo Matté-Trucco.
Plan, north end of car testing track on roof.

Section through north corner. A

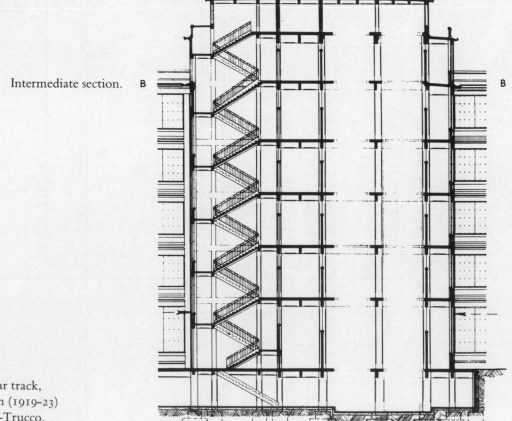

Intermediate section. B

Fiat Works, with car track,
Lingotto near Turin (1919-23)
by Giacomo Matté-Trucco.

45

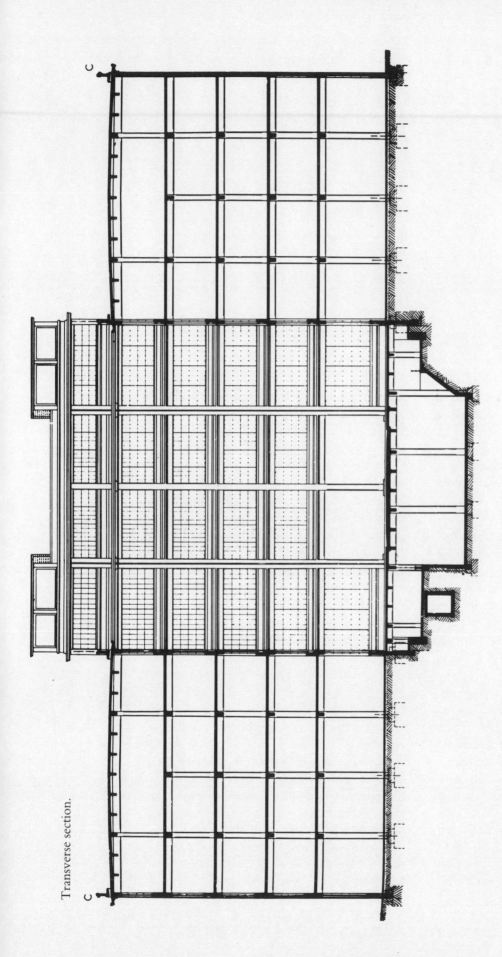

Transverse section.

Fiat Works, with car track, Lingotto near
Turin (1919–23) by Giacomo Matté-Trucco.

Plate 46
Einstein Observatory, Potsdam (1919–21) by
Erich Mendelsohn

Erich Mendelsohn started working on the Einstein Observatory while serving as a soldier in Ilipau. In several letters he referred to it as his 'friendly' project, a contrast to the harsh realities of war. In a letter dated 24 June 1917, he wrote below some sketches, 'Mostly "friendly", tellurian and planetarian'. On 29/30 October 1917 he wrote to Dr Freundlich (the name means 'friendly' in German), the assistant of Einstein, 'My sketches are a record, an outline of a sudden insight I have had. They are architecture, and should be seen as a whole, and they should be kept as such.' Mendelsohn is here voicing a basic expressionist attitude, of which the Einstein Observatory at Neubabelsberg, Potsdam, is a typical example.

The sketches for the building are mostly very small, and executed in chalk, ink or pencil, with an intense moving line. They fully express the dynamic, powerful, streamlined emotionality of the finished building. 'We have defined dynamism in architecture as the logical expression of the movement inherent in building materials; its danger is like the danger inherent in the undisciplined nature of blood . . .', as Mendelsohn himself once put it. When Mendelsohn's drawings were shown in the Cassirer Gallery in Berlin in 1919, they attracted a lot of attention, and

when the building was actually finished, it became the sensation of the time.

It should be remembered that it was the first work of a young architect, still under thirty-two, who had previously been in contact with Art Nouveau artists such as Van de Velde and Obrist, and was an admirer of expressionists like Kandinsky and Marc. He was certainly influenced by the Vienna Jugendstil architects, and probably also by Italian futurists (Sant'Elia). But the new sculptural qualities of the building go well beyond the expressionist visions of contemporary German artists. It was not possible to use very much concrete and brick is the primary building material. But this is used so that it looks like reinforced concrete. This building, and his hat factory at Luckenwalde, are both typical of one fairly short stage of Mendelsohn's development.

The basic form of the building is elongated, ship-like, crowned by a tower containing a telescope. The observatory was built for Albert Einstein, who at the time was developing his theory of relativity, for which he needed to be able to make certain astrophysical measurements. Cosmic rays were led through the telescope down into an underground laboratory. All the interior

Einstein Observatory, Potsdam (1919–21)
by Erich Mendelsohn.
Plan and elevation.

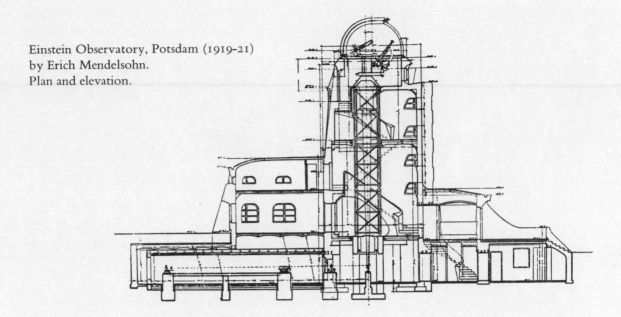

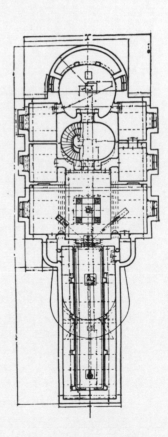

rooms are organized strictly in accordance with scientific requirements, and do not correspond to the sculpturally moulded forms of the exterior, arranged symmetrically, like the bridges of a giant ocean liner. The entrance is a large monumental configuration, a quite superfluous gesture from a functional point of view. Curved windows are recessed into the corners of the building like portholes. Streamlining principles, later rediscovered by industrial designers, are clearly visible here. Adolf Behne, commenting on the importance of the concept of movement in this building, described the entrance as 'sucking', the walls 'leading' and the staircase 'swinging'.

Mendelsohn's own contemporaries stressed the monumental, symbolic nature of the building. Robert Manning said in 1925 that it was, '. . . a travesty of Einstein's contribution and a monument to complication and bewilderment . . .' Einstein himself, however, recognized the building for what it was intended to be. He called it organic, which gave the architect completely new ideas, and led him towards a more disciplined, rational concept of architecture. This astrophysical institute is an architectural and sculptural monument to one of the outstanding men of learning of our times.

Plate 47
The administrative building, I.G. Farben Co.,
Höchst AG, Höchst (1921–25) by
Peter Behrens

It was not only in the works of younger architects (Plate 46), who introduced new attitudes with their visionary projects, that post-First-World-War expressionism was seen, but also in certain buildings by the masters of the older generation, such as Hans Poelzig (Plate 42) or Peter Behrens. It was already clear from Behrens' single-family building on the Mathildenhöhe that he was developing from Jugendstil towards a new form of rationality. His earlier industrial buildings in Berlin, in particular the splendid AEG Turbine Factory (Plate 40), are amongst the best German industrial buildings. In the Höchst building, Behrens showed that he had progressed beyond, and was developing upon, his earlier styles. This building is a powerful example of architectural expressionism.

The new administrative building, with a front 490 feet long, contained offices, design studies, the directors' suite, laboratories, archives, exhibition halls, a large main hall,

and a lecture theatre. It was connected with the existing administrative buildings by a bridge. The dominant feature, crowning the whole complex, is the striking, prismatic lift tower.

The large entrance hall (see plate) is made into an emotionally oppressive space by the use of expressive forms and colours. The bundle-like pillars taper at the base, like stalactites, reminding one of Hans Poelzig's effects in his rebuilt Grosses Schauspielhaus in Berlin. The form of the pillars is emphasized by the flowing range of colours changing from blue-green to orange-yellow. The three octagonal, stalactite-like roof-lights which define the upper limits of the space, provide a white accent, repeated in the central part of the floor mosaics. Behrens' objective was to create unrest, to set clearly organized form in motion by means of light and colour, and thereby to achieve emotional effects comparable to those of Gothic architecture.

47

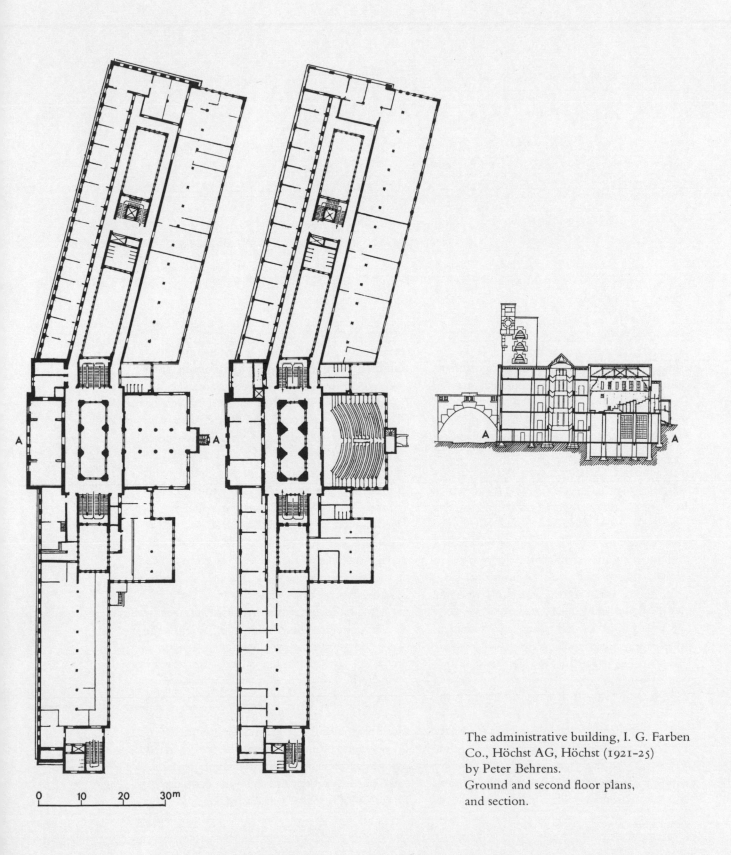

0   10   20   30^m

The administrative building, I. G. Farben
Co., Höchst AG, Höchst (1921-25)
by Peter Behrens.
Ground and second floor plans,
and section.

Plate 48
Cowshed, Gut Garkau farm, Lübeck (1924–25)
by Hugo Häring

Hugo Häring, one of the leading German architects of the twenties, and secretary of the architectural association 'Der Ring', executed few buildings. The most important is the cowshed of the partially completed farm estate at Garkau (1924–25). Häring was not, like Le Corbusier and Mies van der Rohe, concerned to create ideal frameworks by using rectangular reinforced concrete skeletons or industrialized space-cells, but to identify the essential function of a building, and make it fit its function: he wanted to 'unfold the function' of the building.

In the Garkau farm, Häring based the form of the buildings on the function they were required by the farmer to perform. Inside the cattle shed, stalls for forty-one cows are arranged in a pear-shaped layout round the mangers, completely surrounded by a passageway. In the middle there is the feeding table, onto which the hay can be delivered, through a hole in the roof, directly from a barn above. At the western end of the south side of the main building is a tower sloping diagonally downwards, containing the hay-shredder. This runs into a low annexe with a heart-shaped ground plan where turnips are stored (see plate). To the east there is an enclosure for heifers, and to the north a semicircular enclosure for calves. There is a continuous ventilation slit between the windows and the roof which obviates the need to open the windows, whose sole function is illumination. The roof is supported by columns along the edge of the feeding table. The walls are not load-bearing, and only serve to retain heat. The roof, which for reasons connected with ventilation slopes slightly inwards, is a concrete slab three inches thick.

The materials visible from the outside are brick, concrete and wood. It is these which give the building its sculptural structural impact. The brick determines the overall effect, the concrete appears as a system of horizontal bands, and the wood, which is painted green, is used to fill in the walls. This building, with its artistic arrangement of forms and colours, is one of the few finished works of this important architect. It is also one of the few treatments of the problem of farm building worth discussing.

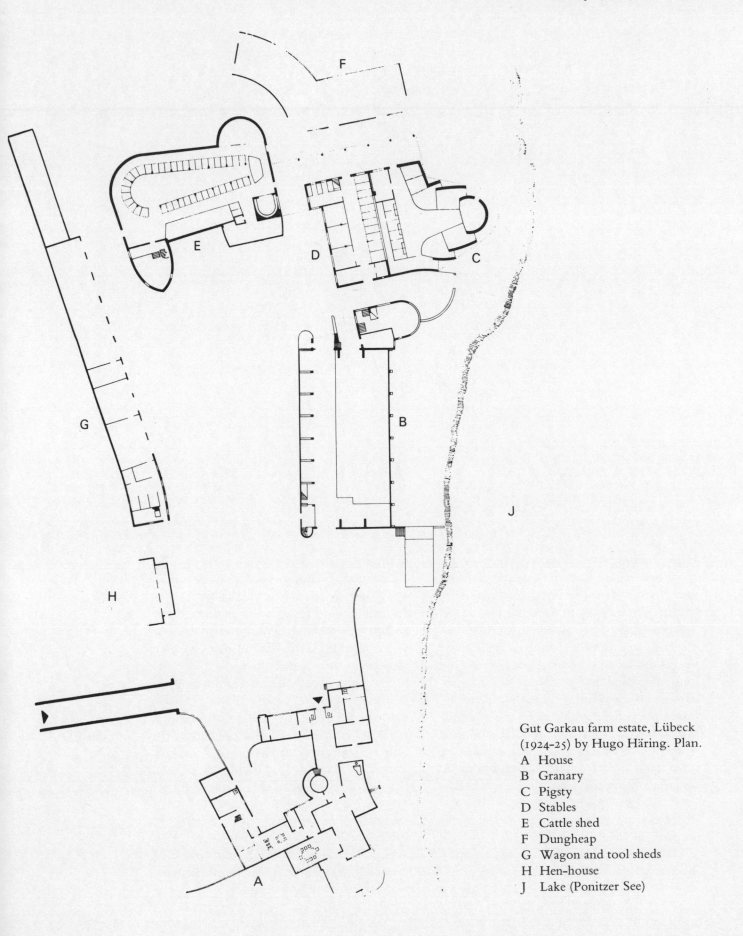

Gut Garkau farm estate, Lübeck
(1924-25) by Hugo Häring. Plan.
A House
B Granary
C Pigsty
D Stables
E Cattle shed
F Dungheap
G Wagon and tool sheds
H Hen-house
J Lake (Ponitzer See)

Plate 49
Schröder house, Utrecht (1924) by Gerrit Thomas Rietveld

This building has a special place in the development of modern domestic architecture. Basic materials and colours are used with rigorous logic to produce new spatial relationships. The architect himself explained, 'we limited ourselves to primary forms, spaces and colours, since they are not only elemental, but are free of other associations. At that time, forms produced by machines were thought to be too cold and hard, and were not yet admired for their economy and cleanness. Steel was therefore used quite openly in this composition in order to show that there need not be any contradiction between structure and beauty.' Even the drainpipes are left visible on the outside, making function obvious.

The two-storey building is composed of horizontal and vertical planes. Open balconies and window-voids are organized according to the same basic planar principles. The resulting contrapuntal play of solids, voids, horizontals and verticals is so successful that photographs of the building were laid on their side and upside down to demonstrate that the same harmonious overall impression was created always.

The lower storey is divided into traditional box-like rooms. Upstairs, however, Rietveld created a room of maximum size and freedom. It opens out from the top of the staircase, which emerges in the middle. Sliding walls are used to divide it into two, three or four rooms. This is the ultimate rational development of Frank Lloyd Wright's earlier 'floating space' (Plate 38), leading to the flowing spaces of Mies van der Rohe. The interior decoration of the house was designed in close collaboration with the owner, Frau Schröder-Schrader.

49

STUDIO WORKING SLEEPING

READING HALL KITCHEN-DINING-LIVING

W.C.

N

0 5 10 FEET
0 1 2 3 METERS

BALCONY WORK-SLEEPING HALL W.C. BATH SLEEPING BALCONY

STORAGE ST. ST.

ST.

WORK-SLEEPING ST. LIVING-DINING ST.

BALCONY

Schröder house, Utrecht (1924) by Gerrit Thomas Rietveld. Plans.

Plate 50
The Bauhaus, Dessau (1925–26)
by Walter Gropius

The Bauhaus building expresses, in both concept and execution, the ideas held by Walter Gropius, the architect and director of the school, about the founding, development and organization of this institution which is so fundamental to the twentieth century. The Bauhaus became a focal point for all those who, ever since the English Arts and Crafts Movement, had been trying to bring together culture and society. The objective was to combine disciplines previously isolated from one other, and to merge crafts and industry into a new unified development. Art was no longer to be divided into higher and lower forms, and the various developments in different countries were to be co-ordinated.

In 1919, in Weimar, the Art Academy and the Crafts School were merged into one institution by Gropius. Gropius, recommended by the previous director of both schools, Henry Van de Velde, as his successor, regarded the merging of the two schools as an essential part of his new programme for educational reform. But it was not until the school, which had by then already become world famous, had to move from Weimar to Dessau, in response to a generous offer from the mayor, that it got its own building. This was designed by Gropius himself, and built in 1925 and 1926 for about 850,000 Reichsmark. The clearly arranged three-part building is not symmetrical in the way that previous buildings by Gropius had been (Plate 43). The main considerations were functional, and it was function which determined the form of the building – the three main functions which Gropius was trying, as it were, to separate and at the same time merge. There are three wings: a school of design with classrooms, a students' hostel, and workshops (model factory). Each stretches out in a different direction. The plan of the Bauhaus is reminiscent of Frank Lloyd Wright's windmill plans.

The school and the workshops were connected by a bridge containing Gropius' own rooms and studio. This bridge spans the road leading into the town. It is like the bridge of a ship, and was intended to express the link between the school's administration, the town, and the outside world. The connector element between the students' hostel and the workshops contained the school hall, the dining hall and a theatre.

The architectonic form of, particularly, the workshop wing shows a consistent development of tendencies already demonstrated in Gropius' previous work, e.g. the Fagus Factory (Plate 43). The structural system is drawn completely into the interior, allowing the exterior of the building to be a curtain wall made entirely of glass. This glass wall, which has since been altered, originally started above a projecting strip of wall and extended right to the top of the building, producing a large interior for the workshops, flooded with light. With no load to bear, it ran right round the corners of the building, emphasizing the dynamic impact already made by the building's asymmetry. The workshop can be seen on the right of the plate. On the left is the school. Major alterations have been made to the workshop. In particular, the curtain wall has been destroyed by revealing the exterior concrete beams.

The six-storey hostel contained twenty-eight rooms, each with its own balcony. The roof formed a terrace.

The Bauhaus, more than any other educational institution, has been responsible for changing twentieth-century attitudes to culture, and has helped bring about many modern developments.

50

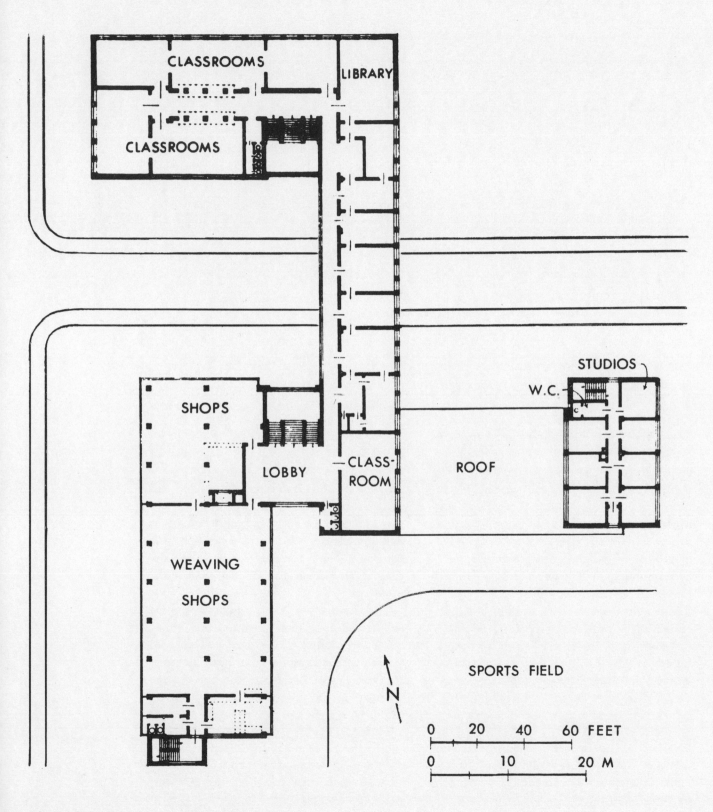

The Bauhaus, Dessau (1925-26) by Walter Gropius.
Plan, first floor.

Plate 51
Housing estate, Hook of Holland (1926–27) by
J. J. P. Oud

The work of J. J. P. Oud represents an early peak in the development of workers' housing estates. In 1918, Oud, like Rietveld a founder member of the De Stijl movement, was in charge of public building in Rotterdam, and in this position was able to be remarkably productive. In 1917 he had already designed a group of single-family dwellings for Scheveningen, but had never executed them. He described them as follows: 'They produced a rhythmic play of straight lines and cubic masses, projecting, receding and interlocking with each other, like pearls strung together.' Frank Lloyd Wright's Francisco Terrace housing estate in Chicago (1895) was a prototype of this type of building, which was socially as well as architecturally revolutionary. In 1924–25 Oud designed the workers' village of Kiefhoek in Rotterdam and the housing estate in the Hook of Holland, built in 1926–27, and described in 1929 by Henry-Russell Hitchcock as 'perhaps the most beautiful example of modern architecture'.

Oud grouped the two-storey single family dwellings so as to make a harmonious, unified whole. A continuous balcony joins the whitewashed houses. The rounded end of each row, some of which contain shops, was lightened by large, ground-floor glass windows, and shaded from the sun by the balconies. These rounded forms soften the strict rectangular character displayed by the buildings.

The majority of the houses have three rooms and a kitchen, although the corner houses are larger. In this estate, Oud freed himself from the influence of both the great Hendrik Petrus Berlage (Plate 20) and the purism of his De Stijl friends. Both influences can be seen in his earlier buildings.

Extreme economy in the use of materials and forms has here produced a new beauty in residences designed on a collective rather than an individual basis. In this housing estate, Oud expresses the striving, typical of the twenties, towards a new kind of architecture.

51

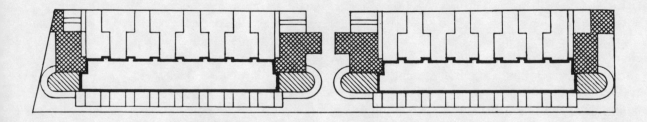

Housing estate, Hook of Holland (1926–27) by J. J. P. Oud.
Plan of two rows of houses.

Plate 52
Lovell beach house, Newport Beach, California
(1926) by R. M. Schindler

Modern architecture in California has been heavily influenced by immigrant architects from Austria who were brought up in the tradition of Wagner and Loos, and in turn influenced by Frank Lloyd Wright. R. M. Schindler, who arrived in America in 1913, and Richard Neutra (Plate 53) are the two most important architects of this school.

After working in Chicago, Schindler joined Frank Lloyd Wright in California, and became his chief draughtsman. The best example of their joint work is probably the Barnsdall house, but it is nevertheless clear that Schindler preferred Wright's earlier buildings. In 1921 he started his own office, and in the years following put up several important buildings in California. His greatest, however, in terms of radicalism and quality, was the beach house built for the Lovell family at 1242 Ocean Avenue, Newport Beach, California. The house is a set of flat horizontal and vertical slab elements making a space which is open and dynamic rather than closed and static. The house is partially supported on columns, and its covered terraces and glass walls are open to the sea. The stairs leading up to the main living room are the only oblique line in the rectangular pattern of the house. The terrace of the second upper storey is held up by supports embedded in the ground, which widen into frames, and lift the shady and airy living room above ground level.

The balanced composition of the Lovell house, which suits its position and climate so well, and is comparable to Gerrit Thomas Rietveld's Schröder-Schrader house in Utrecht (Plate 49), shows, though in a highly individualistic way, the immense influence of Frank Lloyd Wright.

The Lovell house also has several characteristics in common with Le Corbusier's Villa Savoye, built a few years later, including the separation of the living area from the ground, the involvement of the exterior space in the architectural unit, and the play of light and shade on the rectangular pattern of spaces.

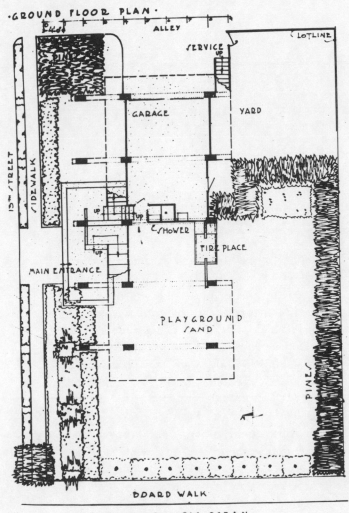

·GROUND FLOOR PLAN·

ALLEY

SERVICE

LOTLINE

GARAGE

YARD

13TH STREET

SIDEWALK

UP

UP

SHOWER

UP

FIRE PLACE

MAIN ENTRANCE

PLAYGROUND SAND

PINES

BOARD WALK

BEACH · PACIFIC OCEAN ·

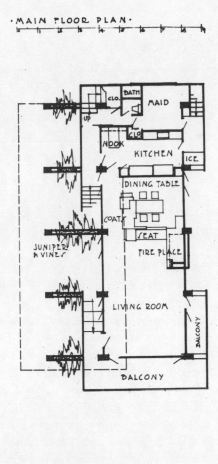

·MAIN FLOOR PLAN·

CLO.   BATH

MAID

UP   CLO.

NOOK

KITCHEN

ICE

DINING TABLE

COAT

JUNIPER & VINES

SEAT

FIRE PLACE

LIVING ROOM

BALCONY

BALCONY

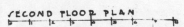

SECOND FLOOR PLAN

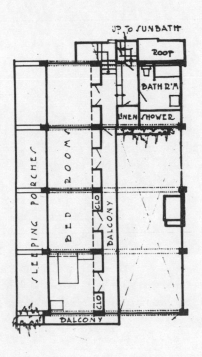

UP TO SUNBATH

ROOF

BATH R'M

LINEN   SHOWER

SLEEPING PORCHES

BED ROOM

CLO

BALCONY

CLO

DALCONY

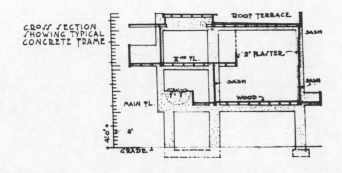

CROSS SECTION SHOWING TYPICAL CONCRETE FRAME

ROOF TERRACE

SASH

II ND FL.

2" PLASTER

SASH   SASH

MAIN FL.

WOOD

4'0"

8"

GRADE

Lovell beach house, Newport Beach, California (1926) by R. M. Schindler.
Plans and section.

Plate 53 (page 265)
Lovell house, Los Angeles (1927–29) by
Richard J. Neutra

Richard Neutra was born in Vienna in 1892, and went to America in 1923 after working in Berlin with Erich Mendelsohn. In Vienna, he was strongly influenced by his teacher, Otto Wagner, as well as by Adolf Loos. In America his early work was clearly influenced by Frank Lloyd Wright, and by his fellow Austrian R. M. Schindler, whose office he joined in 1926. Schindler's influence is particularly obvious in Neutra's early work. In 1927 he built the Jardinette apartment in Los Angeles, and in the same year he began his first large building for the Lovell family, for whom Schindler had already executed some commissions (Plate 52). The luxurious Lovell house in Los Angeles was built with a skeleton frame, and, after Schindler's pioneering work, was a breakthrough for the new technique, and the rational principles on which it was based, into West Coast American architecture. Neutra learnt the techniques of industrial building in Holabird's and Roche's office in Chicago, where he worked in 1924.

The three-storey house has a light steel skeleton which was pre-fabricated and erected in under forty hours on the steep slope of a hill. The frame is filled in by walls made of thin concrete and glass. The balconies are not cantilevered, but suspended from the roof. The particular charm of the house lies in the balance it achieves between steel, concrete and glass, and the alternating solids and voids supported by the fine network of the thin steel skeleton. A glass window, running through two storeys, opens up the staircase and one side of the large living room to the countryside.

Frank Lloyd Wright had already developed in this part of America the principles of the raised living room, the alternation of open and closed areas making space appear to 'flow', and the interpenetration of exterior and interior space. Here Neutra has combined these ideas with new architectural techniques, imported from Europe, stripping them of their emotional pathos, and rationalizing them so that at first sight they are almost unrecognizable. Nevertheless, the Lovell house, which is famous as the forerunner of a new type of architecture on the American West Coast, is a product not only of European but also of American tradition in domestic architecture.

The house also shows signs of the swing in the early 1930s away from the pure rationalism of the twenties towards an architecture which involves in itself nature, the environment, the elements and organic principles. Neutra, who regarded architecture as a kind of applied physiology, called this house, built for the nature-healing Dr Philip Lovell, 'Health House'. The way the glass walls open up to the exterior, and the U-shaped pool contrasts with the strict rectangularity of the rest of the building, are typical examples of organic involvement of man and his house with the surroundings.

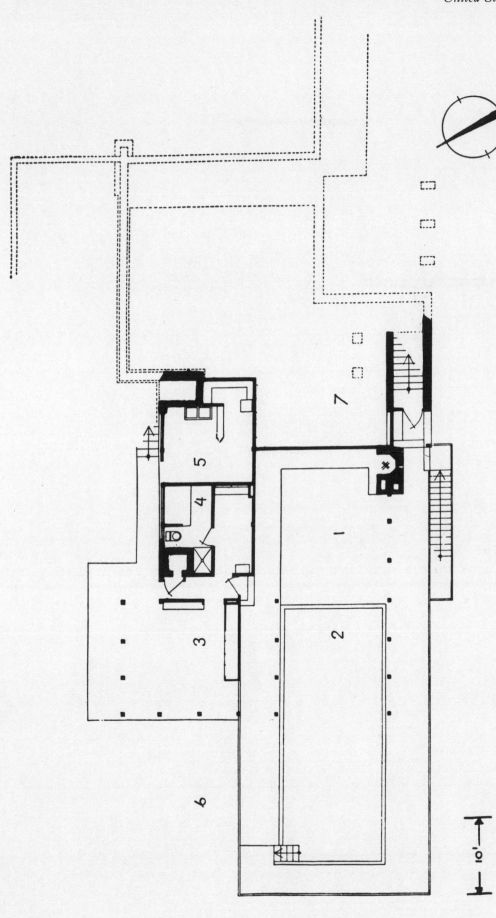

Lovell house, Los Angeles (1927–29)
by Richard J. Neutra.
Ground plan.
1 Playground with view
2 Swimming pool
3 Nursery porch
4 Shower and sitzbath
5 Laundry
6 Gymcourt
7 Not excavated

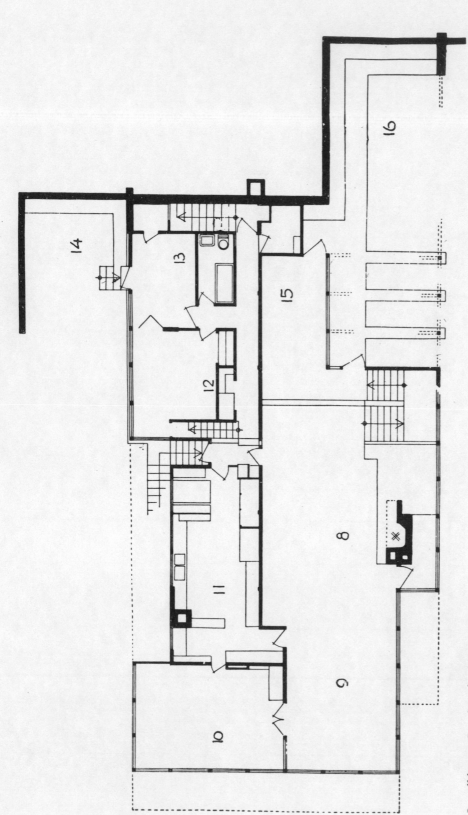

Lovell house, Los Angeles (1927–29)
by Richard J. Neutra.
Lower quarters.

 8 Living room   13 Guest room
 9 Dining room   14 Guest room, patio
10 Porch   15 Library
11 Kitchen and pantry 16 Patio
12 Guest room

53

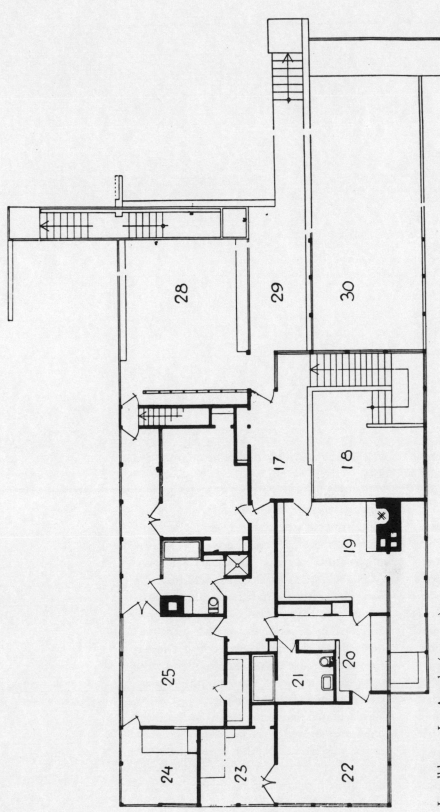

Lovell house, Los Angeles (1927–29)
by Richard J. Neutra.
Upper storey.
17 Entry
18 Open to lower floor
19 Study
20 Dressing room
21 Bath
22 Living room
23 Sleeping porch
24 Sleeping porch
25 Living room
28 Terrace
29 Entrance-terrace
30 Patio

Plate 54
Hermann Lange house, Krefeld (1928) by
Ludwig Mies van der Rohe

Mies van der Rohe built very few buildings in Germany. They include the single-family houses in Guben (Wolf house, 1926) and Berlin (Lemcke house, 1932), and the Esters house (later altered) and the Lange house in Krefeld, both built in 1928. The exterior of the Lange house, only a short distance from the Esters house, has remained unaltered. The house is now a museum of modern art.

For all its individuality, the Lange house has echoes of the work of that great Dutchman, Hendrik Petrus Berlage. Mies van der Rohe was trained by him to accept the standardization and discipline which the special nature of brick imposes on an architect: 'How sensible is the handy little shape of a brick, and how useful for every purpose! How logical is the way bricks fit together, the pattern they make, and their texture! How rich is the simple surface of a brick wall! But what a lot of discipline this material does need.'

The proportions of the Lange house are, as in a few earlier buildings by Mies, determined by the size of the brick. The symmetry of the long street front is broken by a projecting entrance and large windows.

On the garden front of the building (see plate) the top floor has five regularly proportioned windows. Both floors give onto terraces. The ground floor terrace leads into the garden which falls away gently. There is a projecting porch, making the plan of the house reminiscent of the 'windmill' plan, stretching out in all directions.

This luxurious house, with its subdued tones and beautiful proportions, demonstrates, albeit in quite different materials, the great art that Mies van der Rohe subsequently displayed in his glass and steel constructions.

54

Diagrams illustrating Mies van der Rohe's use of the brick as the
smallest basic unit by which the whole structure can be divided.

Plate 55
*Tram Workers' Club, Moscow (1929) by
K. S. Melnikov*

The Tram Workers' Club by K. S. Melnikov (1929) is a climax of Russian architecture of the 'twenties. The new architecture, arising from social changes, created new problems, and produced a new freedom, going further than almost ever before in the exploitation of new techniques. There were many excellent solutions with daring forms. Melnikov, born in 1890, was an independent-minded architect who was not a member of the main architectural coteries of the period. In 1923 he built an exhibition pavilion in Moscow, in 1925 a pavilion for the 'Exposition International des Arts Décoratifs' in Paris. Compared with Le Corbusier's famous 'Pavillon de l'Esprit Nouveau', Melnikov's building is arguably a better solution. He produced a project for a large garage over the Seine, in Paris, at the same time.

The Tram Workers' Club is an important product of this virtually forgotten, but intensely creative, period in Russia, during which Leonidov, the brothers Vesnin, Ginsburg and others, were also working. Melnikov's building is basically geometrical and is impressive for its sculptural power as well as for the impact it makes on its urban environment. It has three wings, each containing a large room. These three rooms open onto two staircases, seen through the two vertical glass window bands in the walls.

The building's exterior is particularly impressive when seen as a sculptural mass in bright daylight, and has a completely functional relationship to the interior. This type of daringly cantilevered construction was not repeated until after the Second World War, and even then, less convincingly.

The building was erected at a time when Russian architecture, and indeed the rest of Russian culture, was undergoing a crisis, evolving from the revolutionary élan of the first years after the revolution towards the long stagnation which followed. Not only did the Russian establishment reject this new concept of architecture, but Western European critics were unable to understand its revolutionary innovations. As recently as 1950, Arnold Whittick, the English art critic, dismissed Melnikov's building as functional, but not architecture. When Melnikov's design for the building for the People's Commissariat for Heavy Industry, in Red Square, was submitted in a competition, his contemporaries condemned it as formalistic and Utopian, although it was a project remarkably similar to the megastructures of today.

55

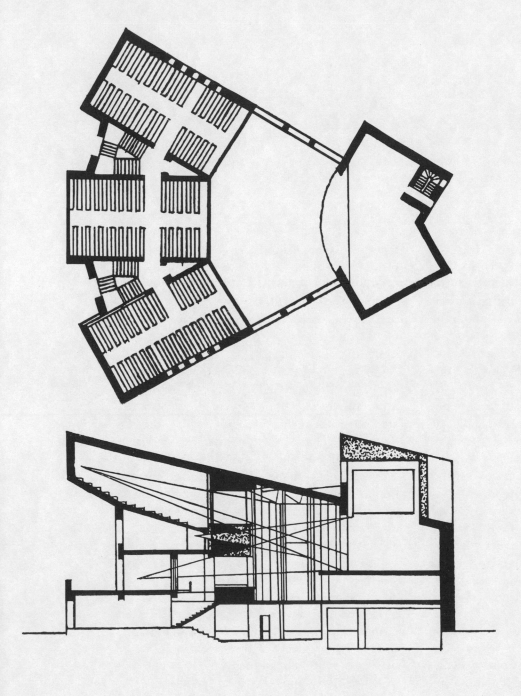

Tram Workers' Club, Moscow (1929) by K. S. Melnikov.
Plan and section.

Plate 56
Tuberculosis sanatorium, Paimio (1929–33) by Alvar Aalto

Finland was one of the countries which achieved international importance in architecture in the 1930s, partly because its special traditions and characteristics particularly suited the changing requirements of the period. These changes in international architecture are clearly demonstrated in both the building problem, and the execution of the Tuberculosis sanatorium in Paimio by Aalto.

The young architect's design for this building won a competition in 1928. Its execution was achieved by co-operation between forty-eight rural councils and four towns, and took place between 1929 and 1933. The building is situated in hilly wooded countryside, well away from towns and villages. It has several wings. Rooms for hospital business and for patients are separated, the latter being mostly double rooms. The main principle underlying the clear and simply composed form of the building is to expose all the rooms to as much light and air as possible. Patients can enjoy both on the many balconies.

This hospital has been taken as a model for many others throughout the world. The main wing (seen in the plate from the west) is for patients. The other wing contains communal rooms (dining rooms, rest rooms, library and a hobby room) as well as rooms for medical examinations, therapy and operations. The main entrance is between the two wings. An east wing, which contains service installations, kitchens, heating plant, etc., is joined directly onto the communal wing. A nearby block contains garages. The houses for doctors and hospital staff are quite separate from the main complex, standing in rows to the west, out of sight of the hospital itself.

The heart of the sanatorium is the patients' wing, which is furnished as practically and as economically as possible. Even the colours are chosen for their therapeutic value; the ceilings are painted in calm, dark colours, and the walls in lighter tones. All lighting is indirect. There are special arrangements for heating air coming through open windows, and the hospital contains some of Aalto's earliest wooden furniture, in the curved, wavy style typical of the 1930s.

Like his subsequent work, the influence of which is now world wide, this building by Aalto demonstrated how architecture was being changed by the application of basic elemental and organic principles. From now on, the requirements of the landscape, the peculiarities of the region and the materials suited to them, and, above all, people and their physical and psychological needs, began to regain their predominance in architectural thinking.

56

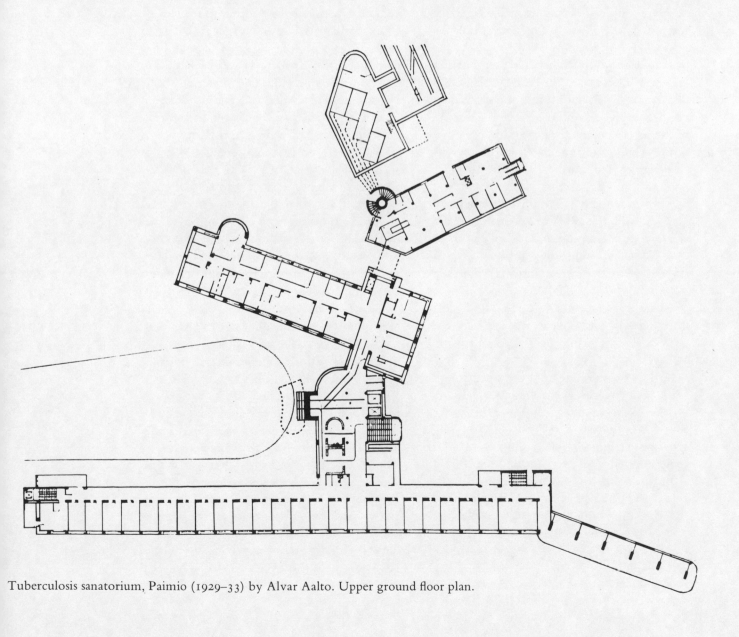

Tuberculosis sanatorium, Paimio (1929–33) by Alvar Aalto. Upper ground floor plan.

Plate 57
Boots chemical works, Beeston, Nottinghamshire (1930–32, 1937–38) by Sir E. Owen Williams

The chemical factory at Beeston, built in two sections between 1930 and 1932 and 1937 and 1938, is the best example of architectural development in England during the 1930s. The huge complex is based on the principle of mushroom-pillar construction and glass filler-walls. The remarkable length of the north and south fronts of the building can be seen in the continuous horizontal wall of the first storey on the north side. The two upper storeys are broken up into pavilion-like masses. The north side of the building has a ship-like appearance.

Above the main hall of the building there is a fourth storey. The enormous hall, covered by a translucent roof made out of glass tiles, has connecting bridges at each storey-level. By using modern building materials, Owen Williams created a space of great transparency and lightness. Glass is the only material which defines the space, as in the workshop wing of the Bauhaus by Walter Gropius (Plate 50).

Sir E. Owen Williams was born in 1889. He was an engineer who, until 1929, always worked with architects. In 1929 he broke away and started on his own, building Dorchester House, in London, and subsequent buildings.

In view of the logical structure, the remarkable transparency and lightness, and the carefully thought-out organization of this enormous building, it is not surprising to learn that Owen Williams also designed aeroplanes and concrete boats, and was a member of both the Royal Aeronautical Society and the Institute of Naval Architects.

The entrance hall on the ground floor of the Boots chemical works leads to the cloakrooms and toilets. Raw materials are brought onto the two ramps alongside the building (on the north side there is a railway ramp) and taken first into the raw material warehouse and then through to the production area. The products are bottled in the central hall with the glass ceiling and then go for packing and despatch and eventually, on a moving belt, to control. The perfume department is completely enclosed by glass because of the smell. On the first floor there are production areas as well as canteens. The smaller fourth storey has a canteen for office workers and a telephone exchange, a medical department, and a rest room. In the basement there are garages, the central heating plant and store-rooms.

In spite of its obvious qualities, this building by Sir E. Owen Williams is still controversial. Arnold Whittick maintained that it was monotonous and lacked variety. Henry-Russell Hitchcock called Owen Williams' work ambivalent. He recognized the brilliance of the construction but found the architectural impact uncertain and confused. There can, however, be no doubt that this building, which basically seems to be an attempt at synthesizing the system of concrete mushroom pillars developed by Robert Maillart with Mies van der Rohe's techniques of glass architecture, is one of the few consistently developed buildings of this size.

57

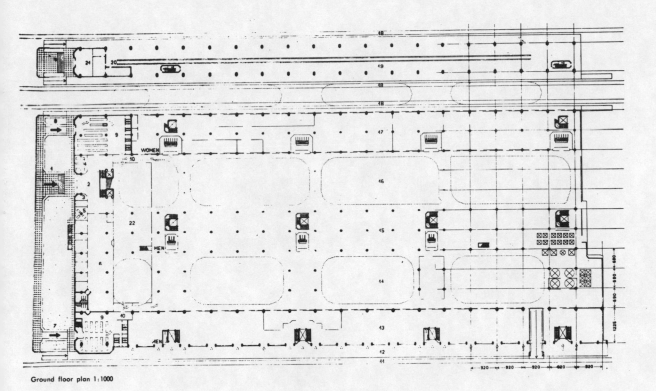

Ground floor plan 1:1000

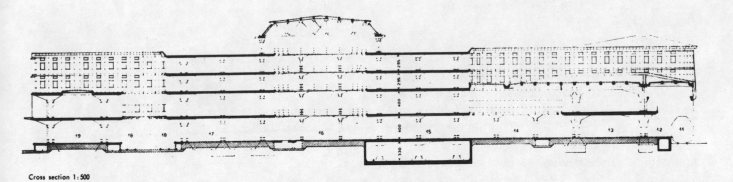

Cross section 1:500

Boots chemical works, Beeston, Nottinghamshire (1930–32, 1937–38)
by Sir E. Owen Williams. Plan and section.

1	Staff entrance	12	Unloading dock
2	Entrance hall	13	Raw materials store
3	Porter	14	Manufactory
4	Women's cloaks	15	Manufactured materials store
5	Men's cloaks	16	Packing hall
6	Office space	17	Stores
7	Works entrance for men	18	Dispatch siding
8	Works entrance for women	19	Dispatch dock
9	Cloakrooms	20	Conveyor
10	Time clocks	21	Dispatch control and checking
11	Arrival siding	22	Perfumery

Plate 58
Open air school, Amsterdam (1930–32) by
Johannes Duiker

The open air school, built from 1930 to 1932 in Amsterdam by Johannes Duiker, is a major example of the new approach to school building, and indeed to architecture, which emerged about 1930. Other revolutionary school buildings of the period include Richard Neutra's Pavilion School in Los Angeles, Ernst May's schools in Germany, the open air school in Suresnes by Beaudouin and Lods, and the school in Villejuif built in 1931–33 by André Lurcat. All these buildings attempted to get away from the traditional, closed type of school, with a playground in front or behind, and to achieve a new, open, looser form which would admit more light and air.

Duiker's school is placed diagonally across a square later formed by new houses. One quarter of its ground-plan, where it faced south, was left open to provide balconies where teaching could be done. The classrooms were opened up, therefore, not only to the light, but to the surrounding space.

This was a common objective at the time, although few architects had the courage to do it.

An entrance building, also by Duiker, leads onto Cliostraat. The whole building, which has recently been renovated, has a four-storey reinforced concrete skeleton which is as revolutionary as that used in the Bauhaus (Plate 50) or the Boots chemical factory at Beeston (Plate 57). Duiker's building is perhaps the most radical modern application of glass architecture. The staircase is in the middle of the building. A gymnasium adjoins the south-east side of the building. The heating, which has worked extremely well, comes through the ceilings.

The open air school in Amsterdam is not only an important example of 1930s architecture, but, with the Gooiland Hotel in Hilversum, and the Cineac in Amsterdam, is the most important building by this architect, who died in 1935 at the early age of 45.

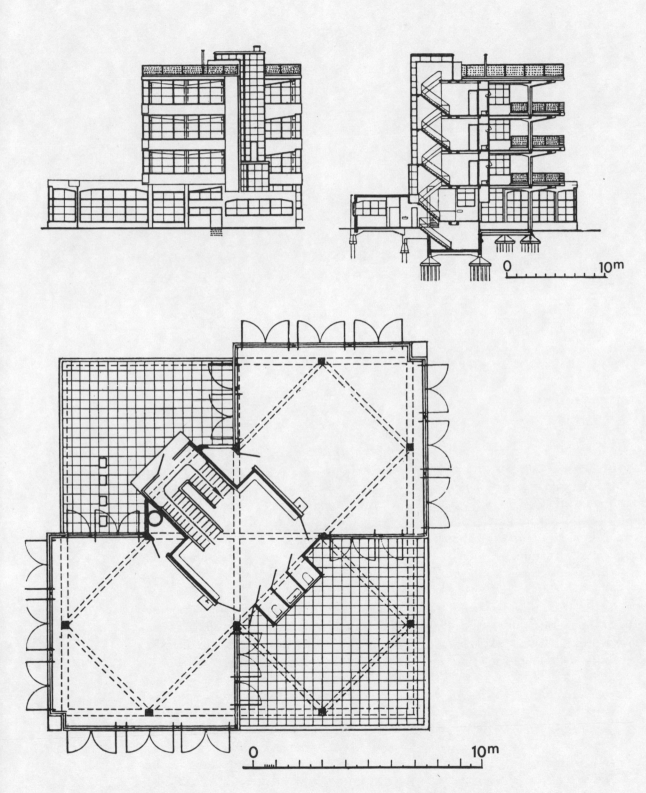

Open air school, Amsterdam (1930–32) by Johannes Duiker.
Plan, elevation and section.

Plate 59
Stadium, Florence (1930–32)
by Pier Luigi Nervi

Pier Luigi Nervi, like Robert Maillart (Plate 60), Bernard Lafaille and Eduardo Torroja (Plate 61), ranks as one of the great engineers of the twentieth century. He was fortunate in being given important public buildings to design throughout his career. One of these was the Stadium in Florence – for which Nervi won a competition – built in two stages between 1930 and 1932. At about this time, architecture was undergoing a change from the rational approach of the twenties toward the dynamic involvement of elemental, organic factors characteristic of the 'thirties.

The Florence stadium, which made Nervi's reputation as a designer in concrete, is built on a ground-plan based on the layout of an ancient circus. It holds 35,000 spectators. The stands, in the form of a huge oval, are only partly covered. The tall, thin, tower with a glass front is known as the Marathon Tower (see plate, on the right). The long track is laid out slightly asymmetrically, which means that the ground-plan of the stadium is also slightly asymmetrical about its longer axis. Access to the stands is by five spiral staircases, which express vividly the true nature of the reinforced concrete of which they are made. The stadium is 900 feet long, and 470 feet wide. The sports field measures 120 yards by 77 yards.

Sigfried Giedion saw a combination of standardization and irrationality as the essence of the new architecture which began to emerge in the early 1930s. In Nervi's stadium both can be seen in the Maillart-like daring of the system of supports on the outside of the stadium, the sweep of the spiral staircases which give direct access to the uppermost seats, and the roofing over the stands; in the rounded inside edge of the tower, the interplay of the colours of the light concrete, the green grass and the red track, and the way the hilly countryside is visually involved in the architectural composition.

59

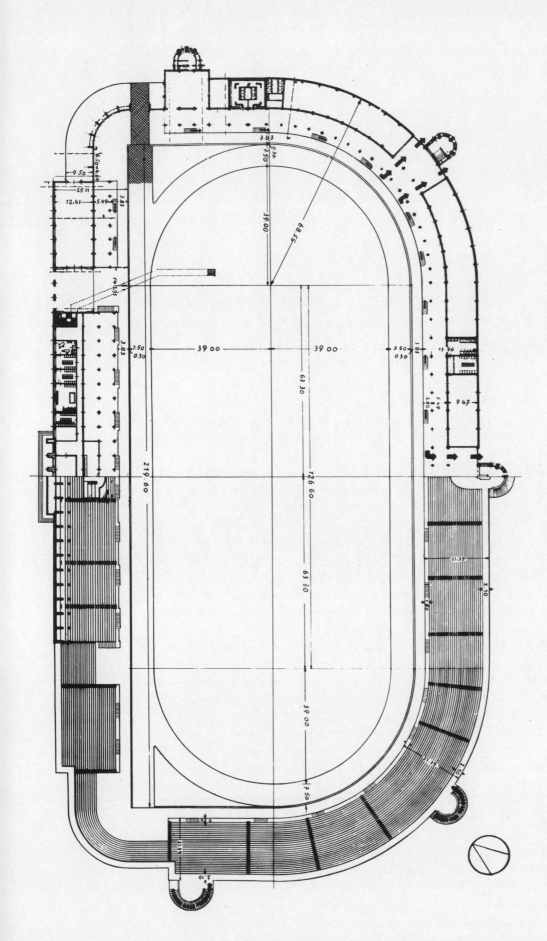

Stadium, Florence (1930-32)
by Pier Luigi Nervi. Plan.

Plate 60
Schwandbach bridge between Hinterfultigen and
Schönentannen, Canton of Bern (1933) by
Robert Maillart

Bridges are a very important part of the work of modern, as well as of nineteenth-century, engineer-architects. In spite of the fact that their form is largely determined by mathematical calculations, there are elements in these bridges which have been interpreted, correctly, as characteristic of a new aesthetic. Among the most convincing twentieth-century examples of this are the bridges by the Swiss engineer, Robert Maillart, which demonstrated more radically than almost any contemporary builder's work the principles of reinforced concrete construction. His bridges show, with incomparable clarity, how, with this material, rigid slabs can be direct, load-bearing elements.

The Schwandbach bridge (1933) and the Salginatobel bridge (1929–30) are the two most uncompromising of Maillart's works (which are not limited to bridges). The former is particularly remarkable, from the technical point of view, in the way it follows the curve of the road. Movement is the essential function of a road, and this bridge fits in organically with this function rather than counteracting it. A curved bridge requires the most unusual structural techniques. Maillart's special genius can be seen in the unity which is made by the span arch over the valley, the upright slabs arranged radially on top of the arch, and the road laid on top of these. Everything is reduced to bare essentials, which gives the structure a purity and beauty. Maillart always tried to keep his buildings as light as possible. He disproved the thesis that massiveness and strength are inseparable and indeed showed that lightness can actually lead to greater strength. The harmony achieved between road and arch in this bridge is not only technically remarkable but also aesthetically pleasing.

The bridge is 146 feet long, and has a span of 124 feet. The total cost of the bridge was only 47,300 Swiss francs, exceptionally low for this type of structure, even in those days. Because they were so cheap, several of Maillart's bridges were built in remote valleys and poor areas, where the local authorities could not afford anything 'smarter'.

Maillart's principle of blending functional structures into the countryside fitted in with a wider movement which was growing at the time and which, after a period devoted to the conquest of technical form, emphasized the importance of man and nature as a determinant of the built-environment.

60

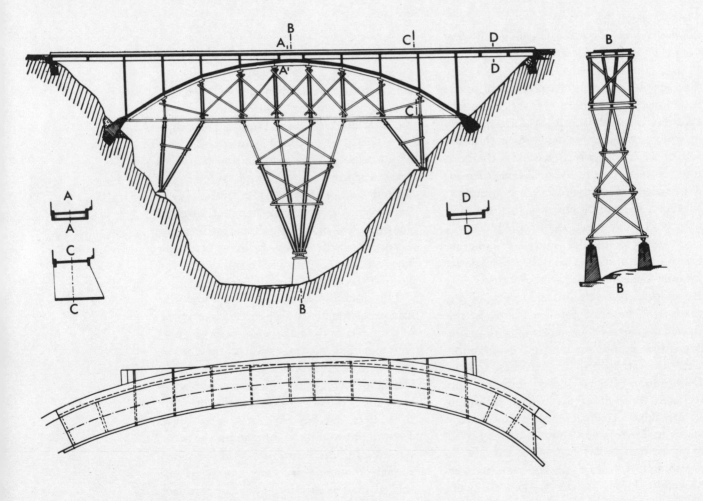

Schwandbach bridge between Hinterfultigen and Schönentannen,
Canton of Bern (1933) by Robert Maillart.
Plan, sections, and elevation showing construction staging.

Plate 61 (page 299)
Grandstand at Zarzuela race track, Madrid
(1935) by Eduardo Torroja

The Spanish engineer Torroja is one of the most inspired builders of the twentieth century. His buildings in Spain have made him world famous. He made advances in the use of concrete, which has recently been used more and more for shell-construction. Torroja was one of the first people to exploit, superbly, the full potential of this material.

In 1934, he founded an institute in Costillares devoted to the study of concrete building techniques. This is today one of the leading organizations in the world concerned with research into and testing of this material. The roof for the stands at the Zarzuela race track was Torroja's first major commission, and was built in co-operation with the architects C. Arniches and L. Dominguez. It has been admired and imitated throughout the world. Although daring, it has a classical simplicity and beauty about it. Torroja said about it later: 'I tried to make the plans look as conventional as possible. If I hadn't, no-one would have looked at them.' In cross section, the plans were indeed simple; the rows of seats in the grandstand slope down from a central gangway towards the track, beneath a roof which is cantilevered a long way out. On the other side, a similarly cantilevered roof covers the betting area, and gives an open view onto the saddling enclosure. During the design stage, Torroja worked towards a freer exploitation of the structural possibilities of reinforced concrete. The roof, fluted in the form of a series of hyperbolic paraboloids, is cantilevered 41 feet from the central upper gangway. It is of varying thickness, between 2 and $5\frac{1}{2}$ inches. This brilliant structure survived the gunfire and bombing of the Spanish Civil War, virtually undamaged.

This grandstand by Torroja (only the middle section can be seen in the plate) is one of the peaks in the achievements in sporting architecture in the twentieth century. As in the works of Robert Maillart (Plate 60) and Pier Luigi Nervi (Plate 59), built at about the same time, the art of construction in concrete here reaches an early perfection. Torroja showed how important he considered a builder's imagination to be when he said: 'Concrete structures cannot be calculated mathematically. They are stronger than mathematics can prove, and we cannot wait for the mathematicians. We must go ahead with our work, and try out what our intuition tells us is possible.'

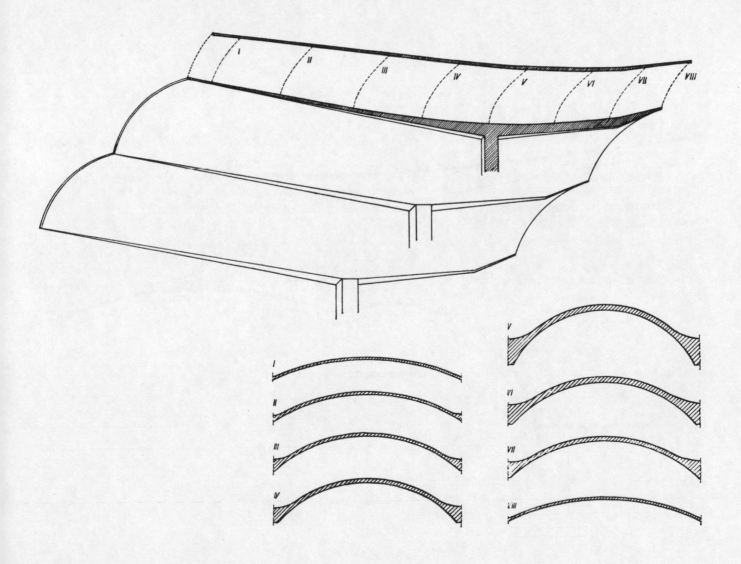

Grandstand at Zarzuela race track, Madrid (1935) by Eduardo Torroja.
Diagram of a cantilevered roof showing sections.

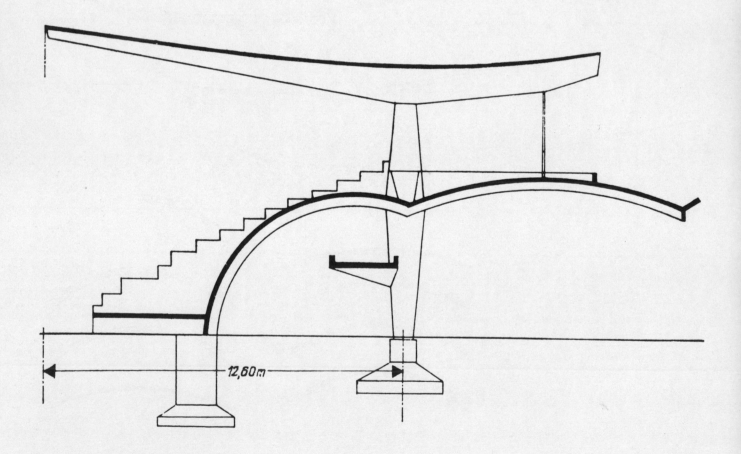

Grandstand at Zarzuela race track, Madrid (1935) by Eduardo Torroja.
Section through stand.

61

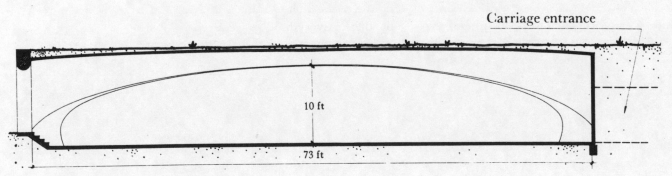

Cross section at ground level.

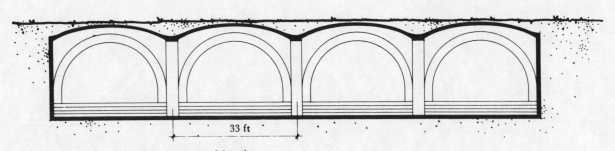

Longitudinal section at ground level.

Grandstand at Zarzuela race track, Madrid (1935) by Eduardo Torroja.

Plate 62
*Casa del Popolo, Como (1932–36) by Giuseppe
Terragni*

The Casa del Popolo, built between 1932 and
1936 in Como by Giuseppe Terragni, has
special significance for Italian architecture,
in spite of being commissioned by and
erected under a Fascist regime, since it
ushers in a new phase.

Antonio Sant'Elia's early death meant that
futurist architecture remained limited to
projects and manifestoes. While the modern
movement forged ahead in Germany, Holland, England, France and Russia, it barely
made any impact in Italy up to the end of the
'twenties. The formation of Group 7, in
1926, by the architects Figini, Libera, Pollini,
Frette, Larco, Rava and Terragni, was the
first sign of change, the effects of which were
to be seen in later years. In this context,
Terragni's Casa del Popolo is an important
building.

It was originally commissioned as a centre
for the Fascist Party, under the name Casa del
Fascio. It has a simple concrete skeleton, and
marble cladding. The building is a rectangle,
106 feet long and 54 feet high, imaginatively
relieved by the play of solids and voids, the
different treatment of the windows according to their functions (i.e. according to
whether they are the windows of rooms,
staircases, etc.), the roof garden, balconies
and an interior courtyard. Terragni originally conceived the building with a courtyard
completely open to one side, but during the
planning stage it became an enclosed space
with a roofed courtyard.

In spite of the fact that the building shows
clear traces of ideas evolved in France and
Germany, it has a peculiarly Italian character,
visible in its easily comprehensible, harmonious proportions, the looseness of its composition, and the sculptural form of the concrete.

62

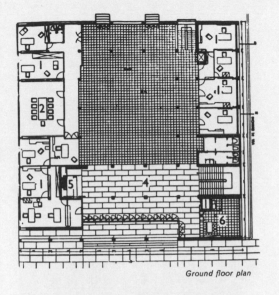

Ground floor plan

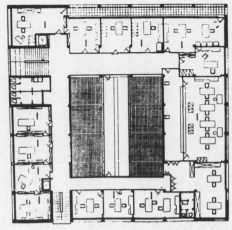

Second floor plan

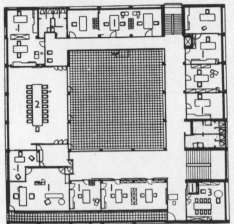

First floor plan

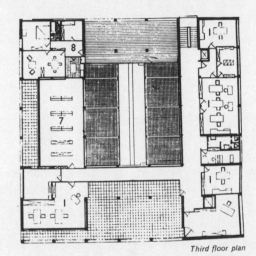

Third floor plan

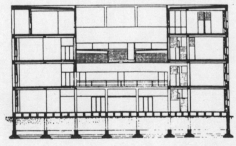

SW–NE section

NW SE section

Casa del Popolo, Como (1932–36) by Giuseppe Terragni.
Floor plans and sections.

1 Offices
2 Committee rooms
3 Waiting room
4 Entry foyer
5 Memorial
6 Caretaker
7 Library
8 Caretaker's flat

Plate 63
Highpoint I block of flats, Highgate, London
(1933–35) by Berthold Lubetkin and Tecton

In Great Britain, where the last major architectural achievements since the nineteenth
century had been the buildings of Mackintosh and other Art Nouveau architects, there
was a retreat from the mainstream of international architecture towards provincial
eclecticism. But in the early 'thirties, England
was affected by the new developments in
other countries, imported mostly by immigrants from Germany and Russia. Peter
Behrens had already put up buildings in
England in 1925. After 1933, he was followed
by Gropius, Breuer and Mendelsohn, who
managed, usually in co-operation with
English architects, to erect buildings which
greatly influenced architecture in England.
After a short stay in France, Berthold Lubetkin arrived in England from Russia in 1930.
He too worked in association with a group
of English architects (Tecton) and put up
some important works, including the buildings at the London Zoo and two tall blocks
of flats. These latter were convincing paral-
lels to the designs of Walter Gropius, the
buildings of Maaskant, Brinkman and Van
der Vlugt in Holland, and of Beaudouin and

Lods in France, all of about the same time.
    The problem here was to evolve a new
approach to urban residential building along
the lines developed in Russian designs in the
'twenties and in the works of Le Corbusier.
Highpoint I was designed by Lubetkin on a
cross-shaped ground-plan, which extended
the four wings into space, rather than making
a block-like, closed complex. This building
had immense influence on reconstruction
plans drawn up after the war. Similarities
between Highpoint I and Alvar Aalto's
Tuberculosis sanatorium in Paimio (Plate 56)
can be seen in the lucid composition of the
building, which rests partly on columns, the
economical use of materials, and the way the
building reaches out into space.
    A little later, another block of flats on the
same lines was built next to this building.
Highpoint II (visible on the right of the
plate) is different from the first building in
only a few details, apart from having two-
storey flats. It is a deliberately Neo-Classical
composition, and instead of steel columns,
has copies of the Erechtheum caryatid in the
British Museum beside the entrance.

63

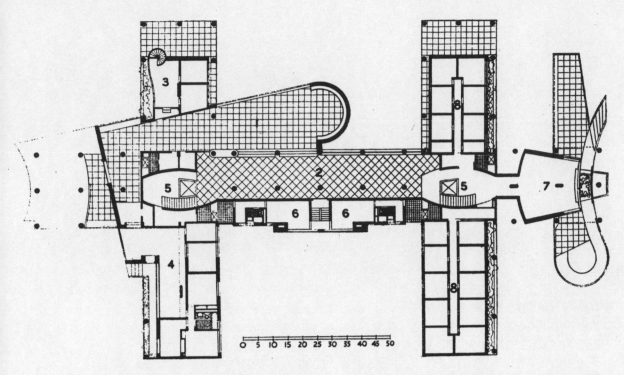

Highpoint I block of flats, Highgate, London (1933–35)
by Berthold Lubetkin and Tecton. Ground plan.

1	Hall and winter garden	5	Lifts and staircases
2	Hall	6	One-room flats
3	Porter's flat	7	Tea-room
4	Large flat	8	Maids' bedrooms

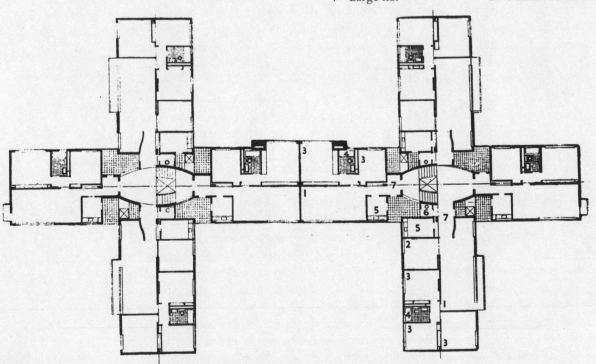

Upper ground floor plan.

1	Living room	5	Kitchen
2	Dining recess	6	W.C.
3	Bedrooms	7	Entrance hall
4	Bathroom		

Plate 64
Edgar J. Kaufmann house, 'Falling Water',
Bear Run, Pennsylvania (1936) by Frank
Lloyd Wright

Frank Lloyd Wright's buildings were in the forefront of the revolution in domestic architecture after 1900, expressed in particular in the Robie house in Chicago, 1909 (Plate 38). Wright concerned himself with this building problem repeatedly in the following decades, each time so individualistically that one might think he was attempting to redefine it on each occasion. In the 'thirties he formulated one of his main themes, which was the combining of architecture and landscape, in a new and elemental way. 'Falling Water' is perhaps his most famous building, and has become a symbol of the international movement. It is in line with the drive in the 'thirties towards a new regionalism and the introduction of natural, elemental, organic factors into the type of architecture founded a generation earlier by, amongst others, Frank Lloyd Wright himself. This building combines both a feeling for nature and for the romance of the machine.

It was originally intended to be a relatively cheap weekend house. It consists basically of two levels of living area, both of which extend over the waterfall, and afford superb views of the surrounding countryside. The entrance drive leads into the main living room, which extends in different directions over the ground floor; the latter is supported on columns. A suspended staircase leads directly to the waterfall. Terraces,

balconies, kitchens, and dining areas all extend in different directions. The bedrooms on the second floor give onto terraces, which, on the side facing the waterfall, are cantilevered out even further than the terrace of the first floor. A second upper storey is set well back, and is much smaller than the first, containing only one bedroom with an adjoining roof-terrace.

If one considers the ground-plans of the three storeys, they can be seen to form a pattern of interpenetrating surfaces, co-ordinated round a single vertical element, which is accentuated by the natural stone tower crowning the staircase. At the foot of this vertical element is the structurally important point of contact between the supported ground floor and the slope of the hill. The precisely thought out spatial composition of the building takes account of practical considerations. The base of the building is made out of natural stone, the individual storeys out of reinforced concrete, and the walls out of glass. The building literally combines Nature and Architecture – the organic and the geometric.

The same principles can be seen in the guest house which was added in 1939. This is connected to the main building by a curved stairway; here again, Wright has combined natural stone and concrete, and intertwined, by means of terraces, exterior and interior, Space and Nature.

64

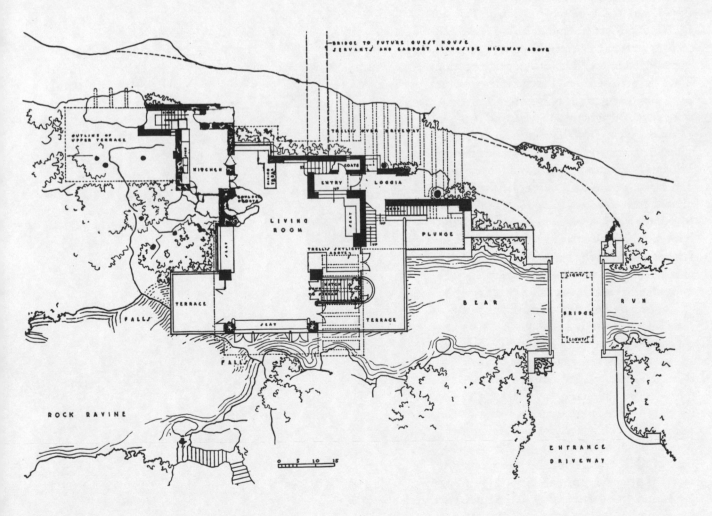

Edgar J. Kaufmann house, 'Falling Water', Bear Run, Pennsylvania
(1936) by Frank Lloyd Wright. Plan.

Plate 65
Taliesin West, Maricopa Mesa, Scottsville near
Phoenix, Arizona (1938–59)
by Frank Lloyd Wright

In 1911, Frank Lloyd Wright built Taliesin I
in Spring Green, Wisconsin; it was his first
house, containing, amongst other things, an
architectural school. This was altered several
times afterwards, but in 1914 it was burnt
down, and had to be reconstructed (Taliesin
II). In 1925, there was another fire, which led
to the erection of a third building. Annexes
were added in the 'thirties and early 'forties.
Thus the architect developed his own home
over different periods of his life.

In 1938, Wright began a second Taliesin
(Taliesin West), for the summer, in Scottsville, Arizona, in the Maricopa desert near
Phoenix. This was a new centre for teaching
and living, in a quite different landscape and
climate from the first. Here Wright was able
to retire from urban civilization. In this
building, he was striving to achieve a basic
relationship with the land and was influenced
in his design by precolumbian ideas as well
as by the desert climate.

The plan is composed of diagonally placed
rectangles, intersected by squares. Wright's
own house is part of a complex consisting of
courtyards, gardens, student accommodation, drawing studios, dining rooms and
sports areas. The basic material used in the
building is red desert stone and wood. The
sloping roof deliberately repeats the motif of
the nearby chain of mountains. The vocabulary of this crystal-line building includes
desert vegetation, open terraces, swimming
pools and the surrounding landscape. Because of the climate, the roof is made of
transparent canvas, which reflects the sun,
but allows air to pass through it.

65

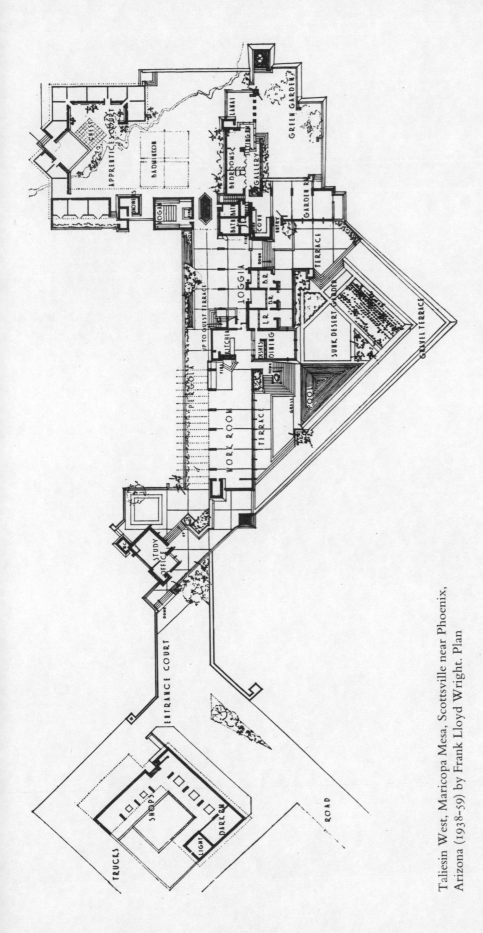

Taliesin West, Maricopa Mesa, Scottsville near Phoenix, Arizona (1938–59) by Frank Lloyd Wright. Plan

Plate 66
House for Dr Edith Farnsworth, Plano, Illinois
(1945–50) by Ludwig Mies van der Rohe

This small villa in Plano, Illinois, by Mies van der Rohe, is one of the most logical solutions to the problem of the single-family house. It was built on a large vacant site on the Fox River. Like the later Crown Hall at the Illinois Institute of Technology (Plate 75), it is a single-volume building. The living functions are put into a pre-formed frame, which can only be rendered serviceable by subdividing the original single space.

The house is raised from the ground on eight steel columns, to which are welded the slabs of the floor and the ceiling, thus making up the structural frame of the building. All the walls are of glass. The services are contained in a solid central unit with wooden cupboards which also serves to separate the living areas and the sleeping areas from the kitchen. There is also an outdoor living terrace, equivalent to the entrance slab in the Crown Hall building, at a slightly lower level.

66

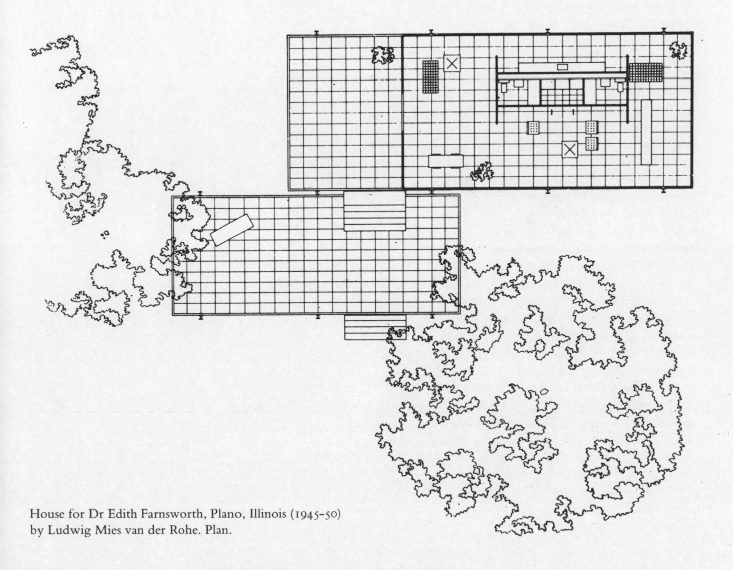

House for Dr Edith Farnsworth, Plano, Illinois (1945–50)
by Ludwig Mies van der Rohe. Plan.

Plate 67
Lake Shore Drive Apartments, Chicago (1948–51) by Ludwig Mies van der Rohe

After having worked in Germany, mainly on single-family dwellings (Plate 54), blocks of flats, and exhibition buildings, Mies van der Rohe's first chance to put his ideas for high-rise buildings into practice came in America. After the Promontory Apartments in Chicago (1946–49), the Lake Shore Drive Apartments were the most important prototype for residential skyscraper buildings throughout the world.

In contrast to the early Dutch high-rise residential blocks built in the 'thirties, and the residential tower blocks erected by Frank Lloyd Wright and Le Corbusier (Plate 68), Mies van der Rohe's buildings are defined by the way he uses the steel skeleton as the framework for the individual apartments. All twenty-six storeys are similarly constructed and the two buildings, which have identical ground-plans, stand at right angles to each other and are connected by a covered path. The two cube-like blocks are related to each other in such a way that they present continuously changing aspects from different viewpoints along the coastal road. The buildings are supported entirely on steel columns. The black painted steel framework contrasts with the glass surfaces, whose narrow rectangles rhythmically punctuate the surfaces of the walls. In 1927, Mies van der Rohe proposed that the inhabitants of a building lay out the plan of each apartment for themselves; here he put the idea into practice.

Mies van der Rohe subsequently built other residential towers, including the Chicago Commonwealth Apartments (1953-56), and Park Lafayette in Detroit, where he combined towers with two-storey row-housing (1955–63) in an area planned by Ludwig Hilberseimer.

67

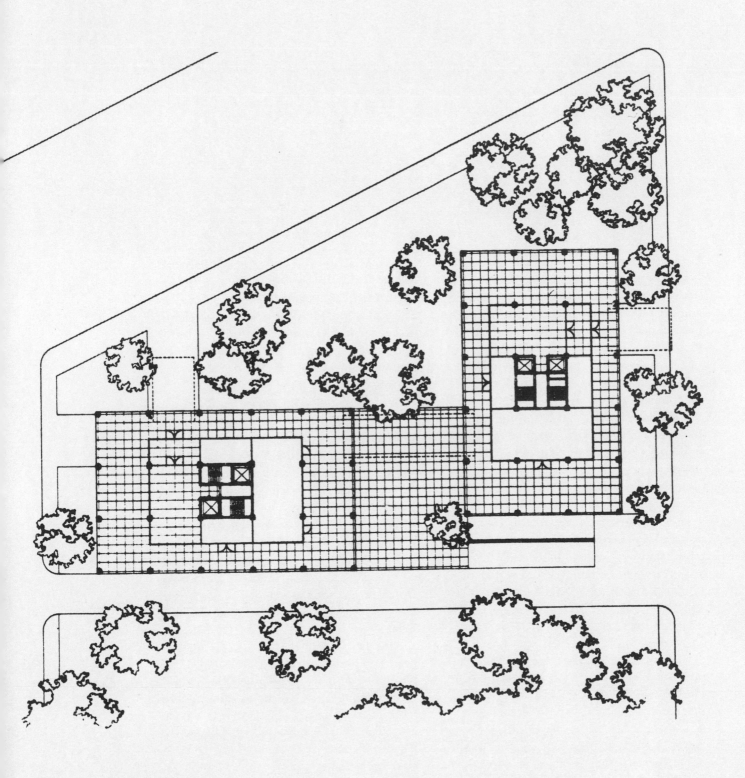

Lake Shore Drive Apartments, Chicago (1948-51)
by Ludwig Mies van der Rohe. Plan.

Plate 68
Unité d'Habitation, Marseilles (1947–52) by
Le Corbusier

Le Corbusier's plans for a vertical town-house, a machine for living which would provide man with the comfort he needed, and offer both privacy and participation in nature, had existed since 1945, and formed part of his ideas for adapting the old concept of the town to modern living conditions.

In this spirit, he designed a town for 2,000 inhabitants under one roof. He used his 'Modulor' system, based on the human body, to determine all the proportions of the building. (The system combines the English duodecimal and the continental decimal system.) This building covers only a fraction of the area that would be covered by a conventional horizontal town for the same number of people. Le Corbusier's first opportunity to realize these plans came in 1947–52 when he built the Unité d'Habitation on the Boulevard Michelet in Marseilles. This was followed by several more Unités d'Habitation in Nantes, Brian-Foret, Meaux and Berlin.

The interior arrangement of the building, which consists of 337 two-storey 'houses', with twenty-three variations, is organized so that pairs interlock. The cross section of each is L-shaped. The lower part of an upper 'house', which is only half as large as the upper part, fits against the upper part of the lower house, which is only half the size of the lower part. The height of each apartment,

where it is two storeys high, is 16 feet and where it is only one storey high is $7\frac{1}{2}$ feet. Apartments are arranged on both sides of an internal 'street'. On the seventh and eighth floors there is a communications centre for the vertical 'town' with a street with shops, laundry, hotel, post office and hairdressing salons. Access to different storeys is by a central shaft, containing stairs and lifts.

The side walls of each balcony are painted in bright colours which accentuate the raw concrete of the building, and have caused it to be compared with a giant beehive.

The often-photographed roof of this building, with its sculpted chimneys and installation elements, is intended for community living. It contains a kindergarten, a swimming pool, a gymnasium and other communal facilities. In sculpting the vertical forms on the roof, the architect tried to make there a park-like environment for the inhabitants.

This first Unité d'Habitation, 163 feet high, 130 feet long and 80 feet deep, led to a revolution in mass-housing and has had incalculable influence, mostly in the southern hemisphere (Japan, India, South America, etc.). The fact that this building, like Moshe Safdie's Habitat '67 (Plate 107) can be criticized in certain respects does not detract from its sociological significance, which led to new trends in the construction of towns.

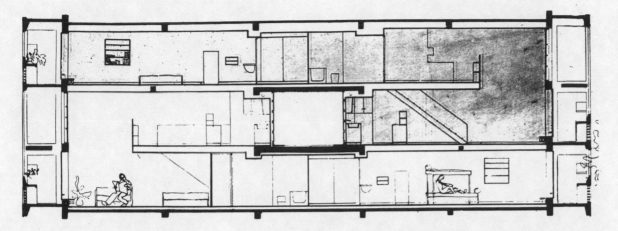

Unité d'Habitation, Marseilles (1947–52) by Le Corbusier.
Longitudinal section through two apartments.

1 Interior street
2 Entrance
3 Living room with kitchen
4 Parents' room with bath
5 Cupboard, shelves, ironing board, children's shower
6 Children's room
7 Upper area of communal room

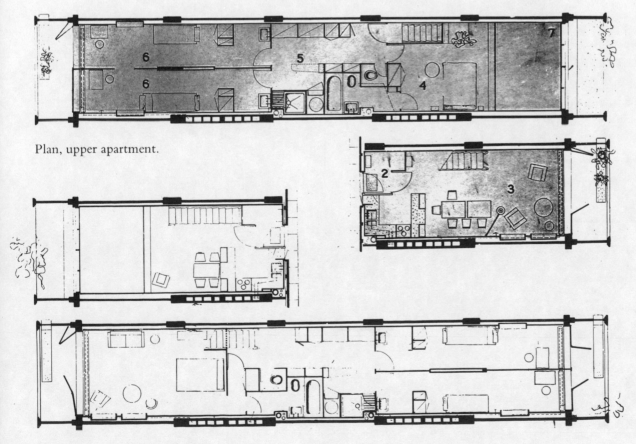

Plan, upper apartment.

Plan, lower apartment.

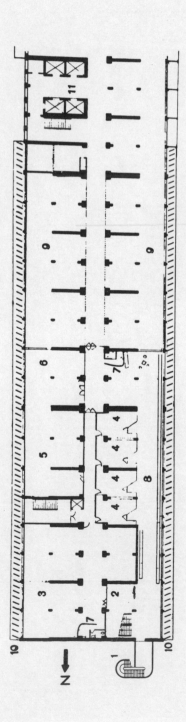

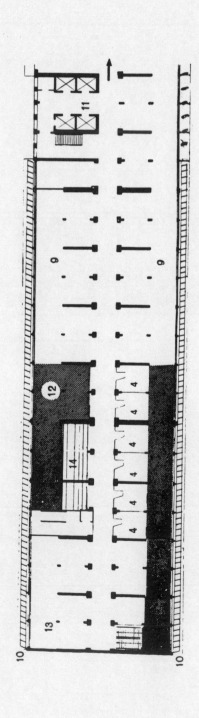

Unité d'Habitation, Marseilles (1947–52)
by Le Corbusier.
Plans, communal services.

1 Emergency stairs
2 Entrance hall
3 Tenants' club, reading room,
  music room, projection room
4 Shops
5 Food depot
6 Food shop
7 Toilets

8 Promenade
9 Studios or workshops
10 Sun-baffles
11 Lifts
12 Open space
13 Laundry
14 Screen

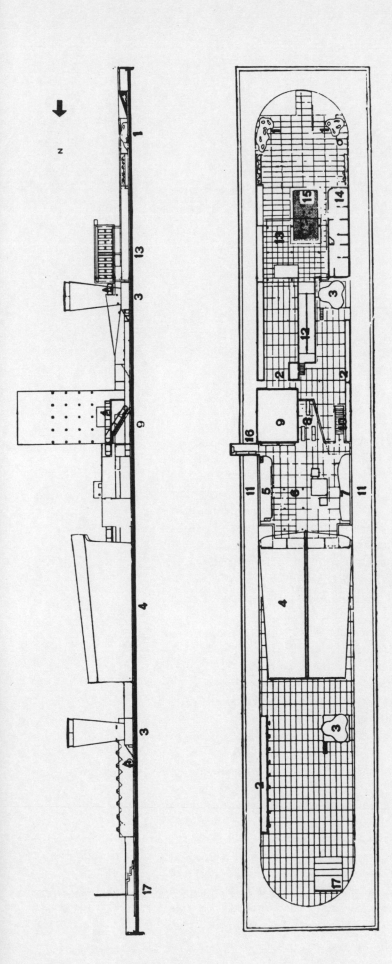

Unité d' Habitation, Marseilles (1947–52)
by Le Corbusier.
Plan and elevation, roof.

1 Artificial hills
2 Flower tub
3 Ventilation shafts
4 Gymnasium
5 East sun-lounge
6 Cloakrooms and upper terrace
7 West sun-lounge
8 Concrete tables
9 Lift with access to terrace and bar

10 External stairs
11 300-metre running track
12 Ramp linking the health-service floor
      (17th) with the terrace and nursery
13 Nursery
14 Kindergarten
15 Swimming pool
16 Balcony
17 Wind-break and open-air theatre

Plate 69
Research Tower for the Johnson Wax Company,
Racine, Wisconsin (1949–51) by Frank Lloyd
Wright

The Larkin Building, Buffalo (1904 – since demolished), reveals that Frank Lloyd Wright's approach to factory building was completely fresh. More than thirty years later, he designed the Administration Building for the Johnson Wax Company in Racine, Wisconsin. This was in the style which he and others had developed at the beginning of the 'thirties. Both buildings have large central spaces, in Buffalo based on crystalline, and in Racine, on organic principles. The Racine building, with its right-angled and curved elements, and its creative use of brick, fits naturally into the organic style of the 'thirties. The building was such a sensation when it was built that it was visited by 30,000 people in the first two days after it was opened. It cost twice as much to build as had originally been foreseen.

In spite of this, Wright's clients commissioned him, in 1949, to design the firm's research centre ten years after he had completed the administrative building. Wright suggested a tower block. This would give a vertical accent to the horizontal form of the rest of the factory, and finish off the composition. An earlier design for the building involved a tower widening towards the top – an 'anti-static' tower, in fact. But this was never executed. Whereas, in the administrative buildings, the main effect is of closed brick walls, in the research tower, brick is only one element of the total composition. This is possible because the fourteen storeys are suspended from a central steel mast, enabling as much light as possible to come through to each floor. The vertically divided walls are broken up by a thin brick band on every second storey. At the top, the final band is rather broader than the others.

The roof elements, which correspond with the forms of the remaining buildings, are rounded and made of brick. The tower is given a spool-like appearance by the way the glass walls and bands of brick are carried round the corners.

This building marks the beginning of Frank Lloyd Wright's later work – that collection of buildings and designs which represents the pinnacle of modern architectural achievement. The main characteristics of his later work are an enormous richness of spatial, structural and functional ideas, the creation of buildings to fit in with a new ideal of living together, and the integration of the individual building into an organically conceived and executed total complex. Hints of all these can be seen in the Tower.

69

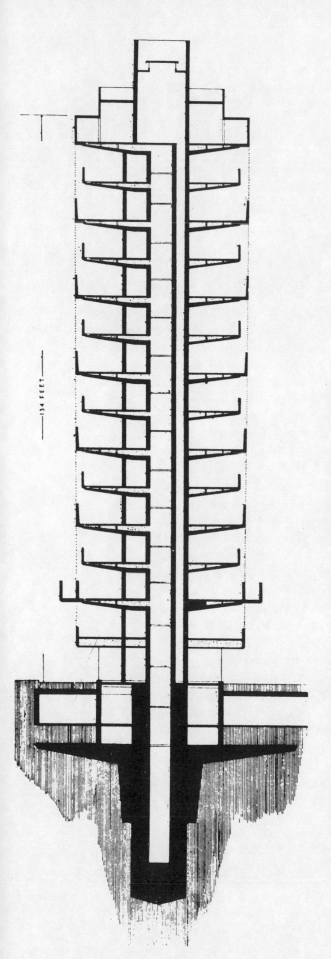

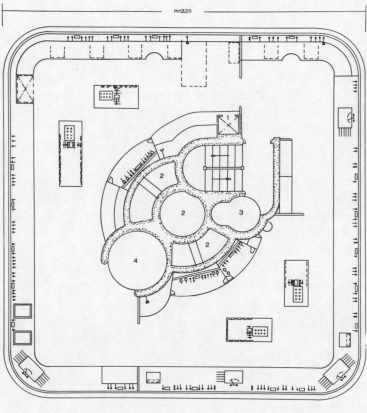

Research Tower for the Johnson Wax Company,
Racine, Wisconsin (1949-51) by Frank Lloyd Wright.
Plan and elevation.
1 Goods lift
2 Air-conditioning ducts
3 Services
4 Passenger lift

Plate 70
General Motors Technical Institute, Warren near Detroit (1949–56) by Eero Saarinen

It is rarely, in the twentieth century, that a whole industrial complex has been so integrally planned and executed by one architect as the General Motors Research Laboratories in Warren, near Detroit, by Eero Saarinen. Similar examples are, perhaps, Peter Behrens' AEG buildings in Berlin (Plate 40), Matté-Trucco's Fiat building in Lingotto near Turin (Plate 45) or Albert Kahn's Ford buildings in Dearborn. In all these cases, there was an opportunity, seized with varying degrees of success, to plan the whole complex integrally from the outset.

Eliel and Eero Saarinen were originally commissioned to draw up the plans for a new General Motors Technical Institute in 1945. However, there were delays in executing the plans. In 1949, Eero Saarinen drew up new plans, upon which the actual buildings were based. In designing the General Motors laboratories, Saarinen used principles established by Mies van der Rohe, including that of designing all the buildings, their proportions and their relationship to each other in terms of a module. It is probable that Saarinen was influenced by Mies van der Rohe's plan of the Illinois Institute of Technology. At all events, their site plans are similar, allocating each building a predetermined place within the complex. There are, however, important differences. As opposed to the almost floating, idealized spaces of Mies van der Rohe, which are produced by the clarity of his structures, here we have a practical, solid, box-like building firmly anchored to the ground, clearly planned and composed.

The individual buildings are arranged in accordance with certain rules of proportion, around an artificial pool. Two building masses punctuate the otherwise regular and right-angled complex: the steel ball of the water-tower (see plate), supported on three slender columns, and the steel dome of the Styling Auditorium, which echoes the round shape of the water-tower. Both are distinguished from the strict rectangularity of the other buildings not only by their shapes, but also their colour. The other buildings are built with brightly coloured tiles (azure blue, tomato red, and sunflower yellow), whereas these two have only the colours of their material. Saarinen was using steel in a new way, to mirror the surroundings, the clouds, the water, the green of the trees, and the colour of the other buildings. This new technique, which anticipated the Steel Arch in St Louis, Missouri, begun in the same year, but only finished in 1966, is only used for a part of the total complex, which is strictly separated into engineer-building and architecture.

This grandiose, well thought-out and perfectly executed set of research buildings for one of the leading automobile manufacturers in the United States has been called 'the Versailles of the twentieth century', and is both an effective and a representative expression of the powers-that-be in modern society.

70

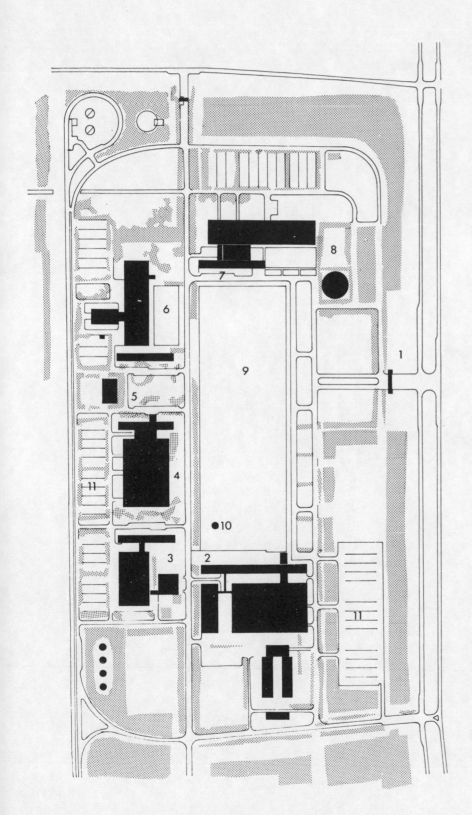

General Motors Technical Institute,
Warren near Detroit (1949-56)
by Eero Saarinen. Plan.
1 Main gate
2 Research
3 Service
4 Manufacturing development
5 Restaurant
6 Engineering
7 Styling
8 Auditorium
9 Lake
10 Water tower
11 Car park

71

Plate 71
Pilgrimage church of Notre-Dame-du-Haut,
Ronchamp (1950–54) by Le Corbusier

Church building in the twentieth century was influenced for a long time by styles and techniques developed primarily for other forms of building, particularly factories. Le Corbusier's pilgrimage church at Ronchamp was a revolt against this trend. This little building represented a breakaway from the strict frame type of building common in the first part of the century, and which Le Corbusier himself helped to develop, towards an architecture of dynamic and imaginative spatial form.

There had been a pilgrimage church on the site, visible for miles, for centuries, dating back to the thirteenth century. The earlier church was destroyed in 1944. Le Corbusier's plans for a new church were submitted in 1950 and approved in 1951. The building, in which some of the stones from the old church were used, was completed in 1954.

The dominant feature is the roof, which is made of two roof-shells on top of each other, $7\frac{1}{2}$ feet apart. The curved roof is supported on similarly curved walls, which, like the roof, are not massive but are given strength by their curved shape. The interior space is only 82 feet long and 43 feet wide, and can seat about 200 people. Three towers, one 72 and two 49 feet, perform the dual functions of crowning the architecture externally, and bringing light into the interior.

The channelling of light is a particularly interesting feature of this church. It is effected partly by a thin opening between the downward-curving ceiling and the apparently massive walls, which relieves the heaviness of the interior space, and partly by the windows and light slits cut into two of the walls, which admit diffused, filtered, occasionally coloured light into certain parts of the interior. The light which comes in from the three towers falls directly onto the altars of the three chapels inside the church.

The pews were designed by the sculptor, Savino. The floor, like all the other forms in the building, is not flat, but slightly curved. The height from the floor to the ceiling, which curves more than 16 feet downwards, varies from $15\frac{1}{2}$ feet to 33 feet.

Outside, the roof projects over the east wall, and makes a covered space, with an open air altar, chancel and dais for religious services. This is particularly important for pilgrims. The hand of the creator of this building can be seen even in the glass paintings and enamel decoration of the main portal. The details of the gargoyles and the treatment of the raw concrete throughout the building clearly betray the sculptural hand of Le Corbusier. The church, visible for miles around, is comparatively small, but its effect is of monumentality.

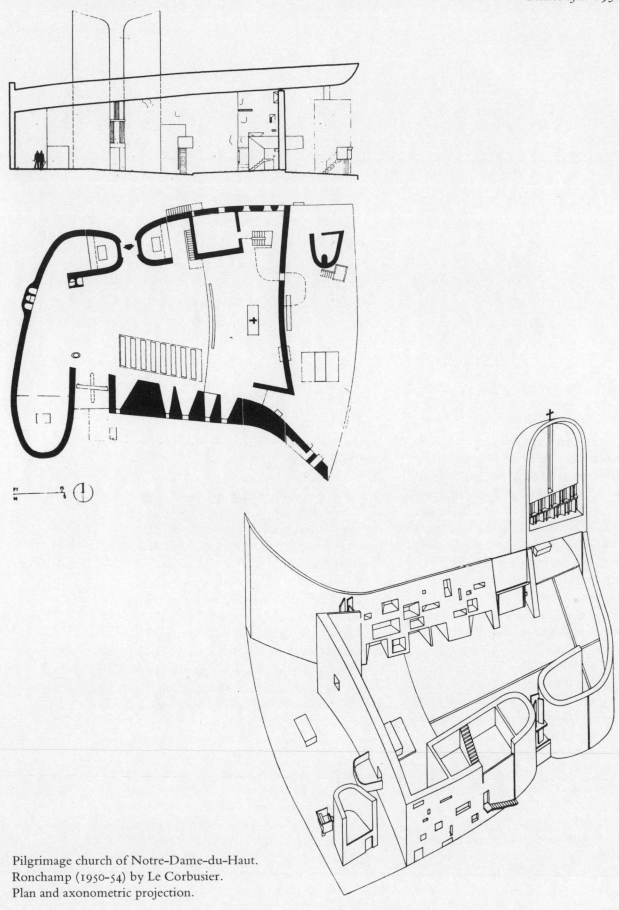

Pilgrimage church of Notre-Dame-du-Haut.
Ronchamp (1950-54) by Le Corbusier.
Plan and axonometric projection.

Plate 72
Administration Centre, Säynätsalo (1950–52)
by Alvar Aalto

Alvar Aalto's Administration Centre in Säynätsalo on Lake Paijanne in Finland was built from 1950 to 1952. It is not only typical of a particular development in architecture at that time, but is also an excellent solution to the needs of a local authority in a small rural district. It expresses, as it were, both the regional and the international.

At the time the building was completed, Säynätsalo had only 3,000 inhabitants. Nevertheless, the local authority had the courage to commission a famous architect to design their administrative building, and prepare a plan for the whole area. Aalto was, therefore, able to design the individual building in the context of a whole area, to make a focal point for the life of the community. The Centre contains the town hall, the library, shops, an enclosed garden with a fountain on the level of the first storey, and a flat for the caretaker. It is therefore a multi-functional unit, and the cultural, social, and economic centre of the town.

Its position, on a tree-covered hillside, enabled Aalto to make clever use of the natural differences of level of the ground, to carry the landscape, as it were, into the architecture. The main materials used are traditional brick and wood. The chief characteristics of the building are its brick walls, the obliquely-rising form of the roof, the closed exterior as opposed to the open interior and the clear contrasts of brick, wood and glass in the predominantly horizontal composition. The complex has two wings: the west wing, with shops on the ground floor and the library on the first, and the east wing, with its step-like cantilever, containing the town hall and offices. Between the two there is a raised, open garden courtyard, which is reached by a flight of steps. The windows of the library are shielded from the low lying northern sun by wooden slats.

The administration and community centre is part of an overall plan for the whole area, and is carefully related to the environment. As Aalto himself said here, '. . . I am trying to achieve integrated architecture'. This building, in particular, not only integrates landscape, region, climate, building materials and structural techniques, but in adapting above all to *human* requirements, it gives man a new importance in architecture.

72

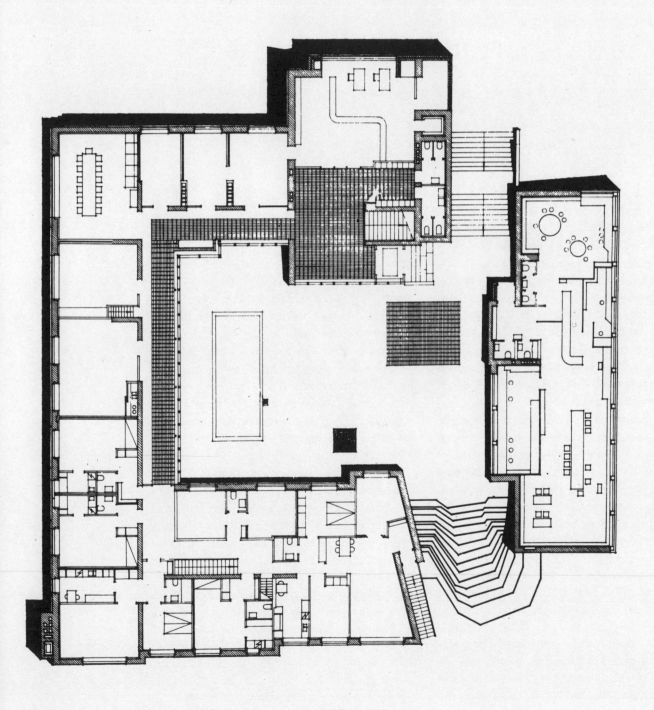

Administration Centre, Säynätsalo (1950-52) by Alvar Aalto. Plan.

Plate 73
Lever House, New York (1950–52)
by Skidmore, Owings, and Merrill

The great prestige of the firm Skidmore, Owings, and Merrill was established with the building of Lever House, at 390 Park Avenue. This building has been copied in several other countries and has become a prototype for administrative headquarter buildings for large companies. As such, it has proved extremely effective.

The basic form was conceived by the firm's chief designer, Gordon Bunshaft. It consists of a twenty-one-storey office tower block, with a skeleton frame and a glass and aluminium skin, and a two-storey podium building, supported, like the tower block, on columns, and designed for public use. The forecourt formed by the adjoining open area is a quiet place cut off from the busy city, open to passers-by. The tower block begins above the two-storey podium. On the third storey (that is, at the bottom of the tower but above the horizontal part of the building), there is a cafeteria and a restaurant. The over-all height of Lever House is 305 feet.

The floor plans of the majority of storeys can, in spite of the uniformity of the exterior of the building, in principle be varied from storey to storey, making open-plan offices possible. The structure is determined by a steel skeleton concealed inside the building, allowing the whole of the exterior to be covered with glass. This uniform glass façade conceals all the interior functions and means that the individual shape of the rooms inside the building cannot be seen on the outside. The glass is permanently closed, and is coloured green to shield those inside from the sun and from public view. The temperature inside the building is maintained by air conditioning units.

The building, which is set 100 feet back from the street, uses less than half of the site, which is on one of the most expensive streets in the world. This creates a pleasant urban court in the middle of Manhattan.

In the nearby Seagram Building, Mies van der Rohe and Philip Johnson tried to achieve a similar 'humanization' of the city-centre (Mies van der Rohe's work clearly influenced the design of the Lever Building). The same ideas in different form can be seen in the Ford Foundation building by Roche and Dinkeloo (Plate 106).

73

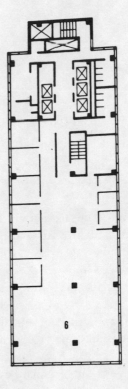

Plan of typical office floor.

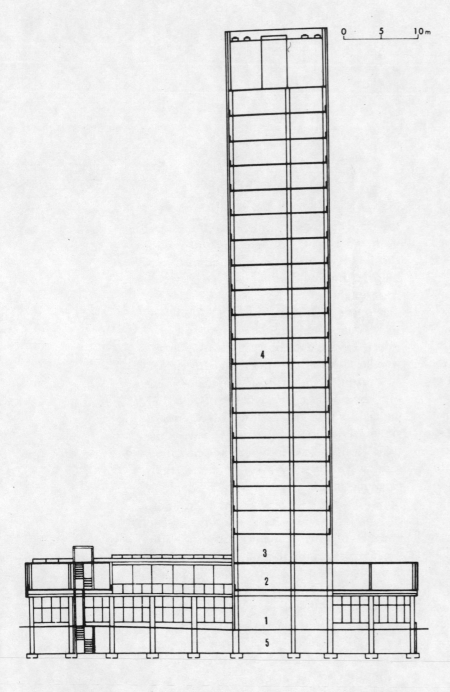

Lever House, New York (1950-52) by Skidmore, Owings and Merrill. Section.
1 Entrance hall
2 Assembly room
3 Dining room
4 Office floor
5 Basement
6 Offices

Plate 74
High Court, Chandigarh (1952–56)
by Le Corbusier

In spite of the fact that virtually all twentieth-century architectural theory is concerned with towns, surprisingly few original towns have been built. Le Corbusier's plans of the 1920s were never realized, and where complete new towns have been built, as in Brasilia, Islamabad, and Chandigarh, compromises have had to be made. Chandigarh, however, the new capital of the Punjab, represents the best that has been achieved so far.

Le Corbusier was commissioned to plan the town in 1950. He produced his designs in 1951. He envisaged a town divided into sectors measuring 880 by 1,320 yards, with a Capitol. The traffic network was split into seven systems. He called it an 'anthropo-morphic' city, regarding the administrative headquarters as the head, and the residential quarters as the limbs, etc. Le Corbusier had to find an idiom which would suit the importance of the project, the country and the people. He had to take into consideration the hostile climate in Chandigarh, with extremes of sun and monsoon, and the need to use minimum resources and primitive techniques.

The High Court, which stands beside one of the three large pools constructed by Le Corbusier, is one of the Capitol buildings, representative of the new state. In order to enable judges and court officials to work regardless of the time of day or the season of the year, the façade faces north-west, so that the sun does not shine fully onto it until late in the afternoon. The different functions in the building are organized within a rectangular frame. The building has a double roof because of the heat and the monsoon. The upper roof, rising from the middle towards both sides, is cantilevered out over the lower, casting a shadow. A channel in the middle leads off the monsoon rain, which runs through pipes at the sides of the building into the pool, helping to keep it full. The upper roof rests on the lower in a series of arches, allowing air to circulate between the two. The half open entrance hall is dramatically accentuated by three concrete walls, reaching right up to the upper roof, defining the entrance, like pillars. To the right of the entrance, there are eight courtrooms, visible in the regular pattern on the outside. On the left is the large supreme court. The windows in the façade are fixed, and cannot be opened. They are shaded by a system of concrete sun-breakers extending up in a curve to the lower roof. Le Corbusier said that his sun-breakers are meant to shield not only the windows, but the whole façade, and to determine the form of the whole structure.

Since access to individual courts is from the outside, something had to be done to protect the waiting public from the weather. It was finally agreed to erect a thin concrete roof, supported on metal columns. This stretches from the right side of the entrance practically to the end of the building, at

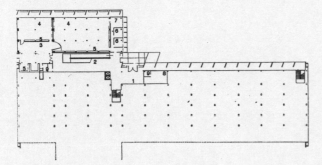

Level 1 : traffic

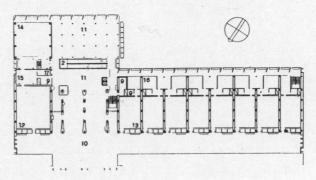

Level 2 : chief concourse

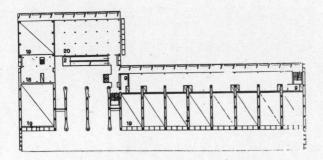

Level 3 : judges' offices

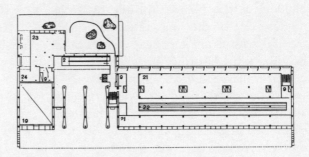

Level 4 : offices, archives and restaurants

first-floor level, and disturbs the overall sculptural composition of the building as little as possible. The courts quickly became too small for requirements, and an annexe for more courtrooms had to be built. This was put, in 1962, behind the supreme court, and connected to the main building by a covered passageway. It is built entirely of brick. This arrangement preserves the finite effect of the main building.

The entrance pillars, which were originally painted white, and harmonized perfectly with the colour of the rest of the building, were repainted by Le Corbusier in spite of tremendous opposition, according to a colour scheme he had worked out in 1958 – black, yellow, green, red and blue. It may be that this was an attempt to counterbalance the triple horizontal lines of the building, emphasized by their reflections in the water. In spite of its much criticized faults, this building, with its powerful plasticity, does suit the climate, its functions, and the country's traditions. It is one of the masterpieces of twentieth-century architecture.

High Court, Chandigarh (1952–56) by Le Corbusier.
1 Entrance
2 Ramps
3 Lawyers' reception room
4 Lawyers' work room
5 Pigeon-holes for books
6 Consultation rooms
7 Librarian's office
8 Police
9 Toilets
10 Entrance from the park
11 Concourse
12 High court
13 Court
14 Library
15 Judges' dining room
16 Judges' rooms
17 Kitchen
18 High court gallery
19 Open space
20 Upper area of concourse
21 Offices
22 Archives
23 Restaurant
24 Office restaurant

Plate 75
Crown Hall, Illinois Institute of Technology,
Chicago (1952–56)
by Ludwig Mies van der Rohe

Crown Hall, the architecture and design
building at the Illinois Institute of Technology, one of the most important architectural schools in America, is the central
building at the Institute, the whole of which
was first planned by Mies van der Rohe in
1939. Mies was the head of the department of
architecture, and was therefore his own
client. Not surprisingly he made architecture
the focal point of the entire Institute.

Here he was able to realize his ideas as
regards both the function and the form of
building to the full. He created a large, symmetrical single space, which could be used
as an open framework for different functions. As a building, it shows how architecture can be not merely the form of a building
but also its content, like Mies' Barcelona
Pavilion in 1929, which hardly needed any
exhibits, since it was itself the prime exhibit.

Crown Hall was designed to house a
permanent exhibition of students' work. Its
plan is symmetrical. Everything is subordinated to the technically determined structure
of the building. The roof, which measures
120 feet by 120 feet, and is suspended from
four girders, is an important part of the
structure, and of the building's total aesthetic
effect. To the sides, the roof slab is cantilevered 20 feet out over the exterior wall.
The exterior walls are curtain walls, and
have no load-bearing function. The work
rooms are in the basement – to avoid breaking the virtually uninterrupted space above,
which can be divided at will. The entrance
is reached by a flight of steps, made out of
slabs of travertine, which appear to float in
space.

75

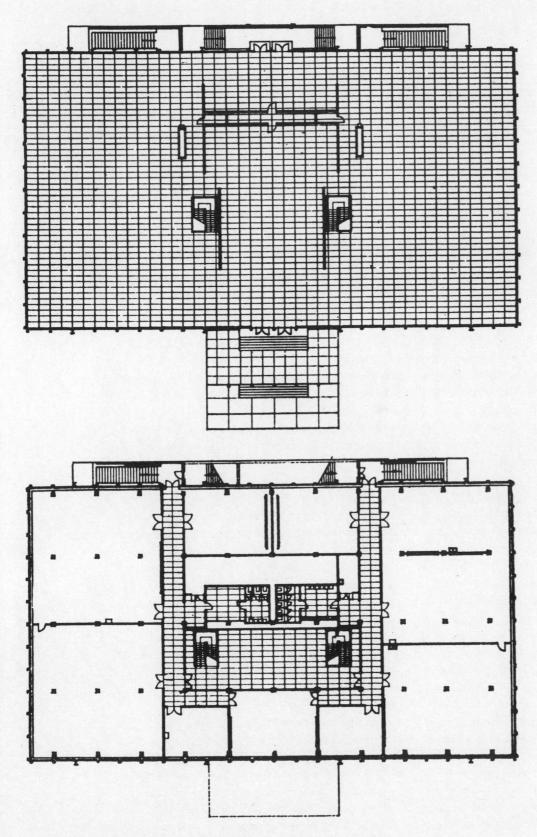

Crown Hall, Illinois Institute of Technology, Chicago (1952–56)
by Ludwig Mies van der Rohe. Floor plans.

Plate 76
Solomon R. Guggenheim Museum, New York
(1956–59) by Frank Lloyd Wright

The later work of Frank Lloyd Wright contains an enormous wealth of forms and ideas of which the originality and significance has hardly begun to be recognized. The Solomon R. Guggenheim Museum, on 5th Avenue between 88th and 89th Street, was completed, after many years of planning, in the year Wright died. It is one of his remarkable later works, and includes several completely new ideas. Plans were first drawn up for this unique building just after the Second World War. A drawing dating back to 1943 envisages a six-cornered design. Another in the same year shows the building as a round shape with an internal spiral. The building site was gradually acquired between 1947 and 1951, giving Wright plenty of time to experiment with the shape. The actual building only began in the later 'fifties.

As so often before, Wright invented a completely new shape for this building problem, creating, for the Guggenheim collection, a sculpture which unfolds into space. The seven-storey building is developed around an open well in the form of a spiral, with a huge skylight as a roof. Individual storeys project ever further outwards at succeeding levels. The visitor is taken up to the top of the building by lift, and then walks down the gentle slope of the spiral ramp to the ground floor, where there is a library and a bookshop. The museum's administrative offices are in a separate building to the north. This also has a spiral shape, a glass dome roof,

and individual storeys giving onto an open internal court. The two parts of the building are connected by a band of concrete.

Wright was trying to develop a new kind of museum in which each work of art was not merely a subordinate part of the wall, but could stand out against a slightly curving surface, and 'float', as it were, on its own. Wright regarded the picture's complete environment, in the widest sense, as its 'frame'. Since not only are the walls curved, but the floor has a continuous gentle slope, any movement on the part of the visitor creates for him continuously changing combinations of forms and colours. Other paintings are always visible when looking at any one of them, since the whole exhibition can be seen from any point on the ramp. Wright attached special importance to lighting. By using both daylight and artificial light, he attempted to achieve 'three-dimensional' light, and create a variety of effects.

Unlike Le Corbusier, who also suggested an 'unending' museum in the form of a spiral, Wright achieved a complete expression of his concept of 'organic architecture'. Le Corbusier had a flat spiral in mind, whereas Wright's concept is three-dimensional, and links the visitor, the picture, and the environment into one unit. The curve of the continuous seven-storey reinforced concrete ramp is based on the principle of the unbroken wave. It makes possible privacy, communication with the individual picture,

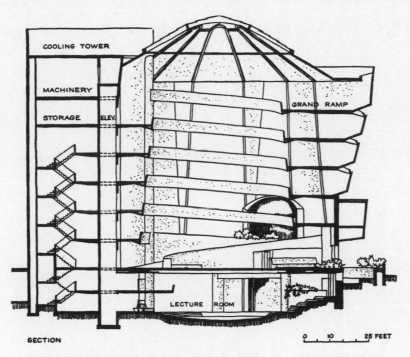

COOLING TOWER

MACHINERY

STORAGE   ELEV.

GRAND RAMP

LECTURE ROOM

SECTION

0   10   25 FEET

participation in the whole, and communication with the total space. Wright has freed himself from traditional limiting rules of form, and has made something entirely original, a product of both discipline and freedom: a new environmental dynamic, a convincing architectural and spatial formula.

During the first nine months after the museum was officially opened, when Frank Lloyd Wright was already dead, it was visited by more than 750,000 people. This was undoubtedly partly due to the outstanding collection donated by Wright's client, Solomon R. Guggenheim, who died in 1949, and was only able to see the early plans for the building. The collection includes major works by Brancusi, Arp, Kandinsky, Cézanne, Klee, and others. But the building itself has been called the most important work in the whole Guggenheim collection.

The first director of the museum, James Johnson Sweeney, had ideas about the museum, with which Wright disagreed, but which eventually produced superb solutions to the problems of lighting and space. In this building, a fresh approach to the concept of a progressive museum has been made; as Frank Lloyd Wright said to Solomon R. Guggenheim in 1949, 'I assure you that anything you desired to happen could happen.'

Solomon R. Guggenheim Museum, New York (1956-59) by Frank Lloyd Wright. Section.

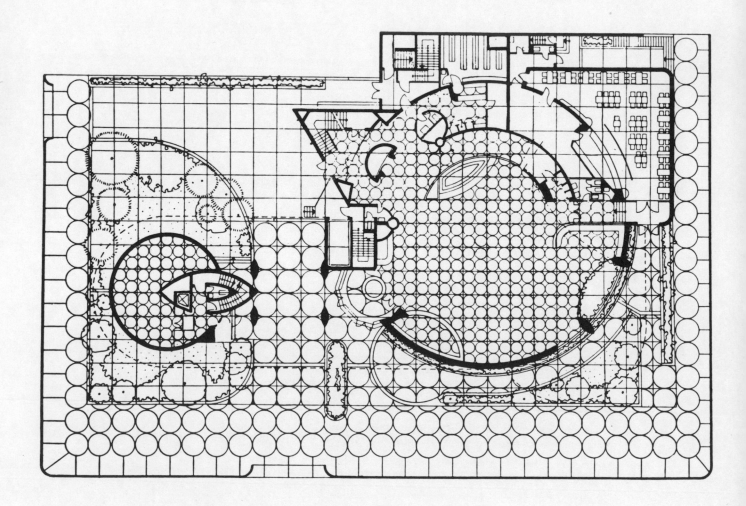

Solomon R. Guggenheim Museum, New York (1956-59) by Frank Lloyd Wright.
Ground plan.

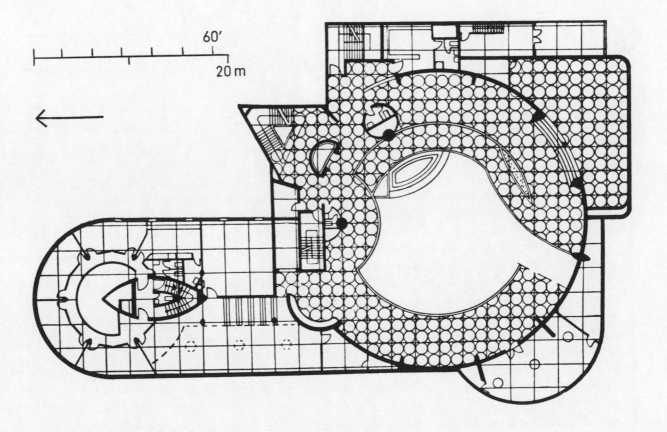

60'

20 m

First floor plan.

Plate 77
Low-cost apartments, Casablanca (1954–55) by
André Studer

Mass housing remains a problem virtually unsolved throughout the world, in spite of the intensive efforts of the younger architects. On the outskirts of towns and cities all over the world can be found the same chaotic agglomeration of temporary and emergency dwellings conflicting with every conceivable principle of modern architecture. The first, surprisingly successful steps towards a solution to the slum problem in developing countries were taken by the French architects Candilis and Woods in North Africa, and by the Swiss André Studer, with his Casablanca tenements.

This Arab settlement in Casablanca was designed by Studer in 1953, and executed in 1954 and 1955, with slight modifications. It is one of the few successful solutions of the problem of mass housing. Studer originally conceived the estate as a coherent unit composed of dwelling systems, in stepped pyramidal form, arranged diagonally around a central market place. The local authorities, however, forced Studer eventually to use a more traditional, block-like arrangement.

Individual building-compartments are placed diagonally, with balconies supported on slender columns. This arrangement shades the apartment underneath, and creates a characteristic play of light and shade; the total effect is both attractive and functional. The most interesting aspect of the building is that mass housing and individuality have been reconciled, and even complement each other. Even on the higher storeys, each family has a completely private open space to itself. It is interesting to notice here that polygamy, usually regarded as a reactionary institution, has produced a revolutionary architectural concept. This solution, specifically adapted to conditions in North Africa, has elements which could well be useful in mass-architecture in quite different parts of the world.

77

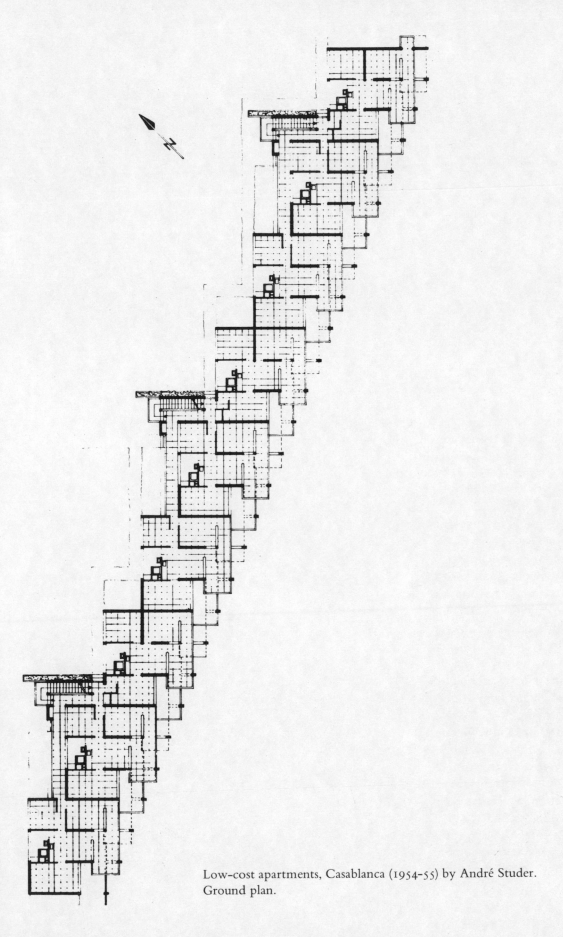

Low-cost apartments, Casablanca (1954–55) by André Studer.
Ground plan.

Plates 78
Swimming stadium in the University town,
Caracas (1957) by Carlos Raul Villanueva

The planning and execution of the University town of Caracas, largely by Carlos Raul Villanueva, began in 1950. The swimming stadium, completed in 1957, is part of this development. It contains a swimming and diving pool, a boxing ring, a fencing room, and rooms for first aid and resting.

The building, with its dynamic cantilever, is made of raw concrete, and is given individuality by its colours, particularly on the lower parts. An almost elemental harmony of colours is achieved by the raw concrete, the occasional dashes of yellow higher up, the brilliant red lower walls, framed in white, and the colour of the water and the surrounding lawns. The structure projects or recedes as required by its function, accentuated by the use of colour, producing a daring, if rather unsubtle play of forces. Perhaps it is this less sensitive, robust approach that is the special attraction of South American architecture.

78

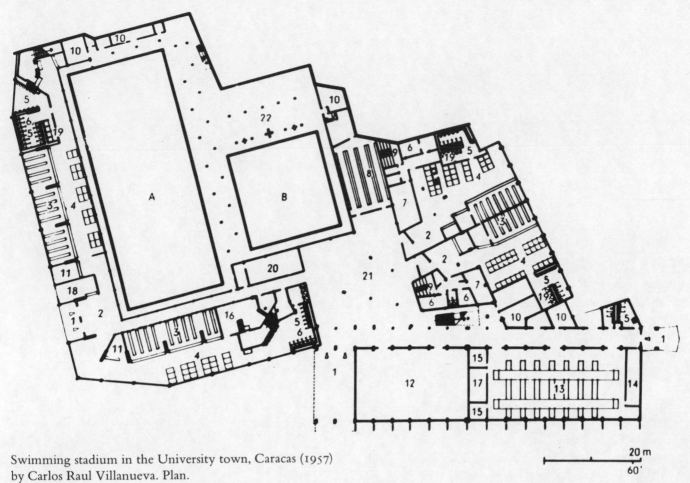

Swimming stadium in the University town, Caracas (1957)
by Carlos Raul Villanueva. Plan.

A   Swimming pool.
B   Diving pool
1   Entrance
2   Hall
3   Cloakrooms
4   Dressing rooms
5   Ambulance stations
6   Showers
7   Rest and massage
8   Lockers
9   Steam bath
10 Storage
11 Control
12 Boxing arena
13 Fencing arena
14 Coach
15 Equipment storage
16 Laundry storage
17 Lounge
18 Guard
19 Baths
20 Pump
21 Underground passage
22 Filter system

20 m
60'

Plate 79
Pirelli Building, Milan (1957–61) by Gio Ponti, Antonio Fornaroli, Alberto Rosselli (architects) and Pier Luigi Nervi, Giuseppe Valtolino, Egidio Dell'Orto, Arturo Danusso (engineers)

Since the Chicago school produced the first masterpieces of this genre (Plate 14), an enormous number of styles of office tower blocks have been developed all over the world. The Italian contribution includes the Torre Velasca and the Pirelli Building in Milan, the latter built by a designer (Ponti) and an engineer (Nervi).

The basic form of the 415 feet high building is an ellipse with two points, flattened at the sides to make it aerodynamic. This corresponds to the laws of function which state that the passages towards the ends of a building will be less used than those in the middle. For this reason the plan is angled, with four triangle apexes at the extremities and four slab-columns in the centre. In cross-section, the structure is like a tree, tapering towards the top. This produces a streamlined, elegant exterior.

The tower stands over a two-storey horizontal podium building fitting most convincingly alongside the park in front of Milan Central Station. The enormous structure is placed so that it forms a vertical accent to the massive revivalist railway station which lies at right angles to its axis.

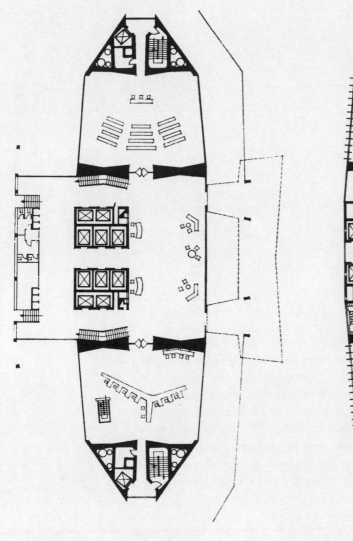

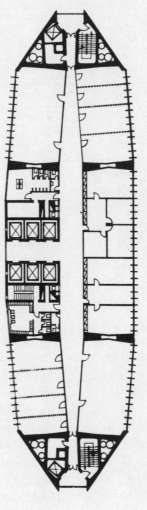

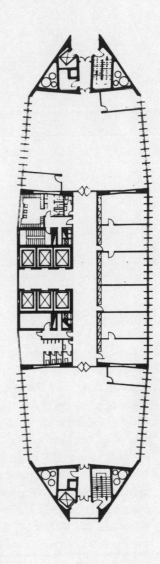

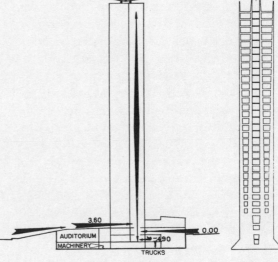

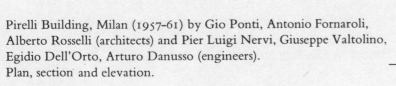

Pirelli Building, Milan (1957–61) by Gio Ponti, Antonio Fornaroli,
Alberto Rosselli (architects) and Pier Luigi Nervi, Giuseppe Valtolino,
Egidio Dell'Orto, Arturo Danusso (engineers).
Plan, section and elevation.

Plate 80
Dulles International Airport, Chantilly, Virginia (1958–62) by Eero Saarinen

The airport of Washington, in nearby Chantilly, is the last, and undoubtedly the most important work of the Finnish-American architect Eero Saarinen (born 1910, died in 1961, before this building was completed). This is one of the most daring engineering achievements of recent years, and was executed in co-operation with the engineers, Amman and Whitney. Basically, the building consists of two rows of sixteen outward sloping pillars supporting the enormous roof, which is inclined to one side. The form of the building is based on the dynamics and tension of 'take off'. Nevertheless, it is the functional way it deals with the requirements of airline traffic, rather than its representation of movement, which is of special note.

Dulles International Airport had to be the main reception building for one of the world's greatest nations, and be suitable for official occasions. It is no exaggeration to say that it succeeds in expressing the greatness of the United States. It is the first, and so far the only airport in the world built exclusively for jets. It was designed to cope with a volume of jet traffic projected decades ahead. Each runway is almost two miles long. Passengers

are taken from the building to the aircraft in groups of ninety, in moving transporters, the best solution so far to this difficult problem. Petrol is pumped to the aircraft through underground pipes. The flows of arriving and departing passengers are strictly separated. If the building becomes too small in its present form, it can easily be extended sideways.

The airport building at Chantilly, about twenty-six miles west of Washington, demonstrates the development of Saarinen's handling of large spaces and suspended roofs. His first suspended roof was in the hockey stadium at Yale University in New Haven. He then went back to a standard concrete structure for his TWA airport building in New York. At Chantilly, he again used the suspended roof, a synthesis of engineering and architecture. The roof, which is reinforced at both ends, is supported like a hammock, and spans a space completely uninterrupted by supports. The resulting transparent, weightless, apparently floating form of this airport building is not merely, as in the TWA building in New York, a representation of dynamics, but is itself dynamic.

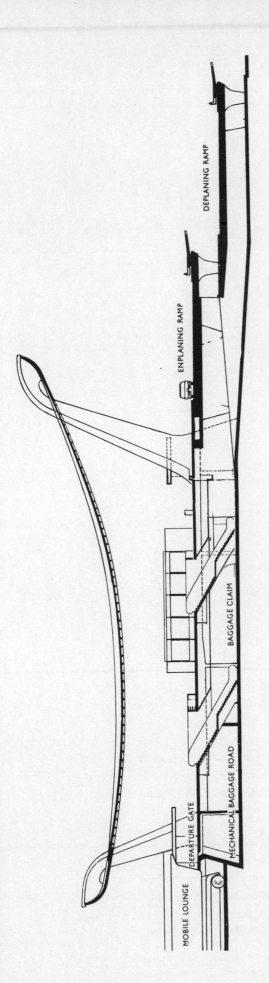

Dulles International Airport, Chantilly, Virginia
(1958–62) by Eero Saarinen. Section.

Plate 81
Richards Memorial Building, University of
Pennsylvania, Philadelphia (1958–61) by Louis
I. Kahn and Alfred Newton Richards

Louis I. Kahn is one of the leaders of modern architectural theory, but his ideas, amounting to a philosophy of architecture, have only been realized in a few, albeit exemplary, buildings. Kahn was born in 1901 in Estonia, but has lived since 1905 in the U.S.A. From 1930 to 1950 he worked mostly with others. Since the 'forties, he has been producing highly original projects and buildings, which put him in the front rank of American architects. In 1957 he moved to Philadelphia, and began working there with Robert Le Ricolais. He has taken up and developed the ideas of Frank Lloyd Wright, Hugo Häring and Alvar Aalto, maintaining that the function of the building should be allowed to 'unfold' itself, and that it should be, as he says, 'what the thing itself wants to be'.

After the Yale University Art Gallery in New Haven in 1955, this research centre in Philadelphia, designed in 1958 and completed in 1961, is Kahn's most important building. It is designed according to his own theories and is a brilliant expression of one approach to modern architecture.

The structure of the building distinguishes clearly between 'served' and 'serving' spaces. The vertical, form-defining towers contain rooms essential for supplying and ventilating the rest of the building, where the actual research is carried out. The plan is based on the square. The towers are built on a small square, and are attached to the main research buildings, which are built on a larger square. The verticals of the towers frame the horizontals, relieved by glass windows. The building's repetitive design means that it can easily be extended. Kahn's co-operation with August Komendant produced some remarkable achievements in prefabrication and on-site assembly of parts of this building. The composition has echoes of medieval structures, particularly of, say, Carcassonne or San Gimigniano, both of which Kahn admires. It is also reminiscent of Frank Lloyd Wright. There are obvious historical references, particularly in the way Wright's principles of form are followed, a tendency which has become accentuated in the later work of Kahn.

81

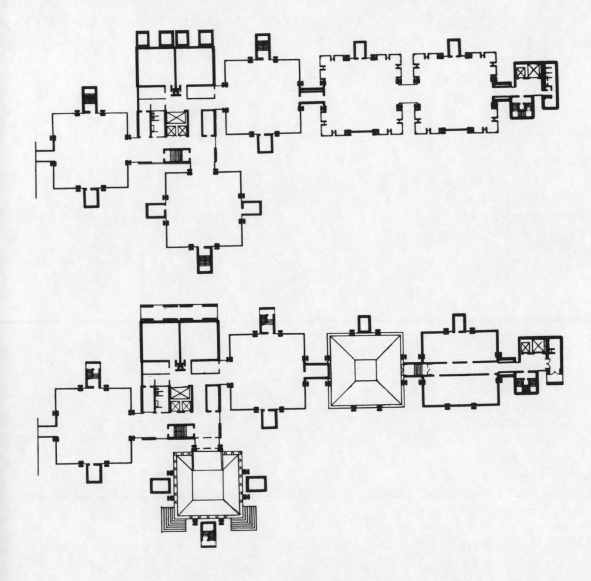

Richards Memorial Building, University of Pennsylvania, Philadelphia
(1958-61) by Louis I. Kahn and Alfred Newton Richards. Floor plans.

Plate 82
Halen Estate, Bern (1959–1961) by Atelier 5
(Erwin Fritz, Samuel Gerber, Rolf Hesterberg,
Hans Hostettler, Niklaus Morgenthaler, Alfredo
Pini and Fritz Thormann)

The planning and execution of the Halen Estate near Bern represented the triumph of an unusual idea in the face of all kinds of difficulties and opposition. A group of young architects managed to build here, in spite of the restrictions on building which exist in Switzerland, an estate of seventy-nine single-family houses as one coherent architectural unit.

The estate is laid out in beautiful landscape, about three miles from Bern. It consists of a number of different types of house arranged like terraces on a south slope, and has a shopping centre, a restaurant, a petrol station, a swimming pool and a central installation for providing heating and hot water. It is inhabited mostly by artists, architects, writers and composers, who own the whole area themselves, including the streets, grassy areas, forest, and all the communal buildings.

The original plans, drawn up in 1954–55, involved prefabrication to a large extent. But they had to be abandoned on economic grounds. The materials which were eventually used were stone, brick and wood. There are two predominant types of house: the multiple-room large house, and the one-and-a-half room smaller house. Careful sound insulation, and considerable, if not entirely complete, protection of each terrace from the view of the neighbours, make Halen an extremely pleasant place to live. Privacy and the need to communicate are reconciled. Solutions of this kind, in an age when terrace-building (see Plates 86 and 107) is to be found everywhere, are meaningful and worthwhile.

82

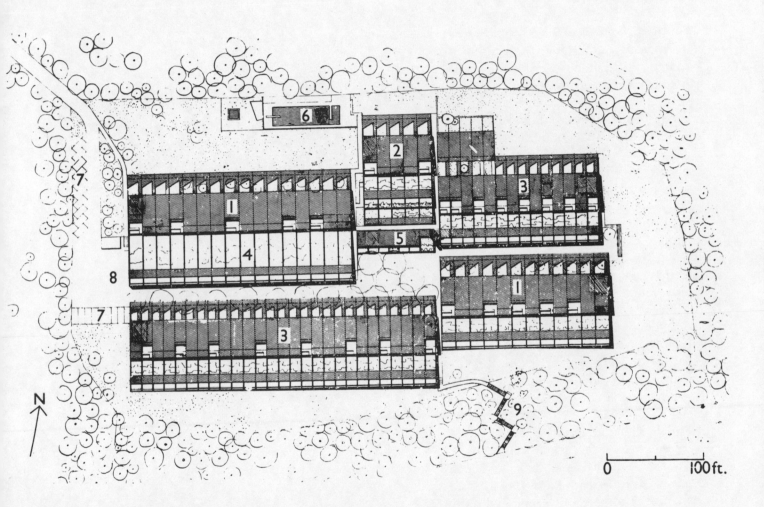

Halen Estate, Bern (1959–61) by Atelier 5 (Erwin Fritz, Samuel Gerber, Rolf Hesterberg, Hans Hostettler, Niklaus Morgenthaler, Alfredo Pini and Fritz Thormann). Plan.
1 Row house with up to six rooms and garden
2 Upper row house
3 Row house with up to six rooms and workshop.
4 Garage built under terraced gardens
5 Restaurant and shop
6 Swimming pool
7 Parking
8 Petrol station and turning circle
9 Stairs to main approach road

Plate 83
Choral Auditorium, Tallinn, Estonia (1960) by
Alar Kotli, Henno Sepman, Uno Tölpus,
Endel Paalman and Helmut Oruvee

The Soviet Republic of Estonia, like Mexico and Rumania, has become a centre for shell-building and its influence extends over the whole of eastern Europe. Several important buildings have been executed there, including the Choral Auditorium in Tallinn, the capital of Estonia, completed in 1960. Another auditorium, based on this one, was built later in Wilna.

The initiator of this experimental building was the architect Alar Kotli, who died in 1963. Kotli built this powerful work with the architects Henno Sepman and Uno Tölpus (died in 1964), the engineer Endel Paalman, and the acoustics expert Helmut Oruvee, after winning the competition for it in 1957 in Tallinn.

The building is basically a huge, open form which serves as seating and as acoustic reflector for a giant open air area for folk singing, which is still cultivated a great deal in this region. To the left of the choir's seats there is a three-storey wing for sound recording and administrative offices. To the right, there is a 138 feet high tower.

The auditorium consists of a metal arch from which is suspended a membrane roof in the form of hyperbolic paraboloids. The roof is made of steel hawsers on to which are clipped wooden slabs (see plate). This technique is based on revolutionary principles first developed by the Polish architect, Matthew Nowicki (who died in 1950), particularly in his main work, the exhibition hall at Raleigh, North Carolina (completed in 1953). It has been used, with modifications, ever since. In Tallinn, this technique produced a vast area spanned without supports for 240 feet.

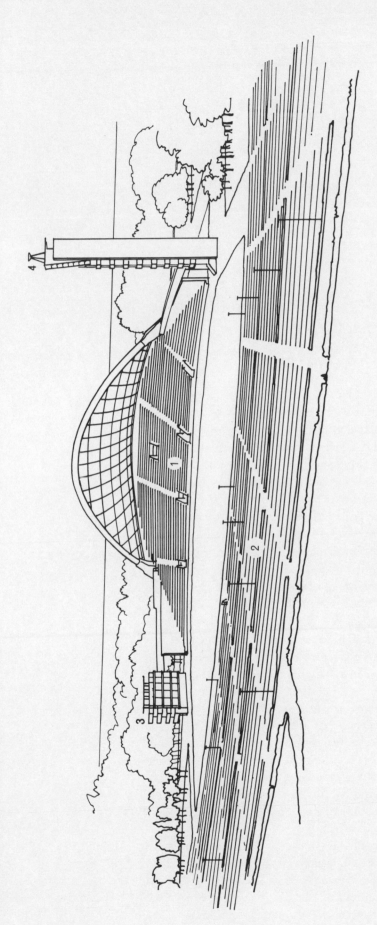

Site of the Choral Auditorium, Tallinn, Estonia (1960) by Alar Kotli,
Henno Sepman, Uno Tölpus, Endel Paalman, Helmut Oruvee.

1 Choir
2 Auditorium
3 Sound recording and administration
4 Ceremonial flame

Plate 84
Concert Hall of the Berlin Philharmonic
Orchestra, Berlin (1960–63) by Hans Scharoun

In 1956 Hans Scharoun won first prize in the competition for the Concert Hall for the Berlin Philharmonic Orchestra, and as a result was commissioned to build it. The decision to build the hall was taken by the Berlin Parliament in 1959. Work was begun in 1960, and in 1963 completed. This much-discussed building with its tent-like roof crowns Scharoun's career. His theory of a strictly functional type of architecture had been developing ever since his work in Insterburg in 1919–23 and in Breslau in 1925–32. He was, however, only able to realize his ideas in a few rare buildings. Like Hugo Häring (Plate 48), whose theories of architecture influenced him considerably, Scharoun believed in a solution to a building task strictly in accordance with the 'nature of the object'.

In the Berlin Philharmonic building, which he worked on with Werner Weber, he was concerned with problems of acoustics, and with fitting the architectural form of the building to its musical contents. The building is symbolized by the triple pentagon, being a unification of three elements (Space, Music, Man). The exterior of the building recedes, following the form dictated by the requirements of the interior. The form of the interior is determined by the 111 feet high concert hall, which makes it necessary to have a roof with three characteristic steps in it. All the other rooms, including foyers, staircases, offices, etc., are fitted into the spaces around the main hall.

The form of the hall itself is determined by the music which is played in it. The orchestra is in the middle. From here rows of seats ascend upwards and outwards asymmetrically. There are 2,218 seats in four blocks in front of the orchestra, three blocks on each side and two behind. The largest dimension of the hall is 245 by 225 feet. Whereas traditional concert halls have long rows of seats, Scharoun arranges the seating in blocks or groups of seats (he himself called them 'vineyards'), making a multiform spatial ensemble without the usual hierarchical organization. The only consideration which determined the arrangement of the seats was the direction from which the sound would come. In this highly individualistic building, every member of the audience can be directly involved in the musical event. No seat is more than 105 feet from the podium. The expressionistic multiplicity of the composition of the interior, and the ecstatic, disturbed effect it gives is counteracted by a symmetry which can only be seen from certain points in the building, and which gives the effect of a single space.

The hall contains the largest concert space in Europe. When it is full, the reverberation lasts a full two seconds. The organ is installed to the left of the dais, which can both be used conventionally and in the round.

84

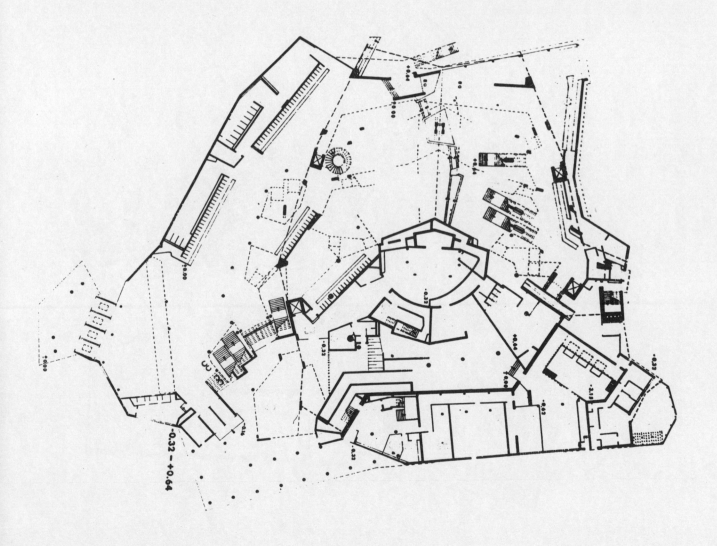

Concert Hall of the Berlin Philharmonic Orchestra, Berlin (1960–63)
by Hans Scharoun. Plan, lower level.

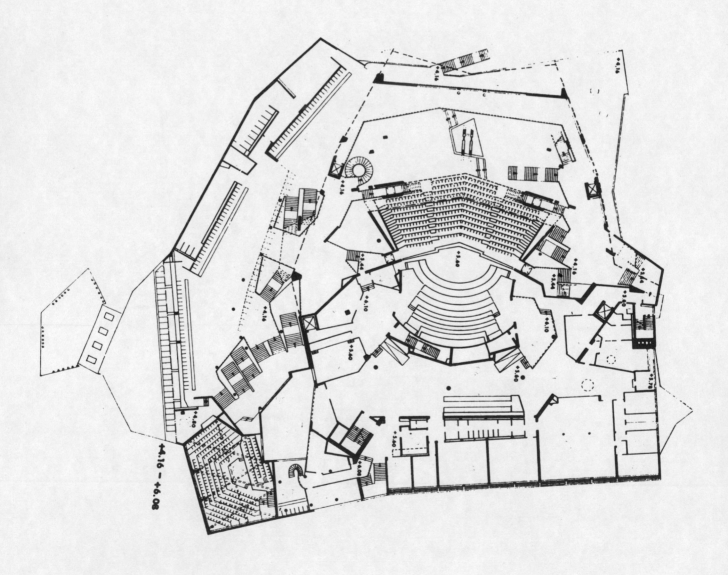

Concert Hall of the Berlin Philharmonic Orchestra, Berlin (1960–63)
by Hans Scharoun. Plan, upper level.

Plate 85 (page 401)
Town Hall and Community Centre, Bat Yam,
Israel (1959–63) by Neumann, Hecker and
Sharon

Some recent buildings in Israel have been outstanding, and demonstrate the country's community spirit and sense of social responsibility. Significantly, this development can be seen not only in housing estates (Plate 86) but also in town halls. This building task requires a specific formulation of the relationship between the individual and the community, as shown by buildings in other traditional societies (e.g. town halls by Kenzo Tange in Japan or Arne Jacobsen in Denmark).

A competition for the town hall of Bat Yam, a rapidly growing industrial town on the shores of the Mediterranean south of Tel Aviv, was announced in 1958. In 1959, the design submitted by the winners, Neumann, Hecker and Sharon, was begun. It was completed in 1963 and contains not only the town hall but also a shopping and community centre.

An open site on the coast of the Mediterranean was chosen for the building, allowing for the town to grow up round it, so that it eventually becomes the centre of the town's community life. Thus the relationship of the building to its surroundings is temporary, and it is not yet performing the urban function planned for it.

This building consists of three increasingly large storeys like an inverted ziggurat. The basic element in the structure is the square, used in the ground-plan and in the individual wall elements, turned so that it stands on one corner. One corner of this town hall protrudes into the extended rectangle of the town centre, and offers a changing, but always impressive, aspect. There is no division in the building between the exterior and the interior, between the skeleton and the building. It all merges into one unified structure called by Alfred Neumann himself 'morphological architecture'. Each storey is cantilevered some way out over the one below it, making a shaded area around the base of the building, which is so important in southern countries. A covered exterior staircase leads to the small amphitheatre on the roof, which is used in the evening.

A covered courtyard is lit and ventilated by the structures on the roof. These roof structures, like all the other building elements, are designed on a system of modules. Bright colours make the striking pattern of forms into a visual and spatial structure. Great importance was attached not only to the application of module techniques, but also to achieving a composition of colours which might enhance the spatial effect. This was described by the architects themselves: 'The horizontal surfaces on the roof are painted in strong Byzantine colours (red, blue and gold) inside and out, while white blocks of silicate are used in the vertical walls. We have not *applied* or *added* colour anywhere in this building, but we have, as it were, actually built individual elements, and even complete structures, *out of* colour. Colour, space, light and shade have all been used as structural and creative elements.' The architects designed a similar building for the town hall in Natania.

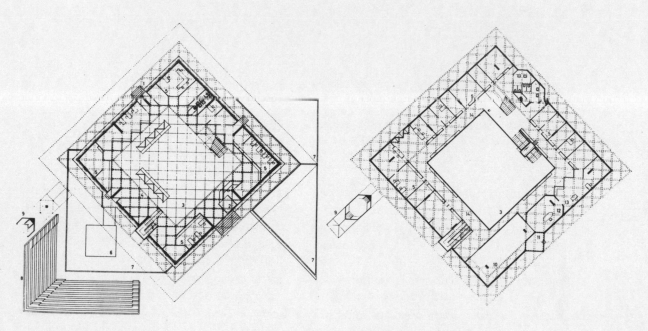

Ground floor plan.   First floor plan

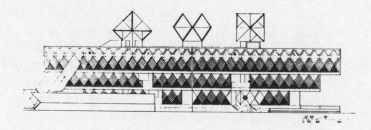

Town Hall and Community Centre, Bat Yam (1959-63)
by Neumann, Hecker and Sharon. Plans and elevations.
1   Entrance
2   Information booth
3   Central court
4   Exhibition space
5   Offices
6   Podium
7   Reflecting pool
8   Amphitheatre
9   Staircase to the roof
10 Council chamber
11 Balcony
12 Mayor's office
13 Secretariat
14 Corridor

85

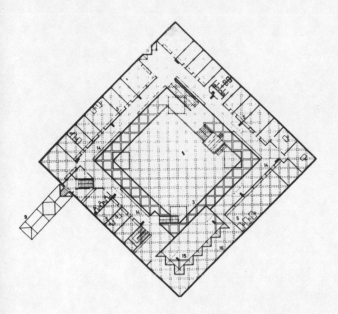

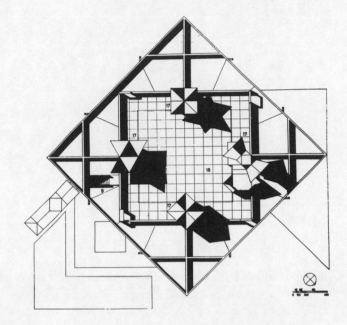

Town Hall and Community Centre, Bat Yam (1959-63)
by Neumann, Hecker and Sharon. Plans.
3 Central court
5 Offices
9 Staircase to the roof
10 Council chamber
14 Corridor
15 Balcony
16 Visitors' gallery
17 Light tower
18 Roof terrace

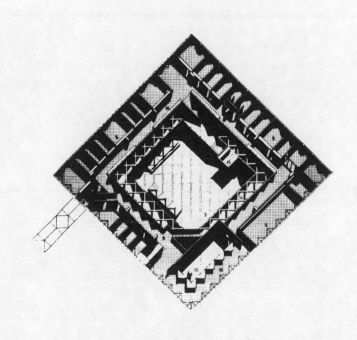

Plate 86
Terraced apartment buildings, Ramat Gan,
Israel (1960–65) by Neumann, Hecker and
Sharon

Since the middle of the twentieth century, architects in several countries have returned to the essentially Oriental and African terraced building forms first revived by Adolf Loos (Scheu house in Vienna). This has led to a new type of residential building, primarily in Algeria, Switzerland (Plate 82), Canada (Plate 107) and Italy. Young architects in Israel have developed some very unusual solutions, which have had international influence.

Outstanding amongst terraced buildings developed in recent years are the dwelling structures by Moshe Safdie for the Montreal World's Fair and the apartment buildings erected a few years earlier by Neumann, Hecker and Sharon in Ramat Gan. This young team is also known for its town hall buildings (Plate 85). Terraced building is suggested by the geographical situation of Ramat Gan, a suburb north of Tel Aviv. This type of building has been developed here entirely logically, in contrast to a number of other examples of it. As the architects themselves have explained, the basic idea of the building overlooking the Mediterranean is a prismatic, hexagonal design. Only the three lower storeys conform to the shape of the hill; the others form a system of overhanging spaces, a conglomeration of the hexagonal forms, making a unit with the lower storeys. There is a bridge to the top of the hill from the top storey giving access to the apartments, although the lower storeys also have separate entrances on different levels. The whole hexagonal space which the building encloses forms a kind of central area with its own climate (shady and cool in summer, sunny in winter), connected vertically as well as across the bridges to individual storeys, and thus accessible to all.

There are two or three apartments on each storey. Each apartment is, like the whole building, based on a three-dimensional, hexagonal form, and has a partly roofed and partly open balcony. Thus there is in this building an interpenetration of open and closed spaces, of interior and exterior, and the possibility of enjoying both privacy and communication with other inhabitants. These principles have been followed with modifications in various types of buildings. Sigfried Giedion has called them the chief characteristics of modern architecture.

86

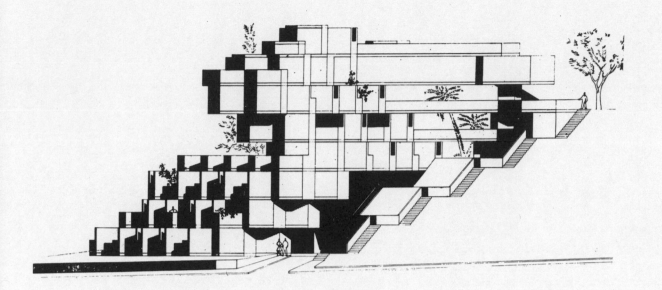

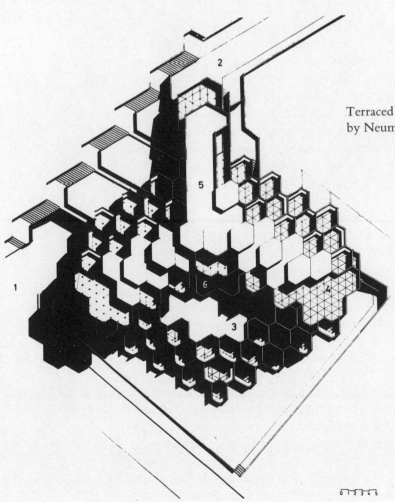

Terraced apartment buildings, Ramat Gan, Israel (1960–65) by Neumann, Hecker and Sharon. Plan and elevation.

1, 2 Passages
3   The first three levels follow the slope of the hill
4   These three levels are partly cantilevered
5   Upper level bridging the gap
6   Piazza

Plate 87
Atomic reactor, Rehovot, Israel (1961) by Philip Johnson

The atomic reactor is one of the building tasks which has only recently fallen into the architect's province. It has created completely new problems. Its objective is not to provide shelter and good working conditions for people, but simply to contain radioactive material suitably and safely. What is essentially new about the problem is that the material inside the building does its own work, and the architect's task is to enable this work to take place. Man only directs and serves. In earlier atomic reactors, for instance in Plainboro (Skidmore, Owings and Merrill), Munich (Gerhard Weber), Switzerland, England and Japan, something approaching a basic style had been evolved, in which the actual reactor, mostly some kind of dome, rises above the offices and research laboratories, which are usually in a flat horizontal wing. Philip Johnson's atomic reactor in Rehovot, completed in 1961, is one of the most striking solutions, still of the same basic type as the others but differing from them in form.

Philip Johnson began his career as an architectural critic and biographer of Mies van der Rohe, and after completing his architectural studies worked entirely in the shadow of the great man. Later, he worked with Mies on the Seagram building. Eventually, however, he broke away from Mies' influence and has recently developed a style which has been called anti-Miesian, and can be regarded as programmatically historicist in a quite new sense. He is the intellectual architect, evolving style from theory.

The complex of the Rehovot atomic reactor is laid out on a rectangular plan, completely enclosed by concrete walls which recede slightly towards the top. Inside, there is an open courtyard, surrounded by concrete pillars narrowing to a point at the base, supporting a projecting roof which shields the glass-fronted rooms from sunshine. This courtyard relieves the strictness of the building (see plate). Next to it is the reactor itself, a dominant vertical on a horizontally composed 'Mesopotamian' ground-plan. The rectangular plan develops into a dynamic polygon at the top, producing contrasting slopes on the sides and creating a huge form, vividly expressive in bright light. Johnson has achieved here a monumental effect, with echoes of sacred architecture, even of a mausoleum.

Philip Johnson's recent historicist tendencies can be clearly seen in this building. The requirements of the building task made him discipline his medium, using Mesopotamian and Egyptian forms, reminiscent of the early expressionist beginnings of modern architecture. The building stands in the desert landscape like a monument to the young state of Israel.

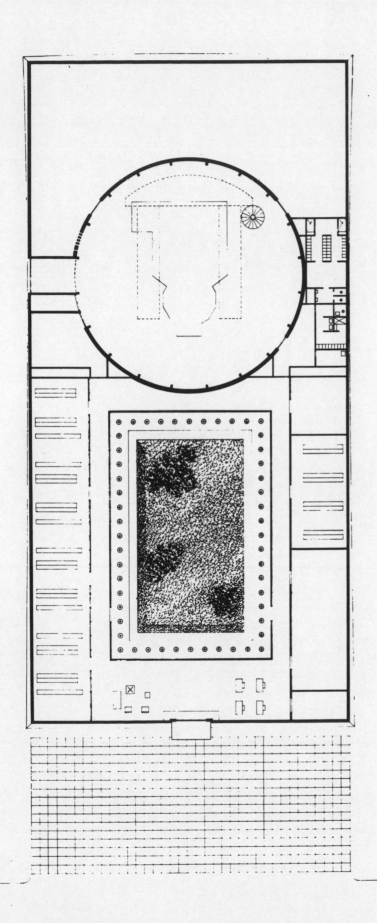

Atomic reactor, Rehovot, Israel
(1961) by Philip Johnson. Plan.

Plate 88
Marguerite and Aimé Maeght Foundation,
Saint-Paul-de-Vence (1961–64)
by José Luis Sert

José Luis Sert has planned or built several luxurious houses on the Mediterranean for contemporary artists including the house for Georges Braque (project, 1960) and the Miró house (built in Majorca, 1955). The original intention of the building in the plate was to create a monument to Aimé Maeght, a Parisian art dealer, while extending the Maeght Foundation so that several artists could live there. The interior and the form of the Maeght Foundation building, completed in 1964, relate to the unexecuted project for a house for Braque. In both buildings, several wings enclose an open interior courtyard, and both have shell-like roofs and closed exterior walls. In this house, Sert tried to develop a theme with which he had been concerned for some time: the connection between painting, sculpture and architecture. The building was constructed in cooperation with the architects Bellini, Lizero and Gozzi. It is an ensemble of open and enclosed spaces, staircases, walls, pools and trees, perfectly situated on a hillside. It is more like a village than an isolated, enclosed house. As in comparable recent buildings (Plates 82 and 94), the principles of group-form are developed. It contains exhibition rooms, a chapel, a library and reading room, a flat for the director, and technical rooms with depots and workshops, mostly underground.

The building is cut off from its environment by a rough stone wall. It is arranged on different levels, partly with right angles, partly with dynamic curves. The pavilion-like parts of the building have different roofs. They are illuminated by concrete shells, which fill the interior with diffused light. The artificial light source is in smaller, cylindrical shells. The particular charm of the building is the continuously changing combinations of interior space and landscape which it affords. The semi-cylindrical shells on the roof are important for ventilation and shade, as well as for lighting. They were known by the building workers as 'half-moons'. They give the building a richly orchestrated spatial movement, which suits both the climate and the contents. The museum contains works by artists such as Calder, Miró, Braque and Giacometti.

88

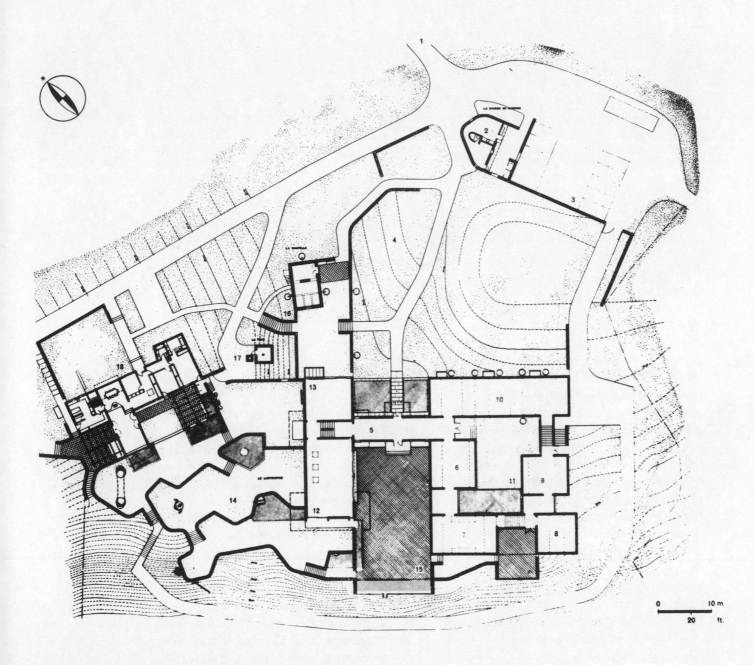

Marguerite and Aimé Maeght Foundation, Saint-Paul-de-Vence
(1961–64) by José Luis Sert. Plan.

1	Entrance	10	Changing exhibitions
2	Watchman's lodge	11	Patio
3	Parking	12	Large exhibition and conference room
4	Entrance patio	13	Library
5	Lobby	14	Terraced garden 'Labyrinth'
6	Braque room	15	Main patio
7	Miró room	16	Chapel
8	Chagall room	17	Transformer tower
9	Kandinsky room	18	Director's house

Plate 89
Art and Architecture Building at Yale University,
New Haven, Connecticut (1961–63)
by Paul Rudolph

Yale and Harvard Universities have two of the most important architectural schools in the United States, and therefore in the world. A kind of architectural open air museum has gradually developed in both these universities, since the most important architects in the U.S.A. have been commissioned to build on their campuses. Paul Rudolph, the Dean of the School of Art and Architecture at Yale University, built the architectural departments there.

The building is on a corner site opposite the art gallery built a few years earlier by Louis I. Kahn. With its precipitous walls, frequently punctuated by balconies and voids, giving a simultaneously open and closed form, and thus an artistically layered effect, the building has become a symbol of Yale University. Its vertical elements seem to be drawn up out of the ground, and the horizontal parts of the building recede so far that they make a contrasting, multiform, mutually interpenetrating system of forms, in the style first exploited by Frank Lloyd Wright half a century earlier. Paul Rudolph can be regarded as historicist insofar as he revived Wright's formal principles. The complicated, disturbing effect of this building is heightened by the contrast of raw concrete and glass, comparable with Rudolph's factory in Garden City (Plate 104).

The Yale building consists of two lower storeys and six upper storeys. Its design allows it to be extended to the north. The second lower storey contains a sculpture studio, the first storey graphic studios, and the ground floor the library. The first storey contains classrooms, recreation rooms for students, and large areas for exhibiting the students' work. On the second storey, there are administration offices, and rooms for the professors; on the third, drawing studios for architectural students; on the fourth, town planning rooms; on the fifth, town planning and painting classrooms; and on the sixth, studios. The top storey is a place for open-air painting, and also contains a café and a guest room. The step-like arrangement of the building extends, therefore, from the rooms devoted to painting, which need a lot of light, to those devoted to sculpture on the second lower storey. Small and large rooms interlock and different storeys overlap each other. Thus structure and space are not separated from each other, in contrast to most buildings with stereotyped alignment.

89

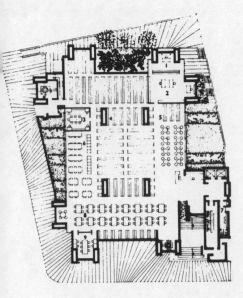

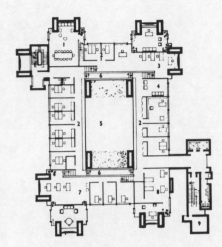

First floor plan.
1 Librarian
2 Workroom
3 Study
4 Stacks
5 Periodicals
6 Files
7 Toilet
8 Reading
9 Study

Third floor plan.
1 Conference
2 Offices
3 Dean
4 Waiting
5 Open to below
6 Bridge
7 Architecture
8 Art
9 Lounge

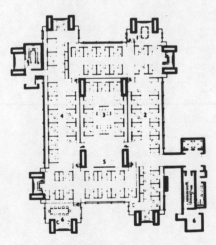

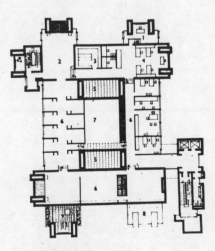

Fourth floor plan.
1 Seminar
2 Architectural design
3 Lounge
4 Rehearsal hall
5 Jury
6 Seminar

Sixth floor plan.
1 Office
2 Drawing
3 Storage
4 Workroom
5 Skylight above
6 City planning offices
7 Painting
8 Roof
9 Terrace

Art and Architecture Building at
Yale University, New Haven
Connecticut (1961–63)
by Paul Rudolph.

Plate 90
Department of Engineering at Leicester University, Leicester (1960–63) by James Stirling and James Gowan

The building of technical colleges and universities, and above all, institutions for training architects and engineers, has become one of the central functions of architecture in the 'sixties. Prototypes can be found in the Glasgow Art School (Plate 22) by Mackintosh, and the Bauhaus in Dessau (Plate 50) by Walter Gropius. Ever since the building of Crown Hall at the Illinois Institute of Technology, in Chicago, by Mies van der Rohe (Plate 75), architects like Castiglioni (Plate 95), Rudolph (Plate 89), Aalto (Plate 91) and Andrews (Plate 101) have looked for new solutions to this building task, in deliberate contrast to Mies' classical architecture. They have been principally concerned with the functions of this type of building, and have come up with solutions which imply a re-appraisal of the role of the professional architect.

In the building at Leicester University, completed in 1963, devoted to the education of engineers, the English architects took technology as the prime objective of education. Therefore technology and efficiency determine the form of the building. The architects were asked to construct a building for 250 students on a fairly small site, containing lecture halls, laboratories, administrative offices, and workshops, making altogether a complete, integrated unit.

The building complex has basically two parts. One is a workshop wing with a roof broken up by projecting triangular glass planes running diagonally across the line of the roof. This wing has three storeys on the south side, and one in the middle (visible in the plate, on the right hand side). The other part is a tower block which itself has two main parts, each of different heights, connected by vertical shafts, one lift and two staircases. The four-storey block to the west contains laboratories ventilated and lit by distinctive, projecting, triangular, vertically punctuated bands of glass, which can be opened at the bottom.

The administrative tower, almost entirely covered in glass, rises from the fifth storey upwards, like a mast on top of the ship-like construction of the rest of the building, composed of verticals and horizontals underpinned by the diagonal of the underside of the cantilevered lecture theatres. These lecture theatres, which have 100 and 200 seats respectively, project in two different directions, cantilevered for half their length and held in place by the weight of the building above. The shape of the individual rooms can in most cases be clearly seen from the outside. The teaching workshops were situated on the north side, with glass roofs in order to achieve the best possible lighting. This gives the whole complex a distinctive, technological, and, when seen from the tower, wave-like form. The materials used are steel, for the basic supports, and concrete, covered with Dutch terra-cotta tiles.

Although the total effect of this building is to reflect the technical reality of our time, in many ways it is reminiscent of the earliest developments in modern architecture (e.g. the Russian constructivists, Plate 55; Sant'Elia; Owen Williams, Plate 57; and Frank Lloyd Wright, Plate 69).

90

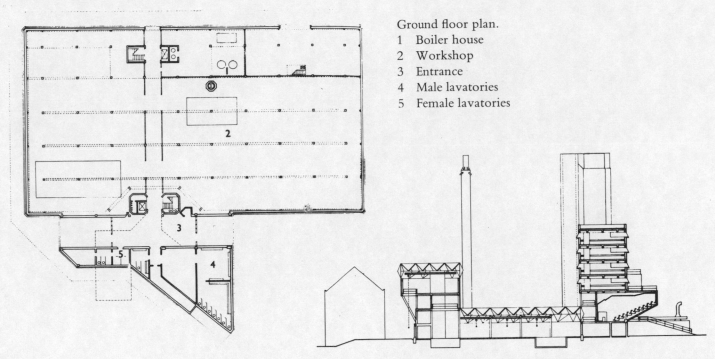

Ground floor plan.
1 Boiler house
2 Workshop
3 Entrance
4 Male lavatories
5 Female lavatories

Section through small lecture hall
with laboratories over.

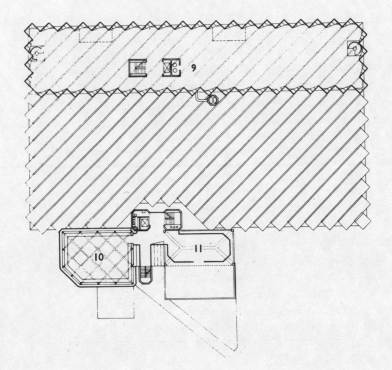

Third and below, sixth to ninth floor plans.
9 Aerodynamic laboratory
10 Laboratory
11 Periodical room
13 Offices

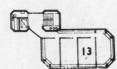

Department of Engineering at Leicester University,
Leicester (1960–63) by James Stirling and
James Gowan. Plans and section.

Plate 91
Auditorium Maximum of the Technical
University, Helsinki-Otaniemi (1962–64)
by Alvar Aalto

The whole of the Helsinki Technical University has been moved to the Otaniemi area, on the outskirts of the town. Aalto won the competition for the design of the whole campus in 1949, but never intended to build more than the main building himself. This was actually executed in 1962–64, and contains the Institute of Technology, the Department of Architecture, a sports hall, shops, and a student hostel. It is exactly in the middle of the large campus, which consists of institute buildings, laboratories, student hostels, dining hall, church, sauna baths, and communal buildings (including the Dipoli Student Union by Reima Pietilä, Plate 102). The Aalto building dominates the whole complex, which is designed to fit in with the wooded and slightly hilly surrounding countryside. The main building was always intended to stand at the top of a hill, and to be the central point of the campus. The lecture theatres, as the centre of the faculty, are stressed in such a way that they can be seen clearly to form a central point for the whole university. The building, for functional reasons, is an amphitheatre. As usual, acoustic and lighting considerations have been carefully taken into account by Aalto. The unusual shape of the building is unique in modern architecture. The materials used are brick, copper and glass, a combination found in many recent Finnish buildings.

We can see here precisely what Sigfried Giedion meant about the new Finnish architecture being the product of a combination of standardization with irrationality. Giedion explained, 'this means making use of standardization, not being used by it'.

The Auditorium Maximum is flanked by the central administrative offices of the Rector and by other lecture theatres and laboratories. Between these rectangular blocks, Aalto's building opens like a fan on one side; thus he has used a standardized, rational building technique to create a building following a particular formal idea. The exterior form corresponds to the interior function of the big auditorium.

91

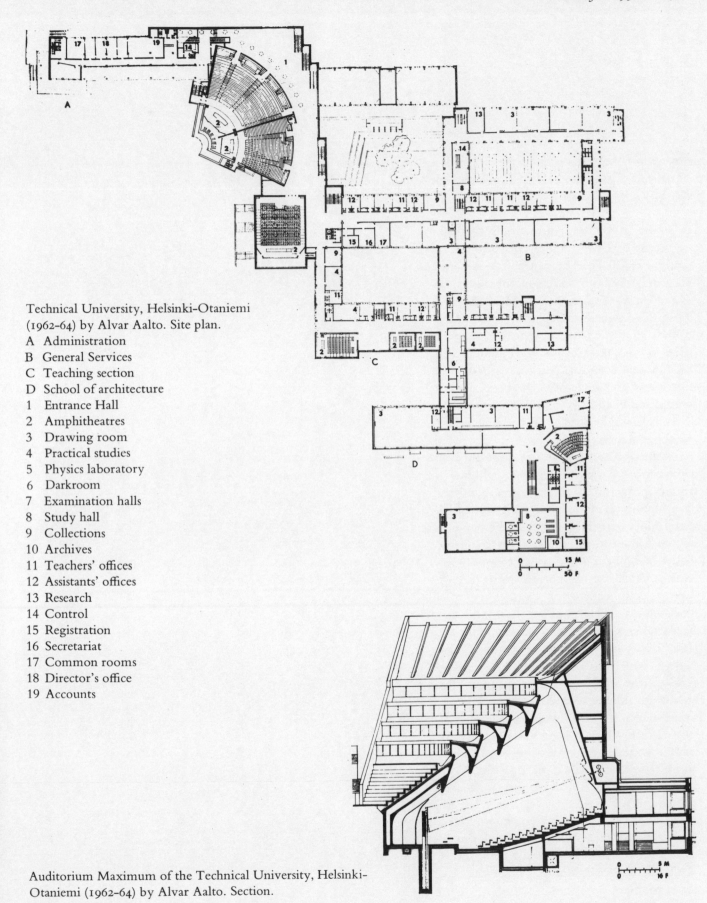

Technical University, Helsinki-Otaniemi
(1962-64) by Alvar Aalto. Site plan.
A Administration
B General Services
C Teaching section
D School of architecture
1 Entrance Hall
2 Amphitheatres
3 Drawing room
4 Practical studies
5 Physics laboratory
6 Darkroom
7 Examination halls
8 Study hall
9 Collections
10 Archives
11 Teachers' offices
12 Assistants' offices
13 Research
14 Control
15 Registration
16 Secretariat
17 Common rooms
18 Director's office
19 Accounts

Auditorium Maximum of the Technical University, Helsinki-
Otaniemi (1962-64) by Alvar Aalto. Section.

Plate 92
St Mary's Cathedral, Tokyo (1962–65) by
Kenzo Tange

In 1961, a limited competition was announced for the design of St Mary's
Cathedral in Tokyo, to replace the old
cathedral, built in 1889 and destroyed in
1945. Kenzo Tange, Kunio Maekawa and
Toshiro Taniguchi took part in the competition. Tange's tent-like design won the first
prize in 1962. He executed the building with
his Japanese assistants Akui and Sasaki and
the Swiss architect, Max Lechner. It was
completed in 1965.

In Japan only about 0·5 per cent of the
total population is Catholic. The Episcopate
has existed since 1928, and in this cathedral,
subsidized by donations from Cologne, it
found powerful architectural expression.
The building is in the form of a cross, which
determines the arrangement of the building
in the ground-plan, and is repeated in the
bands of light coming through the roof. The
walls, which run together towards the top
like a tent, consist of eight hyperbolic
paraboloids. Their polished sheet steel surface makes a tremendous impact. There is
also a 195-foot high, free standing bell
tower, which cannot be seen in the plate
(off to the right). This accentuates the
deliberate silhouette-effect of the building,
and connects it to the lower, annexed buildings. Of these, a crypt and a sacristy already
exist, but the competition specified that it
should be possible to add on, at a later date, a
building for the bishop, a monastery, accommodation for visiting priests, a convent
and a kindergarten. Kenzo Tange's Olympic
buildings, in the middle of the Japanese
capital (Plate 93) are stylistically comparable
with this church building, which can seat
1,500 people.

92

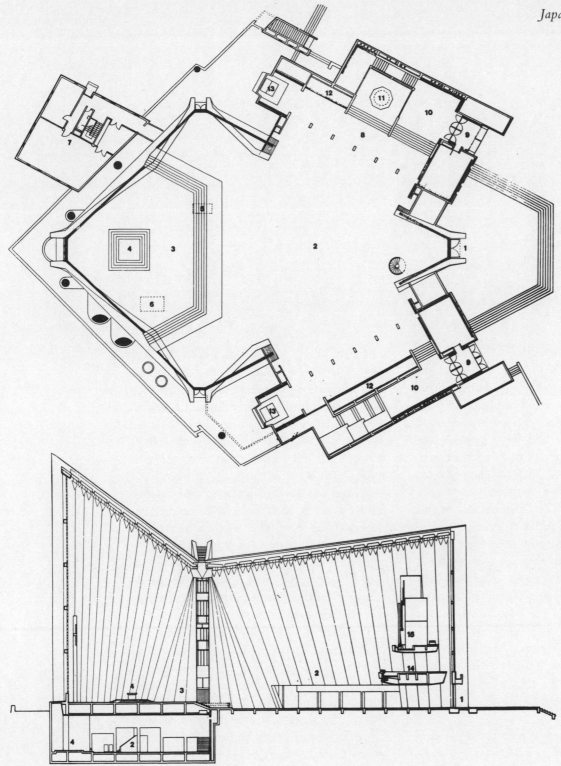

St Mary's Cathedral, Tokyo
(1962–65) by Kenzo Tange.
Plan and elevation.

1 Main entrance	9 Side entrance
2 Nave (pews)	10 Side entrance hall
3 Sanctuary	11 Baptistery
4 Altar	12 Confessional
5 Pulpit	13 Side altar
6 Cardinal's seat	14 Choir
7 Sacristy	15 Pipe organ
8 Side aisle	

Plate 93 (page 435)
Olympic Halls, Tokyo Yoyogi (1963–64) by Kenzo Tange (architect, assisted by Kojo Kamiya), Yoshikatsu Tsuboi, Uichi Inoue (engineers)

The buildings for the XVIIIth Olympiad in Tokyo are one of the greatest achievements of world architecture. The existing sports facilities in Tokyo needed extension to cope with the 1964 summer Olympics. A large swimming stadium had been planned for some time. The Ministry of Education gave the huge project to the architect Kenzo Tange, who worked with the engineers, Tsuboi and Inoue. The building was begun in January 1963 and the two great halls were opened for the Olympic Games in the autumn of 1964, after the sensationally short time of one and a half years. The two halls are organized along a north–south axis parallel with that of the Meiji shrine. This means that the area has a harmonious unity even from the air. The main entrance to both halls is from the south. The architect allowed for possible extension at a later date. The two buildings are linked by the park and promenades.

The larger hall, at the rear in the plate, is for swimming, skating, judo and other competitive events. The roof is suspended from cables stretched between two enormous pillars. The hall can seat 13,246 for swimming events, and 16,246 for judo. The two centres of the semicircles of the plan form points, and the taut cable which supports the roof is also used to make a roof over the entrance, to ensure trouble-free entry and exit of large numbers of people. The roof of the building is made of a steel net suspended from the reinforced concrete pillars. It is insulated on the inside with an asbestos lining, and is painted on the outside to reflect the heat. Its curvature presents virtually no flat surfaces to the wind. Light comes in through a band running between the two pillars, which lets in vertically filtered daylight, and also contains artificial light sources. Visitors enter and leave the building at ground floor level. The actual sports area is below ground level. The swimming pools can be covered to create a skating rink or an area for judo and other sports. The multiplicity of function is one of the great achievements of the architect.

The smaller hall, in the front of the plate, can seat in all 3,931 people for basketball and 5,531 for boxing. It is a development of a circular form. It, too, has a suspended roof, but in this case, suspended from only one pillar. The structural achievement is even more fascinating in this building, since all the forms point towards one central source of support and light. Whereas the interior of the larger hall is mainly defined by the material used – concrete – and by the openings at the sides, the smaller hall has a closed character and takes its overall effect more from the wooden seats and the surface of the floor. A connecting underground building contains administrative and communal rooms, and training pools on both sides.

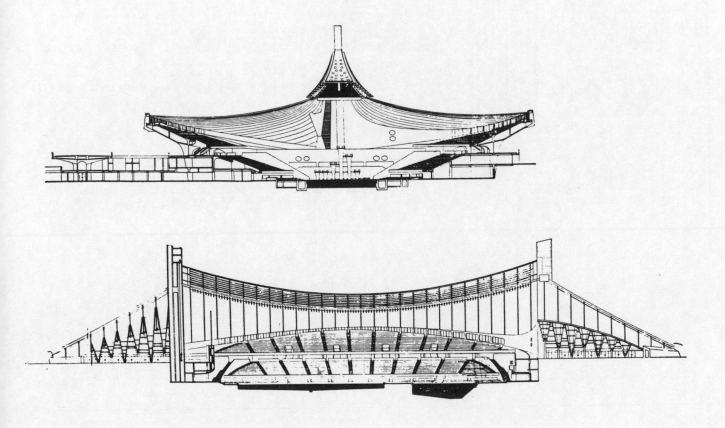

Olympic Halls, Tokyo Yoyogi (1963-64)
by Kenzo Tange (architect, assisted by Kojo Kamiya),
Yoshikatsu Tsuboi, Uichi Inoue (engineers).
Longitudinal and cross sections through main gymnasium.

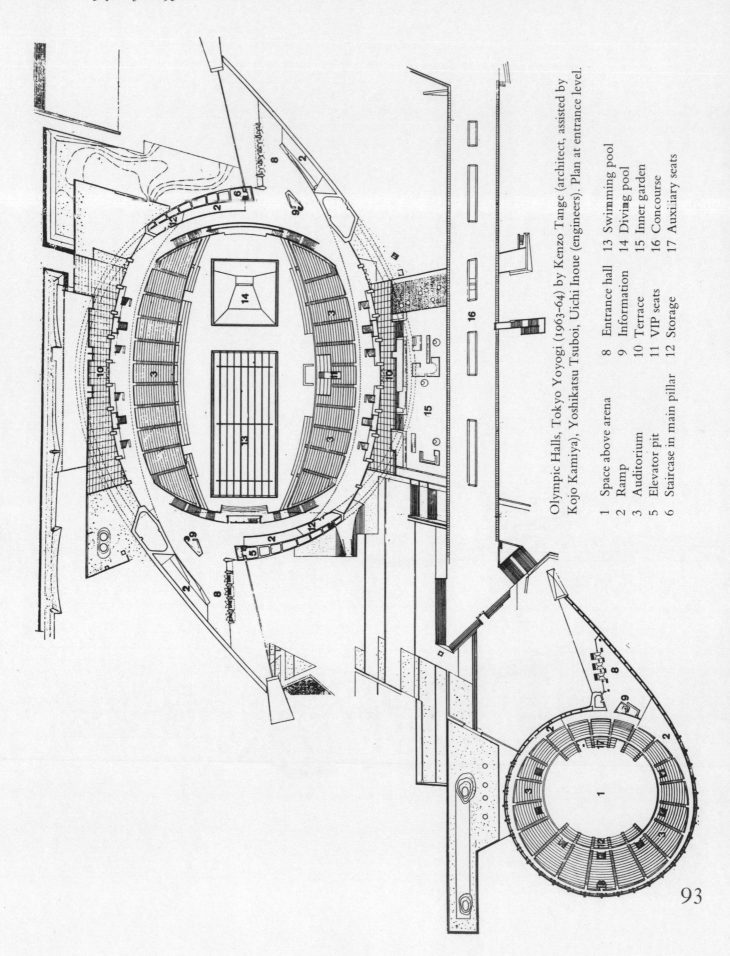

Olympic Halls, Tokyo Yoyogi (1963–64) by Kenzo Tange (architect, assisted by Kojo Kamiya), Yoshikatsu Tsuboi, Uichi Inoue (engineers). Plan at entrance level.

1 Space above arena
2 Ramp
3 Auditorium
5 Elevator pit
6 Staircase in main pillar
8 Entrance hall
9 Information
10 Terrace
11 VIP seats
12 Storage
13 Swimming pool
14 Diving pool
15 Inner garden
16 Concourse
17 Auxiliary seats

93

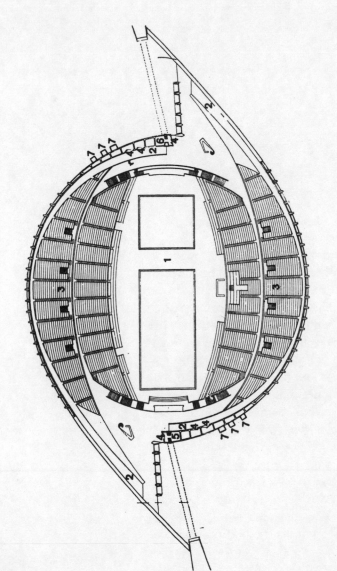

Olympic Halls, Tokyo Yoyogi (1963–64)
by Kenzo Tange (architect, assisted by Kojo Kamiya),
Yoshikatsu Tsuboi, Uichi Inoue (engineers).
Plan at first floor level of main building.

1 Space above arena
2 Ramp
3 Auditorium
4 Duct
5 Elevator pit
6 Staircase in main pillar
7 Air exhaust

Plate 94
Student apartments, Urbino (1963–66) by Giancarlo de Carlo

Urbino, a town which has long lived in the past, has taken on a new significance with its University, which has doubled the number of inhabitants. The historic centre, with its ducal palace, was not disturbed by the new settlements, since they were separated from it by two hills, on the far side of which they were built. At first the University used two abandoned palaces. More recently, it has begun building for the students, beginning with these student apartments by Giancarlo de Carlo, built in 1963–66 on the Capucino Hill. They are connected to the old Capucino Monastery by a path. This monastery is also soon to be used as part of the University.

The complex stretches out from a central, organically formed building, containing the communal rooms (dining and recreation rooms, library and reading rooms, administrative offices, kitchens, a flat for the director and an assembly hall) in concentric rings over the hill, star shaped to one side. So far, 150 apartments have been completed, but this can be extended to 200 at any time. The central building is formed of three cylindrical masses, with balconies at all levels, connected by ramps and staircases to each other and to the passages leading to individual apartments. The entrance is on the highest level, where the assembly hall is. Two dining halls are contained in the storey below. The kitchens and all other communal installations already have the capacity to cope with 200 apartments.

The apartments themselves consist of groups of identical cells. Each unit contains two two-storey apartments, each with an entry hall. These entry halls form covered terraces through which the apartments are reached. The cells are built up on a modular system, and are a few degrees off the rectangular, to fit the curve of the hillside. The two-storey individual elements can therefore be displaced both horizontally and vertically. The materials used are concrete and local clinker stone, the manufacture of which goes back to ducal days. The staircases which lead to the terraces have concrete balustrades which merge into the terrace balustrades. This gives the whole complex an appearance of unity, taking its distinctive form from the contrast between the rectangular and sculptural rounded elements, and between brick and concrete. The organic, partly closed, partly open, central building, like a castle over an old town, surmounts the whole complex, which stretches in waves over the hill.

The student apartments in Urbino are an important step in the direction of a contemporary architectural approach to group-form. Each individual unit is related to the whole, to the environment and to the landscape.

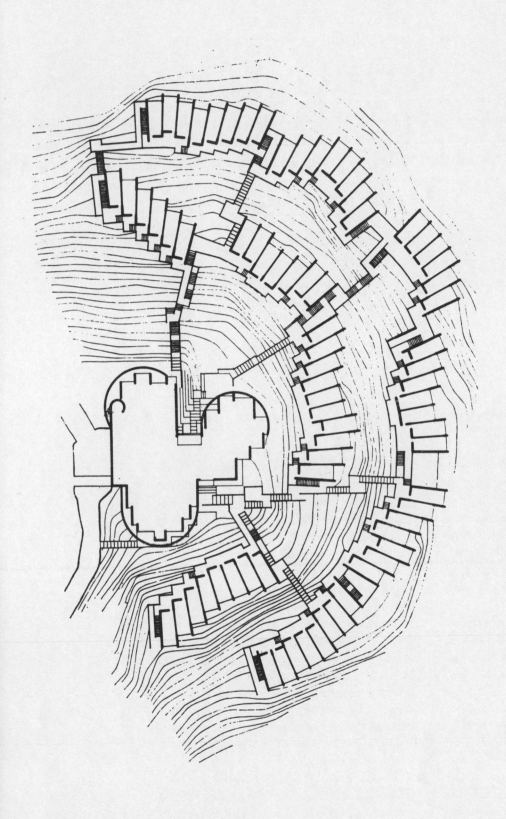

Student apartments, Urbino (1963-66)
by Giancarlo de Carlo. Plan.

Plate 95
Technical College, Busto Arsizio near Milan
(1963–64) by Enrico Castiglioni

Enrico Castiglioni is one of the architects responsible for the change in direction of architecture from the limited to the unlimited, from the static to the dynamic, from the rational to the irrational. His various buildings since 1950 show this quite clearly. The fact that Castiglioni is an architect, an engineer, a painter and a sculptor probably helps explain his achievement.

The Technical College in Busto Arsizio, a little town to the west of Milan, where Castiglioni lives and where most of his buildings are to be found, is only partially complete in its present state. Only half of the daring design for a symmetrical concave, twin-winged building, which was to be connected together by a central mass, has been executed. Nevertheless, this alone does show how important Castiglioni's work is. The form is basically a set of curves organized in distinct relationships to each other. Upward sweeping curves round off the two vertical sides of the building, connected together by

the slender glass band of the staircase. Horizontal curves determine the form of the ground-plan, and the shape of the workshops, connected to the two long façades and arranged one behind the other, making for excellent illumination.

The design gets its dynamic from the slight difference between the levels of the two similarly shaped buildings, which stand as it were, back to back, giving the distinctive form when seen from the side. This dynamic is emphasized by the splendid sweep of the horizontal curved façade, with its vertical concave concrete pillars between the windows. The dry brightness of the raw concrete in the southern light gives a specially striking effect to the vertical and horizontal swing of the building.

The Technical College at Busto Arsizio is important not only for the nature of the problem but also because of the brilliance of the functional architectural solution which has been achieved.

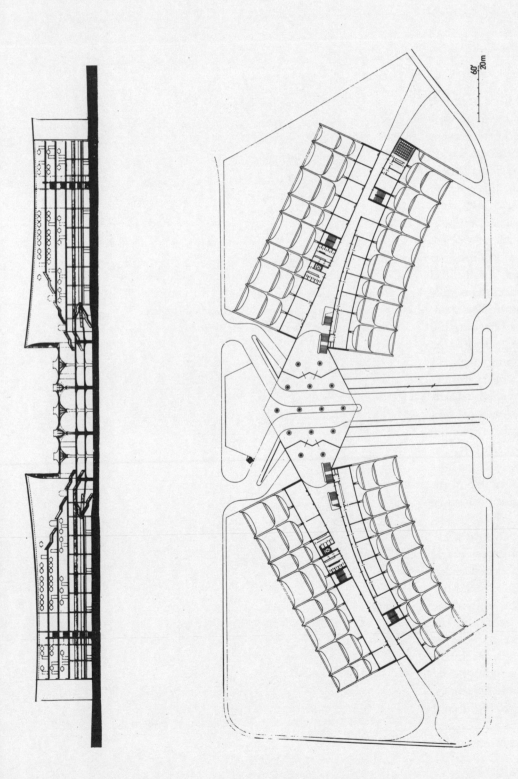

Technical College, Busto Arsizio near Milan (1963–64)
by Enrico Castiglioni. Plan and section.

60°
20 m

Plate 96
The Izumo Shrine, Izumo-Taisha-Chonoya
(1964) by Kiyonori Kikutake

This small building by the Japanese architect
Kiyonori Kikutake is one of the most important religious buildings in Japan erected
in recent years. Since it is a Shinto building,
the architect has used old Shinto forms which,
while expressing the striving of this religion
towards purity and variability, also have
much in common with modern architecture.

The architect has followed ancient Japanese
tradition in constructing his building in
accordance with a three-stage, methodical
plan; starting with the ancient 'ka' (the basic
idea, still in the mind); then using the 'kata'
(the technical process needed to execute the
idea); and finally achieving the 'katachi' (the
expression of functions in architecture). An
elongated building is used for this new
Izumo Shrine, with walls sloping outwards
in a trapeze-like system of horizontal and
vertical struts. The horizontal slats make the
enclosed space seem almost transparent, like
a weightless, immaterial continuum. The
broad, horizontal beams extending right
across the building, projecting at both ends,
are reminiscent not only of ancient traditional Japanese forms, but also of the masterly
use made of Japanese techniques by Frank
Lloyd Wright (who has himself had much
influence on modern Japanese architecture).
The diagonal decoration on the ends of the
building repeats the basic theme of the
sloping walls. By using new materials while
following ancient principles the architect
has managed to create here a sacred building
in which horizontals, verticals and diagonals,
massiveness and weightlessness, light and
shadow, interior and exterior, tradition and
modernity are all intimately combined.

96

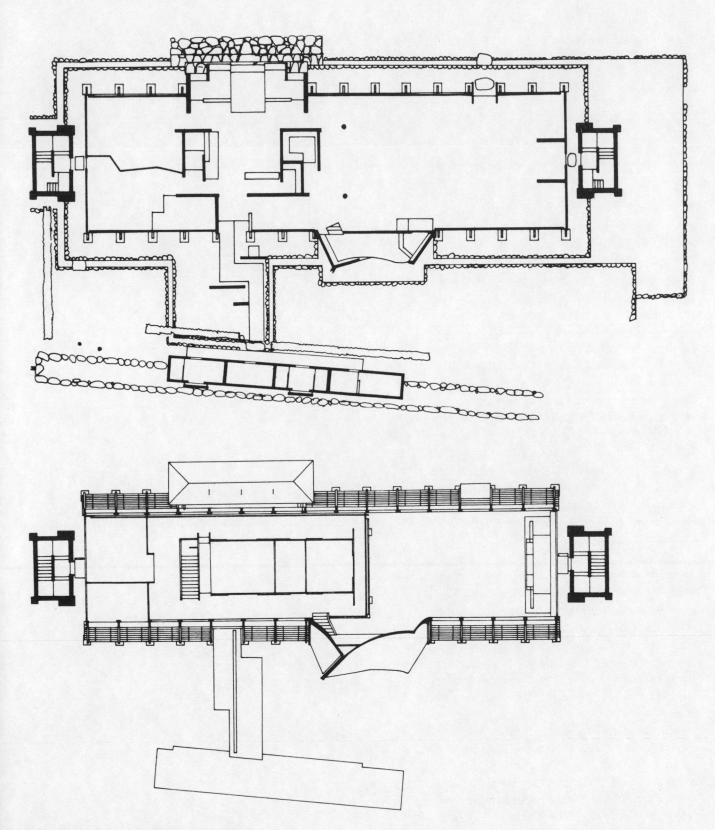

The Izumo Shrine, Izumo–Taisha–Chonoya (1964)
by Kiyonori Kikutake. Plans.

Plate 97
International Conference Centre, Kyoto Matsu-
gasaki (1964–65) by Sachio Ohtani

In 1964–65, near Kyoto, a big international
centre was built to provide conference and
congress facilities for people from all over
the Pacific.

The young Japanese architect, Sachio
Ohtani, who had previously worked in
Kenzo Tange's office, built this huge complex for about £3,250,000. The fascination
of the six-storey, reinforced concrete, steel-
framed structure lies in its trapezium shape,
which puts the building – which marks a new
stage in Japanese development – alongside
the great traditional buildings of Japan. As
with Kenzo Tange and other young Japanese
architects, it is an individualistic, creative
development of the traditional wooden
Japanese building.

The complex is basically a multi-layered
assembly of large and small trapezoid forms
with inverted trapezoids in between. The
upright trapezoids provide the space for conference rooms, while the inverted trapezoids
contain annexes needed for preparing for
conferences. The building takes its vitality
from the artistic combination of these two
basic forms and is completed by a few vertical
towers.

The Centre demonstrates, in the materials
used and the technique in the details, the
intimate acquaintance of young Japanese
architects with Western architecture, as well
as their inclination to refer back to traditional
Japanese concepts of form and space. It is
typical of the new phase of Japanese architecture, independent of the West.

97

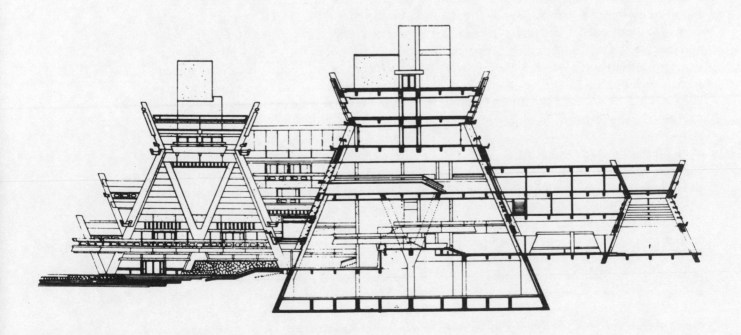

International Conference Centre, Kyoto Matsugasaki (1964–65)
by Sachio Ohtani. Section.

Plate 98
Marina City, Chicago (1964–65) by Bertrand
Goldberg

Residential and business architecture in the major cities of the world needs continuous reappraisal and renewal, and for this reason fresh approaches to this central theme should be generally welcomed. In his Marina City in Chicago, Bertrand Goldberg has designed and executed a building which represents just such a fresh approach. It is the result of ideas developed by Goldberg over several decades and is an entirely individualistic variation on the theme of American residential architecture.

Goldberg studied under Mies van der Rohe in the Bauhaus in Berlin, and, from the expressionist office tower blocks which Mies van der Rohe designed for Berlin in 1920–21 (the connection between two round towers in the ground-plan is similar in both), Goldberg has here developed a practical urban feature which combines office, residential and parking spaces, all of which are included in the two round towers and the link between them. The complex also contains restaurants, banks, a theatre, and a quay. Since 1964, Bertrand Goldberg has had his own office in Marina City.

Each of the 580 feet tall reinforced concrete towers has sixty storeys and 900 apartments of varying size. The towers are situated at the edge of the Chicago Loop, between State and Dearborn Street. The eighteen lower storeys have parking areas for cars. The segmented pattern of the ground-plan gives the apartments in the upper storeys a special feature – the kitchens and bathrooms are situated at the rear, in the narrow part of the segments, while the living room expands towards the outside edge of the building. The large, roofed balconies afford a marvellous view of Lake Michigan.

Four thousand people can live in each of the towers. They all share common services, including laundry, servants' apartments, parking lots, restaurants, and medical and cultural facilities. This project represents an important idea – that of the 'house-town' – for solving the problem of the big city. Harry Seidler's skyscrapers in Australia, using the same circular form, are similar to these buildings; so are the designs of younger architects in South America and Japan, which are some way in advance of even Marina City.

98

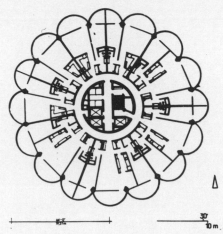

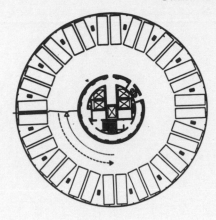

Plan of an apartment floor.

Plan of a garage floor.

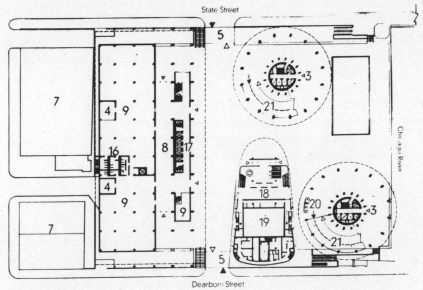

Plan of the 'Plaza'.

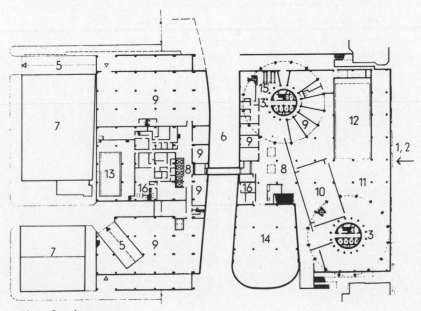

Plan, first basement.

Marina City, Chicago (1964-65)
by Bertrand Goldberg.

1 Marina (below)
2 Storage space for pleasure craft (below)
3 Centre of tower block
4 Ancillary premises
5 Ramp
6 Railway line (below)
7 Existing buildings
8 Passage
9 Shops
10 Kitchen
11 Restaurant
12 Skating rink
13 Swimming pool
14 Exhibition hall
15 Post office
16 Lavatories
17 Lobby of office building
18 Theatre foyer
19 Upper part of exhibition hall
20 Petrol station
21 Up and down ramps of the multi-storey garage

Plate 99
Candle Shop, Vienna (1964–65)
by Hans Hollein

Modern architecture in Vienna is typified by consistent development of tradition, and adjustment to the facts and the requirements of an old town. Hans Hollein's candle shop is comparable to the American Bar by Adolf Loos (Plate 37) built in 1907. Both are characterized by extreme economy and imagination in the use of very small space and optical and spatial effects. Mirrors, light and their psychological effects play an important role.

The street façade of the Retti Candle Shop has neither the window nor the name-fascia of the normal shop. Hollein preferred to try, by opening up the façade above the entrance door, to let the interior of the shop shimmer enticingly through. This is intended to stimulate the interest of the passer-by and draw him into the shop. The effect is enhanced by the windows, which are not set face on to the street, but at an angle to it, and thus confront the passer-by as he walks towards the shop.

The façade is strictly symmetrical. The horizontal opening in the wall above the entrance is chiefly designed for passers-by on the other side of the street, since cars are almost always parked immediately in front of the shop. This opening and the doorway look like a huge keyhole, and the shop is popularly known as the 'keyhole shop'. The proprietor's name is written up at eye level in the small passage leading to the door and is therefore first read by the customer once he has decided to go into the shop. The material used for the exterior wall is aluminium. Hollein used it here so well that he was given the Reynolds Memorial Award, which is regularly made for the suitable application of aluminium in architecture. For the first time in the history of the prize, it was awarded for a project costing less than the $25,000 prize-money.

The most significant feature of the building is the arrangement of the interior space. The shop consists of two rooms with square floor plans, connected by a passageway. After walking through the narrow entrance passage and doorway, one enters the first room at a right angle to its greatest width, which means that, although it is a comparatively small room, it seems remarkably big after the narrow entrance passage. This illusion is heightened by mirrors on both sides. This first part of the shop, in which, again, symmetry is dominant, is used as the showroom.

The second room, also reached by a narrow passageway, has a similar floor plan but with its longest dimension at right angles to the length of the first room. This is the sales room. Here again, Hollein uses mirrors to expand the room optically, and pays great attention to the interplay between colour, space, the texture of materials, and the illusion-giving elements. All the details help make up the total concept, from the simple lamps to the prism-shaped aluminium blocks specially designed by Hollein for displaying candles, the cupboards, the tables, the shop windows, the door handles, and even the shop's promotional material which uses the shape of Hollein's façade. Thus, light is the content of the shop, and not only does it determine the basic form of the interior, but it also attracts attention through the hole above the entrance.

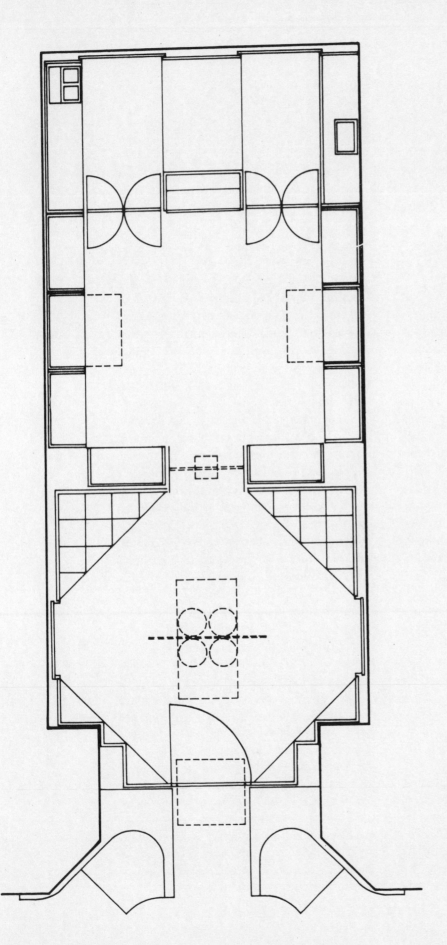

Candle Shop, Vienna (1964–65)
by Hans Hollein. Ground plan.

Plate 100
City Hall, Boston, Massachusetts (1962–68)
by Kallmann, McKinnell and Knowles

The new City Hall in Boston is the central feature of the local government's recently developed Centre Urban Renewal Plan for downtown Boston. Architecturally, it is intended to be the centre of the urban landscape, and symbolically, the heart of urban community life. The winners of the competition for this project, announced in 1962, Gerhard M. Kallmann, Noel McKinnell and F. Knowles, subdivided the complex into three parts. The lower part contains large offices for the majority of public business. Above this, supported on enormous concrete pillars, there is a rectangular part which the architects call the 'crown', beneath which are suspended rooms for official or ceremonial functions. This middle part of the building, which seems almost like something inserted afterwards, also contains the mayor's rooms (which extend round the corner) with ceilings of varying heights, and the Council Conference chamber. Office annexes are attached to both. There is also a public library.

The building dominates a square covered with brick. The walls of the lower part of the building, on both the outside and the inside, are also made of brick. Thus the brick surface of the square extends through the entrance, bridging the boundary between exterior and interior and bringing the square into the inside of the building.

Since the 'crown' rises clear of the brick base, a series of covered open air terraces is created at ground level, and can be reached from all sides of the square, as well as from the entrance. This makes an impression of easy access to the building, almost of participation in government. The three office floors which form the 'crown', project further out at succeeding levels, and do not quite run all the way round the building on all sides. They are regularly subdivided, giving an ornamental finish to the upper part of the structure. Some of the parts of the building suspended beneath the crown recede even more than the lowest of the three upper storeys and some project further out, with frames to provide shade. This gives the building alternating receding and projecting parts, and there is an interplay of horizontal rows and vertically rising elements which creates a multilayered spatial effect. The chamber of the Council is directly over the main entrance, and is emphasized, as the most important part of the ensemble, by the system of projecting frames round its windows and a brick staircase tower.

The upper parts of the building are executed in concrete and glass. The concrete pillars were partly prefabricated and partly made on the site. Electric cables, drains and the air conditioning system run through ducts in the supports. This building, which reminds one of the sculptural quality of Le Corbusier's buildings, is equipped in the most modern possible way. It has a data processing centre, two computers, and a centre of operations with a radio broadcasting unit in case of disaster.

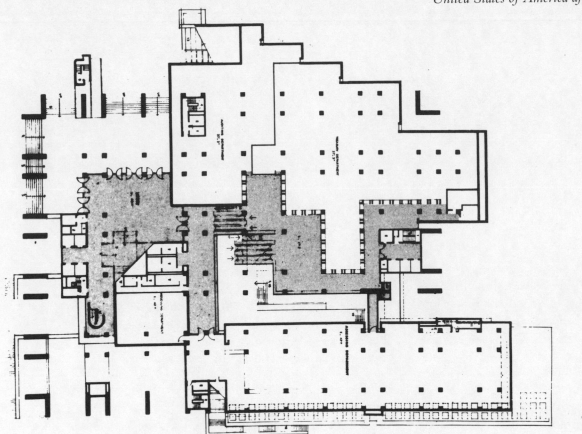

Third floor plan.

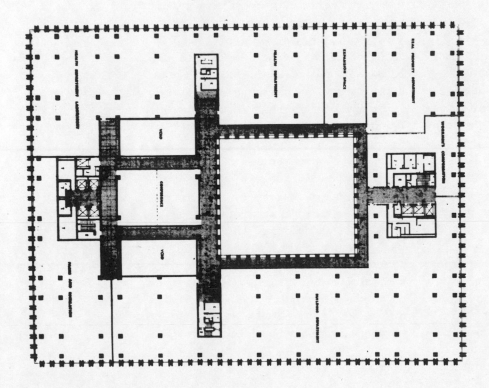

Eighth floor plan.

City Hall, Boston, Massachusetts (1962–68)
by Kallmann, McKinnell and Knowles.

Plate 101 (page 469)
Scarborough College, Toronto (1964–66) by
John Andrews

Scarborough College in Toronto, built by John Andrews in co-operation with Page and Steel, is one of the three pioneering buildings which have recently attracted international attention to Canada. First came the forceful City Hall built by Viljo Revell, also in Toronto. This was followed by Scarborough College, designed and executed by John Andrews, and then came the dwelling complex known as Habitat '67 in Montreal, by the young architect Moshe Safdie (Plate 107). All three have attracted a great deal of attention.

The most important feature of the building in the plate is its special function. It is an educational building which the architect has adapted to new ideas about education. Andrews designed the whole complex as 'group form', i.e. it consists of independent but interconnected units and, like Giancarlo de Carlo's student apartments in Urbino (Plate 94), it was designed from the outset to allow for subsequent extension, which would spoil neither its appearance nor the educational functions performed inside it.

A pavilion-like arrangement was not suitable because the climate in Toronto tends to extremes. Andrews, therefore, developed a complex stretching outwards some distance into the surrounding countryside from a central administration block. All parts of the complex can be reached by a pedestrian way connecting the administration block to the other buildings, called by the architect the 'artery' of the campus. This makes the administration block (which for the time being also serves as a library until the planned library block is built) into the point of origin of the whole complex. To one side of it stretches the Science block, to the other, the Arts block. There are plans to build, later, to the north-east, a theatre, a swimming pool and two sports halls, loosely arranged. The library block will be to the north-west.

The rows of buildings stretch zig-zag along the edge of the hill. The Science block, after running zig-zag for some distance, takes a sudden bend to the north-east. Its four upper storeys facing outwards from the slope recede upwards like steps. Each 'step' is pitched like a roof and covered with glass bricks which let in light. The ventilation shafts (see plate), which punctuate the horizontal line of the stepped blocks, give the building an appearance reminiscent of earlier town designs by Antonio Sant'Elia.

The four upper storeys of the central administration block and of the arts block, with its three bends, are cantilevered out from the hillside in steps corresponding to those of the science wing. The whole complex, which is built of a raw concrete, is composed in several layers to fit into the landscape, and it uses the hilly environment superbly. The design of the building takes into account the needs of the continuously growing modern education industry. Its carefully thought-out, powerful construction, and its use of expressive and yet insensitive materials makes this educational building one of the few important buildings which is really adapted to the likely requirements of the future.

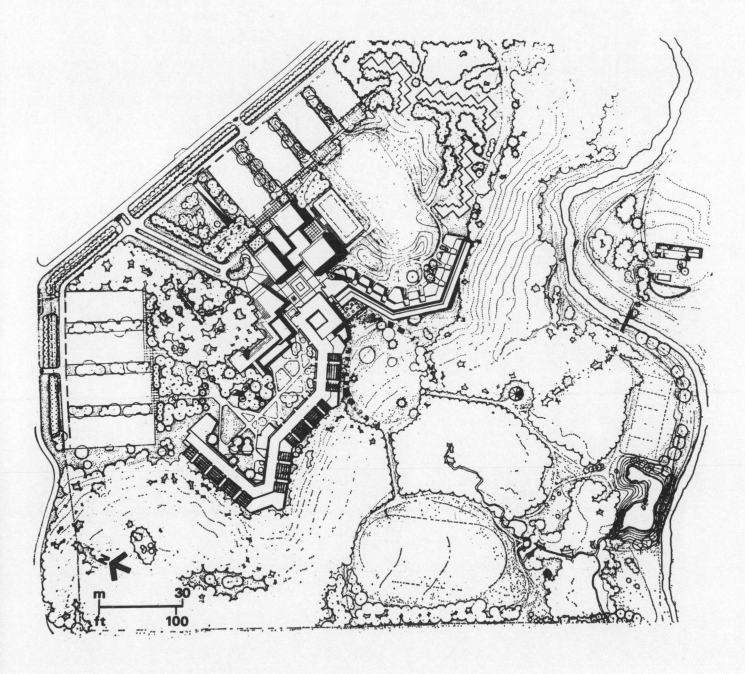

Scarborough College, Toronto (1964–66) by John Andrews. Site plan.

Scarborough College, Toronto (1964–66) by John Andrews.
Plan at levels 2, 3.

1 Meeting place
2 Pedestrian route (humanities)
3 Cafeteria
4 Lecture theatre
5 Undergraduate laboratories
6 Master television studio
7 Lorry tunnel
8 Service entrance
9 Boiler room
10 Main entrance
11 Pedestrian street (science)
12 Meeting place
13 Lecture theatre (upper level)
14 Undergraduate laboratories
15 Television studios
16 Pedestrian street (humanities)
17 Dining room
19 Lecture theatre

Scarborough College, Toronto (1964-66) by John Andrews.
Plan at level 5.
18 Faculty office
20 Meeting place (upper level)
21 Council room
22 Administration offices
23 Mechanical
24 Graduate student lounge
25 Graduate laboratories
26 Faculty laboratories and offices

Plate 102
*Student Union 'Dipoli', at the Technical
University, Helsinki-Otaniemi (1964–66) by
Reima Pietilä and Raili Paateleinen*

Reima Pietilä's Student Union 'Dipoli' at the
Otaniemi Technical University, for which
he won the competition in 1961, was built
from 1964–66. It is an important example of
the general swing which has been taking
place in international architecture from the
fixed to the unfixed, from form to action,
from good taste to emotional impact, from
narrow schematic compositional laws to
openness, freedom and new formal principles
– the latter albeit 'still' concerned with
composition. Prior to this building, Pietilä
and Paateleinen had only built the Finnish
Pavilion at the Brussels World's Fair in
1958, a church in Kaleva, and apartments in
Suvikumpu.

Admitting the novelty of the building,
Pietilä has himself said, 'we are building
ourselves'. Since the complex had to be
added onto the existing University buildings,
the student hostel is related on three sides to
earlier buildings, including Alvar Aalto's
Auditorium Maximum (Plate 91). On the
fourth side, to the east, it is a freely unfolding
architectural sculpture. The different functions are co-ordinated with each other on
two levels. On the ground floor, the main
entrance leads into the foyers and thence
into a theatre. This, like the beer cellar leading off the entrance to the right, the bar and
the seats round the fireplace, is in the
'dynamic' half of the building. The other,
'geometric' half of the ground floor contains assembly rooms, a library, and various
technical installations and offices. Both parts
are connected together by the students'
foyer. On the upper storey are the main hall,
with a stage, the students' restaurant, a
cafeteria, and various other rooms. Behind
the large hall, directly accessible from the
beer cellar on the ground floor, there is a
restaurant open to the public. On the other
side, there are several large assembly rooms.
The main part of the upper storey in the
'geometric' part of the building is reserved
for the kitchen which can supply food in
three different directions. The maximum
capacity of the building, with all facilities
being used simultaneously, is three thousand
people. The main restaurant can seat 2,000
people at once.

In the structure of the building there is an
organic combination of curves (particularly
on the entrance side) and geometrical,
basically rectangular, forms. Both are effective within the closed whole. There is order
without symmetry, indeed without any
determining structural principle. The combination of different formal principles is
paralleled by the combination of different
building materials, e.g. reinforced concrete,
copper, wood and glass.

102

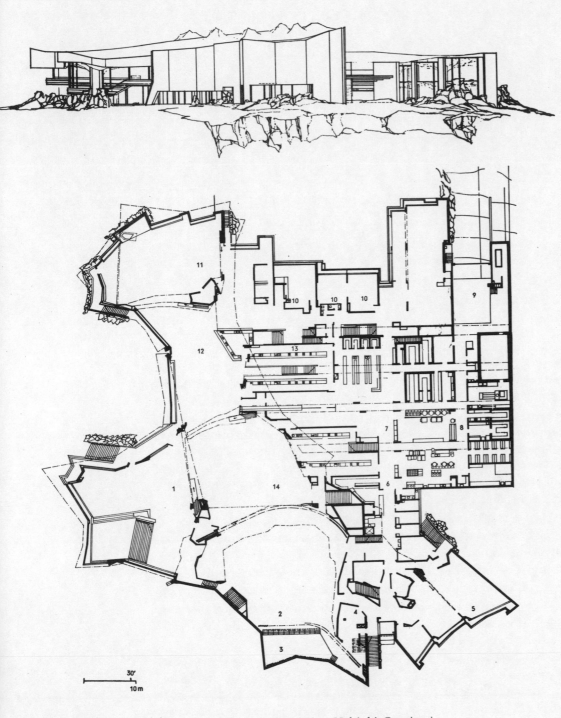

Student Union 'Dipoli' at the Technical University, Helsinki-Otaniemi
(1964-66) by Reima Pietilä and Raili Paateleinen. Plan and elevation.

1 Foyer
2 Large conference and lecture hall
3 Stage
4 Property room
5 Public restaurant
6 Meal service
7 Kitchen
8 Stores
9 Goods delivery
10 Conference room
11 Cafeteria
12 Students' restaurant
13 Buffet
14 Restaurant with dance floor

Plate 103
Shrine of the Book in the Israeli National Museum, Jerusalem (1965) by Frederic Kiesler and Armand Bartos

One of the most important places in the new state of Israel is the Israeli National Museum completed in 1965 by the Israeli team of architects, Alfred Mansfeld and Dora Gad. Frederic Kiesler, Armand Bartos and Isamu Noguchi also worked on the museum complex, which was designed as a cult centre. It contains, amongst other things, the treasures of the Bezalel Museum (founded in 1908) and of the Archaeological Museum. Kiesler and Bartos built the Shrine of the Book to contain the priceless Dead Sea Scrolls. The sculptor Noguchi made the west slope of the museum hill into a sculpture garden.

The area planned and laid out by the architects lies to the north-west of the north-south axis of the Museum grounds. It contains a rectangular entrance building, in which is the library and an office, and the central room, with a square ground-plan and a white dome, in which the scrolls are exhibited. In the domed building there are also a rest room and a souvenir shop. The two buildings are connected by a passage-like building, in which the Nahal Never and Masada documents are kept. To the north of the entrance hall there is a black basalt wall which rises up opposite the white dome (on the right in the plate).

The passageway to the precious documents, which in case of danger can be lowered with their glass cases into the ground, leads at an angle downwards. In the interior room, the light from the centre of the dome picks out the concentric sculptural rings of the roof and falls onto the 'Shrine of the Book', raised like an altar.

The strong symbolic content of the building, as the central point of the new Israeli cultural centre, is expressed not only in its organic form, in contrast to the other basically cubic parts of the museum, and its situation to the east of the north-south axis, but also in its colours – the white glazed concrete dome, a hugely magnified imitation of one of the lids which originally covered the scrolls, is set off by the black basalt wall. Even its name differentiates this building from the rest of the ensemble and underlines its sacred character.

103

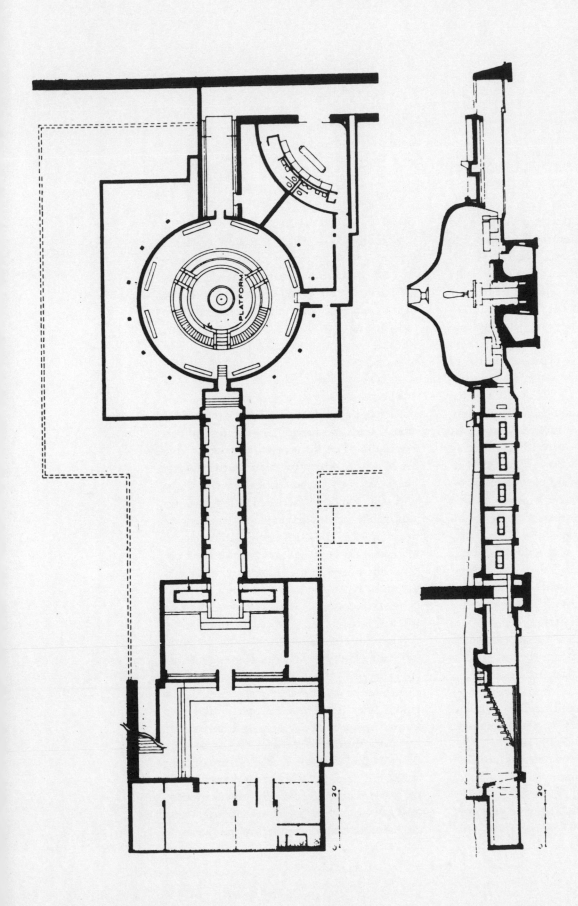

Shrine of the Book in the Israeli National Museum, Jerusalem (1965) by Frederic Kiesler and Armand Bartos, Plan and section.

Plate 104
Endo laboratories, Garden City, New Jersey
(1962–64) by Paul Rudolph

Recently, factory building has occasionally returned, as in the nineteenth century, to historical building forms. This contrasts with the totally functional and basically rectangular transparent factory architecture used by Walter Gropius in Alfeld (Plate 43), E. Owen Williams in Beeston (Plate 57) and Brinkman and Van der Vlugt in Rotterdam (Van Nelle factory). A typical example of the new historicist trend is the headquarters of the Endo Chemical Works in Garden City, a castle-like building by Paul Rudolph. The firm specified an attractive building for specially trained employees to be carefully designed to fit the functions required of it, and also to present a favourable public image. Rudolph's solution was a striking, formal building, divided, as is usually the case with classic factory buildings, into three parts: production, research and administration. Since the site was limited to a spit of land along Meadowbrook Parkway, the three different functional areas of the building are laid out one above the other.

The highly specialized production areas for individual products are on the ground floor, with the other parts of the building above. Since different branches of production need rooms which differ in height and width, the building has a very carefully planned arrangement of interlocking rooms, at the end of which there is a functionally situated, common packing area, storeroom and despatch department.

The factory is approached over a series of changing levels and a sweeping, curved staircase, with, on the administration side, very broad steps. The entrance lobby, and the roof lobby above it, give a view onto the flowering terraces, and from the administrative office, there is a marvellous view onto the Parkway. An entrance on the south side of the building, which can be reached from the parking lots, is used by the employees. On the roof, the open glass cafeteria is surrounded by a carefully laid out roof garden, with curving lines.

The basic material of the building, visible both from outside and inside, is raw concrete, with a rough aggregate, ribbed externally. The little concrete towers give the building, which is closed on the outside like a castle, its characteristic defensive shape with the windows between them looking almost like arrow slits. In some departments these towers also function internally as niches for desks or as places to sit, behind the finishing tables. Some have plastic domes through which the tables are lit. The other projecting concrete parts, corresponding to the little towers, are for ventilation.

The whole of the interior was also designed by Paul Rudolph. He used materials for covering the floor and the ceiling which contrasted with the raw walls. The Endo laboratories have become one of the best known features of the area and are visited by a large number of people. This accurately thought-out factory, reminiscent of the sculptural lines of Wright's Johnson Wax Factory (Plate 69), is an example of the new historicism which has come mainly from architectural schools in the United States of America.

104

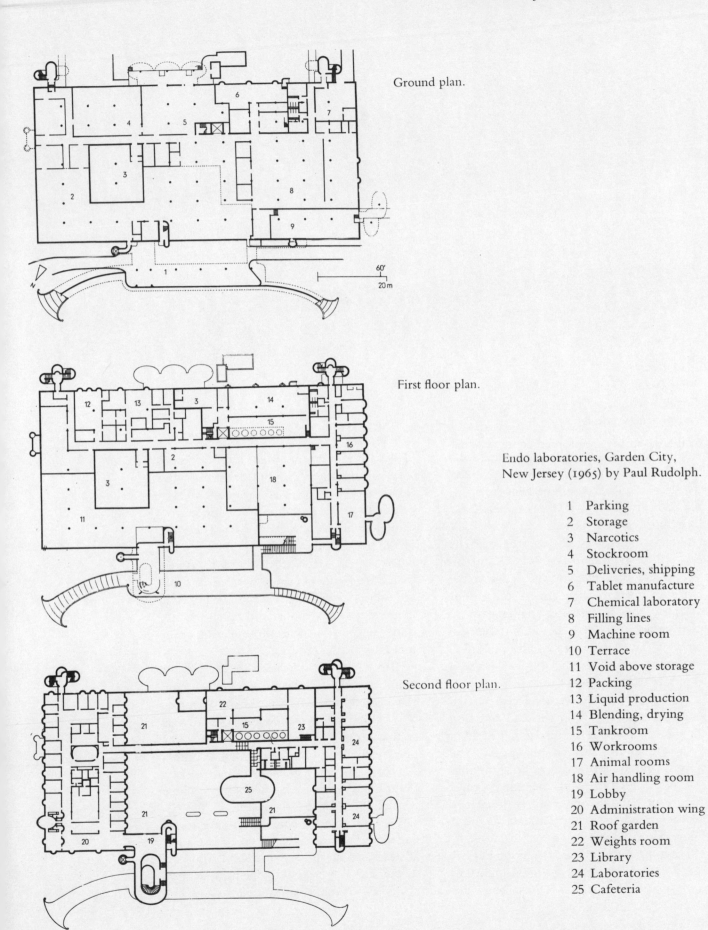

Ground plan.

First floor plan.

Second floor plan.

Endo laboratories, Garden City,
New Jersey (1965) by Paul Rudolph.

1 Parking
2 Storage
3 Narcotics
4 Stockroom
5 Deliveries, shipping
6 Tablet manufacture
7 Chemical laboratory
8 Filling lines
9 Machine room
10 Terrace
11 Void above storage
12 Packing
13 Liquid production
14 Blending, drying
15 Tankroom
16 Workrooms
17 Animal rooms
18 Air handling room
19 Lobby
20 Administration wing
21 Roof garden
22 Weights room
23 Library
24 Laboratories
25 Cafeteria

Plate 105
Kline Biology Tower at Yale University, New Haven, Connecticut (1965–66) by Philip Johnson and Richard Foster

Philip Johnson is one of the most individualistic of contemporary American architects. The buildings he has designed since rejecting the path pioneered by Mies van der Rohe, have repelled some people. His more recent buildings, like the atomic reactor at Rehovot, Israel (Plate 87), the museums in Utica, Fort Worth and Bielefeld, and the theatre in the Lincoln Centre in New York, show a range of approaches to historical building form, often going back to the early twentieth century. The laboratory of the biological department at Yale University in New Haven is an example of this tendency.

The seventeen-storey tower rises on the south-west corner of an enclosed court on the top of a hill, and is intended to provide a visible focus for further buildings of the science department (also designed by Philip Johnson), which are to include an auditorium and an anthropology building. In the nearby geology building, Johnson repeats the motif of the Kline Tower.

The appearance of the biology building is characterized by the drum-like supporting columns of reinforced concrete. These are clad in brick in contrast to the flat, horizontal line of the stone spandrels, beneath the windows. The glass surfaces of the deeply recessed windows almost disappear, as though behind a set of iron bars. The form of the tower is simple, and yet subtle – the narrower end façades reach out more vividly than the broader ones, and of these, the east one more vividly than the other. The materials used are clinker and Longmeadow stone, which fit in with those used in other buildings on the campus.

The building is served by central lift shafts, and the cylindrical columns contain the ventilation shafts for the laboratories. The library is in the basement of the tower, so that it can be extended at any time. The glass wall of the reading room looks onto a sunken court. The entrance hall and staircase of the library extend over two storeys. There are club rooms on the top storey.

This disciplined, superbly proportioned and thought-out building is clearly historicist in its formal means of expression. And yet, in the way it merges into the campus, it is also unmistakably contemporary.

105

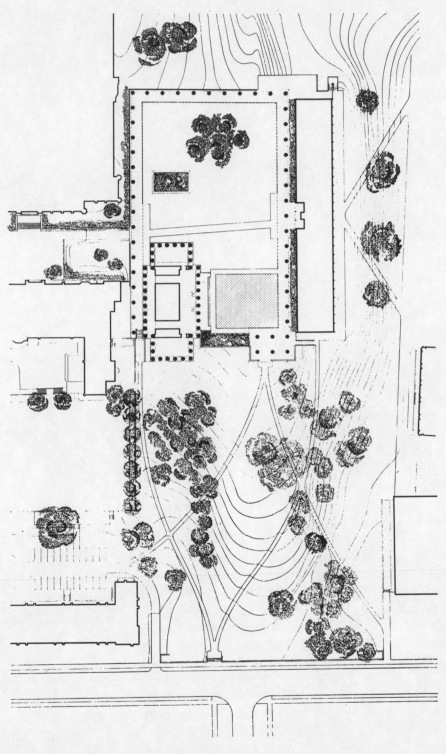

Kline Biology Tower at Yale University, New Haven, Connecticut (1965–66) by Philip Johnson
and Richard Foster. Ground plan.

Plate 106
Ford Foundation Administration building, New
York (1966–67) by Kevin Roche
and John Dinkeloo

In refraining from using the whole of the site and making some of it available to passers-by, Lever House (Plate 73) introduced a new concept in urban office architecture. The Ford Foundation building in New York uses the same idea, but here the public space is inside the building, protected from the weather.

The architects, Kevin Roche and John Dinkeloo, had previously worked with Eero Saarinen (who died in 1961), and had cooperated closely with him on various projects (Plate 80). The Ford Foundation building was the first important work of the new firm, which was formed after Saarinen's death.

The Ford Foundation covers the block between 42nd and 43rd Street, near the United Nations building. From the outside the complex looks like one unit, although on the inside it contains offices and an enclosed urban area. The offices are on two sides of the 12-storey building, arranged in an L-shape around an air-conditioned interior court. On the other two sides there are glass curtain walls ten storeys high. The glass is supported by vertical granite-faced concrete pillars and horizontal steel elements. Most of the offices, which were furnished by Warren Platner, give onto the interior court. The cafeteria on the 11th storey, and the directors' office, are suspended, so that they appear to float in the space at the top of the building. The folding glass roof above the court keeps out the weather, and, like the glass curtain walls, admits enough daylight to illuminate the inside.

The use of air conditioning for the whole of the enclosed urban area is the most revolutionary feature of the building. Although only a comparatively small experiment, it shows that air conditioned urban spaces are possible. This makes the building an important indicator for the future.

106

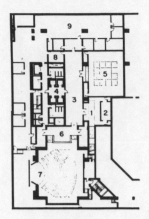

Basement level plan.

1	Public entrance	6	Balcony
2	Cloakroom	7	Auditorium
3	Reception	8	Servery
4	Lift lobby	9	Data processing
5	Boardroom		

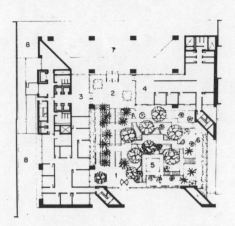

Ground plan.

1	42nd St. entrance	5	Pond
2	43rd St. entrance	6	Sitting area
3	Reception	7	Set down
4	Employment	8	Service areas

Typical floor plan.

1	Directors' offices	4	Stair tower
2	Reception	5	Services tower
3	Secretarial offices		

Tenth floor plan.

1	Reception	4	President's office
2	Balcony	5	Conference room
3	President's reception	6	Vice-president

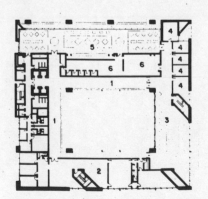

Eleventh floor plan.

1 Balcony
2 Chairman's suite
3 Executives' dining rooms
4 Private dining rooms
5 Staff dining
6 Kitchen

Ford Foundation Administration building, New York (1966–67) by Kevin Roche and John Dinkeloo. Floor plans.

Plate 107
Habitat '67, Montreal (1966–67) by Moshe
Safdie and others

Moshe Safdie's mass housing complex, Habitat '67, built for the 1967 Montreal World's Fair, is a first step in the direction of actually realizing some of the many suggestions made in recent years for mass town housing. Safdie was born in Israel in 1938, and came to Canada at the age of 15. He started planning this type of housing while still a student at the McGill University School of Architecture. In essence, his idea is to bring people out of the suburbs back into the centre of the town, and to make available to them the pleasures of the large city, as well as the natural surroundings of the suburbs.

Safdie's original design envisaged 900 dwelling units for about 5,000 people in two separate blocks of different sizes. In the event, only a section of the smaller block was actually built, with 158 apartments for 700 people.

Habitat '67 is a pile of equal-sized prefabricated concrete boxes all fitted together in a different way. Each pair of boxes is joined vertically with a taut cable. This means that the boxes can be organized in almost any arrangement. Each unit is about 37 feet long, 19 feet wide, 11 feet high, and weighs 90 tons. The units were prefabricated on the site, sand-blasted, and equipped with walls, floors, services and kitchens before being lifted into place by crane. The bathroom units are one-piece moulded glass fibre shells, prefabricated in a factory.

There are three different sizes of apartment. The smallest is a single box, about 2,430 square feet. Larger apartments consist of two or three boxes, and usually have two storeys. Every apartment has a balcony formed by the roof of the box below. On the rail of each balcony there is an automatically watered flower box. On the ground floor there is a hobby room and parking space for cars. There are two 'streets' at the fourth and eighth floor level, from which staircases lead to the individual apartments. Interior playground terraces can be used by all the inhabitants.

The 'piling-up' of 158 'houses' made out of 354 boxes with fifteen different floor plans, in twelve storeys, is reminiscent of a Mediterranean mountain village. Habitat has also been compared to a Pueblo Indian cliff dwelling, and even to the Minoan Palace of Knossos in Crete.

Since only a limited number of apartments were actually built, the average cost of each apartment, at about $100,000, was far too high. The costs, which were more than twice as high as originally envisaged, include, however, a giant crane which had to be built specially ($750,000) and which can be used again. The pile of apartments is arranged in such a way that something like a façade is created on one side, and it looks quite different from the rear.

In spite of all criticisms which can be levelled at Habitat '67, it remains the first

107

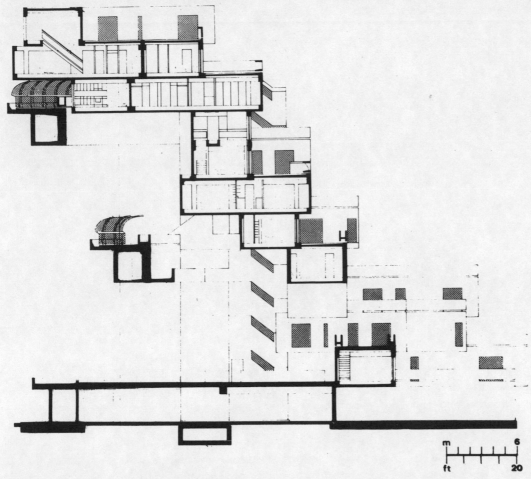

Habitat '67, Montreal (1966-67)
by Moshe Safdie and others. Section.

realization of an idea which has been studied
by young architects throughout the world
with increasing interest, viz. Kenzo Tange's
Japanese designs, the work of the Meta-
bolists, or Yona Friedman's projects for mass
urban dwellings. These ideas have, until
recently, remained in the realm of theory.
Moshe Safdie was the first architect to get
the opportunity to show how it was possible
to make mass housing compatible with
individual dwellings. Le Corbusier's Unité
d'Habitation in Marseilles (Plate 68), the
Halen Estate near Bern (Plate 82), the Ramat
Gan Estate, in Moshe Safdie's own country,
by the Israeli architects Neumann, Hecker
and Sharon, are all prototypes of this type
of building, though none of them went as
far as Habitat '67. Besides, nobody can dispute the unusual effect made by the sculptural ensemble of raw concrete boxes, and
the play of light and shade on the units, as
they project and recede in space, almost as
though they were trying to draw space into
the block.

Plate 108
German Pavilion at the 1967 World's Fair,
Montreal (1966–67) by Rolf Gutbrod
and Frei Otto

The German Pavilion at the 1967 Montreal World's Fair is the finest achievement to date of the German architect and engineer, Frei Otto. After a development lasting more than ten years, progressing from smaller buildings like the Tanzbrunnen in Cologne (1957) to the important official German Pavilion in Montreal, Frei Otto was finally able to demonstrate internationally the uses of his flexible and adaptable building techniques.

The pavilion consists of a taut cable net, suspended from eight tubular steel masts, under which is stretched a polyester skin covered with PVC. This covers an exhibition platform made out of prefabricated steel frame parts, and arranged in terraces forming two spirals. There is also an auditorium with a gallery, covered with a shell made up of wooden slats. Seven of the eight masts stand on the corners of one larger and one smaller square, with a corner in common. The eighth mast stands on an island, enabling the tent to extend over the water. The masts are cylindrical in the middle and conical at the top and bottom, coming to a point. They support a roof with a surface of 107,640 square feet, covering a ground area of 83,000 square feet. This roof is extremely light and the strength of the structure comes from its suppleness. In a wind the enormous roof surface yields like a tree.

All the parts of this extremely cheap building were made in Germany, individually packed, and shipped to Canada, where they were assembled on the site. The cost of the whole building was about £250,000, of which transport and packing accounted for about £20,000. The building actually cost less than the original estimate.

The elegant lightness of this exhibition tent had already attracted attention even before the exhibition was opened. The transparent skin of the lower saddle surfaces bathes the interior in a diffused greenish light. Individual parts of the exhibition were highlighted by eye-like plastic openings in the roof. The whole exhibition area is visible from almost any point on the platform. On warm days, the tent was left open at the edges. Wind vanes directed air onto the places where the visitors walked and stood. Warm air was automatically extracted by fans at the top of the masts. Only the enclosed parts of the building, such as the offices, the auditorium, the restaurant, and the kitchen, were actually air-conditioned.

The significance of this building is that it was the first opportunity Frei Otto had to demonstrate his ideas about 'Grosshülle' ('large-scale coverings'), which could be used for much larger buildings. In fact this, his first official national commission, has brought him in further, larger commissions. One can imagine a building like this being used to protect a dry area from the sun or to shield a place against the vagaries of a very unpleasant climate. The buildings underneath a covering like this could be very light and flexible. Thus the real significance of the German Pavilion at the 1967 Montreal World's Fair lies in its relevance to the future.

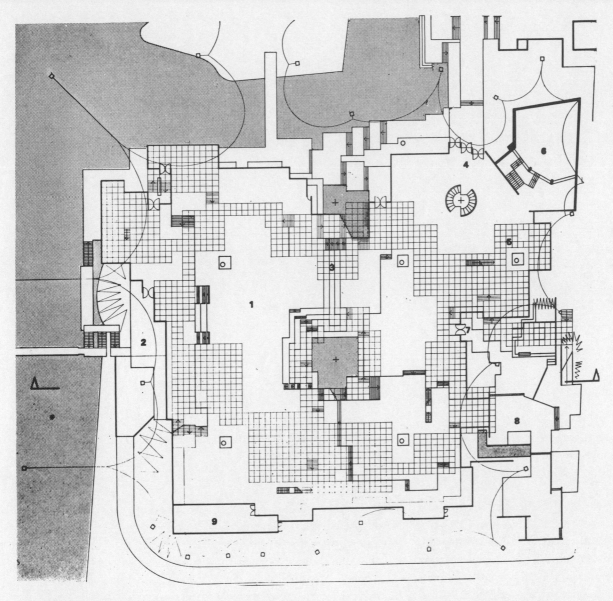

German Pavilion at the 1967 World's Fair, Montreal (1966-67)
by Rolf Gutbrod and Frei Otto.
Plan, ground level and gallery level superimposed, and section.

1 Exhibition area	6 Auditorium
2 Terrace	7 VIP entrance
3 Library	8 Sculpture court
4 Main entrance	9 Store
5 Information	10 Air conditioning

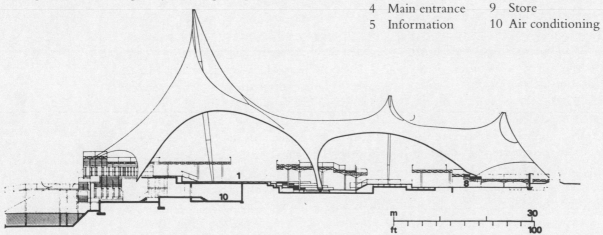

Plates 109 (page 503)
U.S.A. Pavilion at the 1967 World's Fair,
Montreal (1967) by Richard Buckminster Fuller

Since the 'twenties, Richard Buckminster Fuller has tried to build economical and industrially manufactured buildings adapted to the needs and materials of our times. After decades of rejection, this important architect and teacher has, since the Second World War, been given major commissions. He has worked for American authorities and private firms, and extensively for clients elsewhere.

His most important building to date is the U.S.A. Pavilion in Montreal. Here he has used the results of his experience with his remarkably cheap geodesic domes. Knot joints link the outside net of thick struts, which carries most of the weight, with the thinner, inner net, on which 2,000 acryl-painted caps are mounted. Motors at the joints react automatically to the sunlight, moving a system of sunblinds, and a number of hexagonal caps contain a ventilating system. The dome does not therefore cut off the interior space entirely from the exterior,

but merely shields it from undesirable external effects, producing a pleasant temperate climate inside.

The building, described by Buckminster Fuller as a 'geodetic skyscraper dome', has a spherical diameter of about 250 feet and a maximum height of 200 feet. Its surface measures 141,000 square feet. Under the shell, through which the exhibition train ran, the exhibition floors were arranged independently on several different but connected levels, joined by escalators.

The possibility of air-conditioning a large space is more dramatically demonstrated here than in the Ford Foundation building in New York (Plate 106). Like Frei Otto (Plate 108), Fuller has taken the concept further. The building is demountable, reusable, cheap, and can be replaced in parts. In this sense, it is less architecture than a sign of what the future may bring, like several exhibition buildings since the Eiffel Tower.

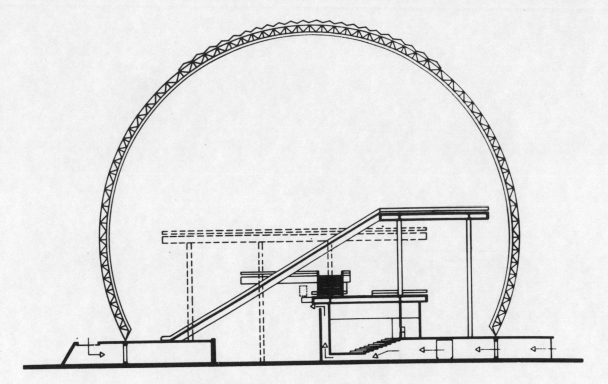

Cross section in the north–south direction, with the
123-feet long escalator leading to the highest platform.

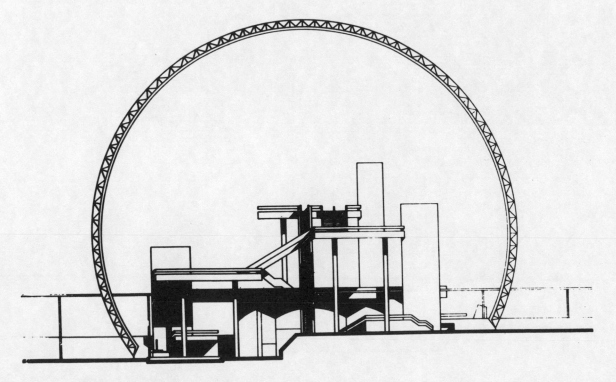

Indoor equipment seen from the south.

U.S.A. Pavilion at the 1967 World's Fair, Montreal (1967)
by Richard Buckminster Fuller.

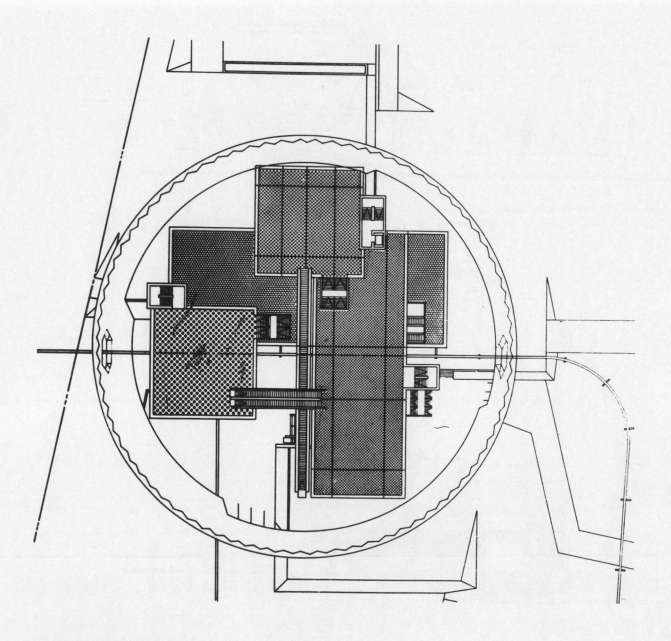

U.S.A. Pavilion at the 1967 World's Fair, Montreal (1967)
by Richard Buckminster Fuller.
Plan with the four upper platform levels.

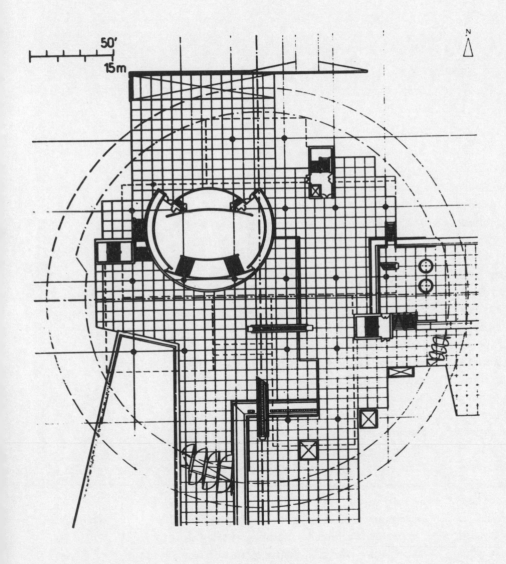

U.S.A. Pavilion at the 1967 World's Fair, Montreal (1967)
by Richard Buckminster Fuller.
Plan with the three lower platform levels.

Plate 110
Sports Palace (Palacio de los Deportes), Mexico
City (1966–68) by Felix Candela, Antonio
Peyrí and Enrique Castañeda

Felix Candela is the most important exponent in the world of the shell building techniques. In 1966, a limited competition was announced for the large Olympic Hall in Mexico City. A number of entrants proposed shell constructions in the style of Candela; but Candela himself proposed something quite different – a copper roof suspended from a steel structure on the hyperbolic paraboloid principle. The latter serves as a space frame, and provides the required span of 545 feet, which would have been economically impossible with reinforced concrete.

The building is situated on the Calle Lorenzo Boturini, and was completed in 1968. In the Olympic Games it was used mostly for the basket ball matches. It is an example of mammoth architecture comparable to Kenzo Tange's Hall for the 1964 Tokyo Olympics (Plate 93).

Candela designed the building to be able to be erected quickly, using local facilities and equipment. It is, therefore, based on a concrete structure, with four anchors with bridge-like spans. The space frame of the roof grows out of this with a steel framework and skin of shiny golden-copper plates, visible from a considerable distance. The building lies directly under the line of flight of aeroplanes landing in Mexico City.

The maximum height of the dome is 140 feet. The arena, which is unconnected to the roof structure, measures 295 feet across. There are 22,370 seats, of which 15,458 are fixed and 6,912 demountable. All light sources are in the roof, which is attached by sloping struts to the concrete base. This enormous roof also covers a promenade, a restaurant, a cafeteria, a radio and television station, and various technical installations. The economy of this vaulted, wave-like roof, with its glistening sweep only slightly interrupted by thin side struts and its enormous support-free span, makes this sports building one of the most significant communal buildings of the 'sixties.

110

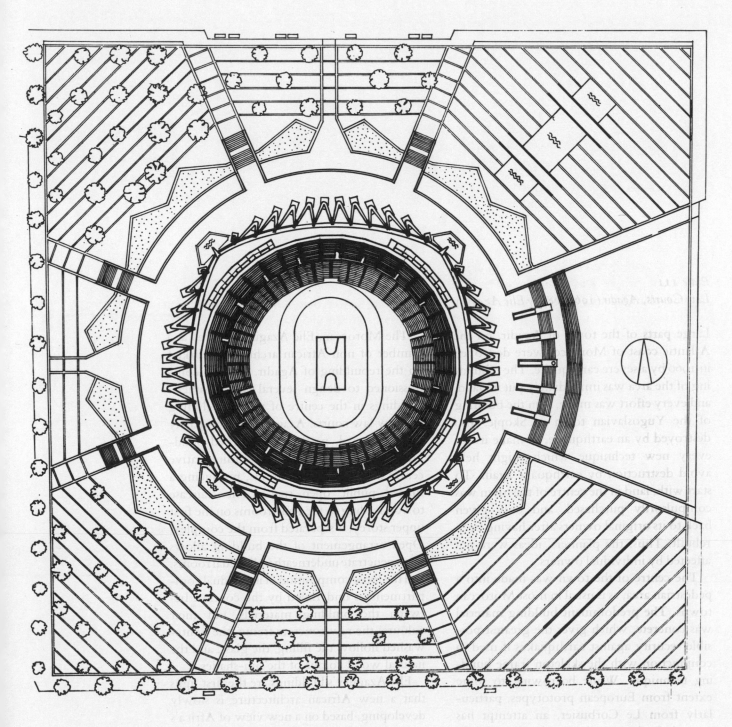

Sports Palace (Palacio de los Deportes), Mexico City (1966–68)
by Felix Candela, Antonio Peyrí and Enrique Castañeda. Plan.

Plate 111
Law Courts, Agadir (1967–68) by Elie Azagury

Large parts of the town of Agadir, on the Atlantic coast of Morocco, were destroyed in 1960 by a severe earthquake. The rebuilding of the area was immediately put in hand, and every effort was made, as in the building of the Yugoslavian town of Skopje, also destroyed by an earthquake, to make use of every new technique which might help avoid destruction by earthquake again. To start with, land in the centre of the town was compulsorily purchased, and only given back to its original owners after having been rebuilt. Thus, the planners' ideas were not affected by individual owners.

The centre of the town was made into a pedestrian area, as is usual in most Moroccan towns. The predominant building material was concrete, which gives the greatest possible security against earthquakes if used in conjunction with the skeleton frame building technique. While borrowing to some extent from European prototypes, particularly from Le Corbusier, an attempt has nevertheless been made to achieve specifically African forms.

The Moroccan, Elie Azagury, as well as a number of non-African architects, worked on the rebuilding of Agadir. He was commissioned to design several of the official buildings in the centre of town, including the new law courts. Azagury put this partly three-storeyed, partly one-storeyed building, which is part of the administrative centre of Agadir, on columns, producing a shaded public open space. The staircase tower, leading to the courtrooms on the first upper storey, is separated from the complex. Open arrangement of the building allows air to penetrate underneath individual rooms, and the loose composition of individual compartments is underlined by the contrast between the building materials and their colours: the raw concrete frame, the whitewashed hollow tile filling, the glass, and the natural wood colour of the sun-shades.

Elie Azagury's buildings are the first signs that a new African architecture is slowly developing, based on a new view of Africa's own traditions as well as the influence of European architecture.

III

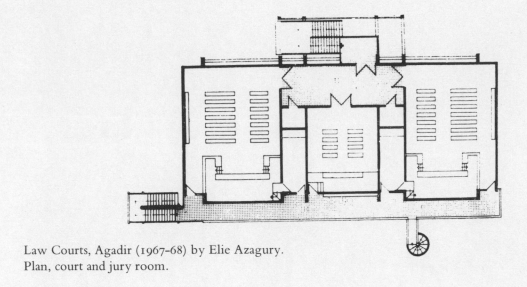

Law Courts, Agadir (1967-68) by Elie Azagury.
Plan, court and jury room.

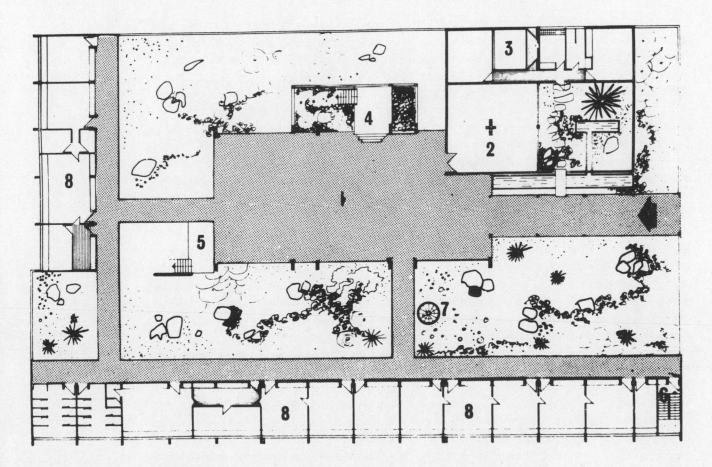

Ground plan.

1	Concourse	5	Magistrates' staircase
2	Notary department	6	Staircase leading to the cells
3	Caretaker's quarters	7	Prisoners' staircase
4	Public Staircase	8	Offices

Plates 112
*Yamanashi Communication Centre, Kofu
(1964–66) by Kenzo Tange*

The radio and television centre at Kofu represents the first examplar of a new theory. Designs of this type have so far not progressed beyond the drawing board in other parts of the world. The plan for building was developed from earlier plans for various projects which were never executed (e.g. The Tokyo Plan, 1960). It is the first time a major city administrative centre has been raised above the ground and set in a frame-like spatial structure which can be extended in almost any direction in the future.

The building consists of a reinforced concrete structure, with 16 towers, each 17 feet in diameter. Horizontal planes and office storeys are suspended from this frame as required. All the basic installations are in the towers, three of which contain staircases, two passenger lifts, two goods lifts, three toilets, and six air conditioning ducts. These functional rooms 'serve' the horizontal floors, in much the same way as in Louis I. Kahn's towers in Philadelphia (Plate 81). The towers can be built higher if necessary. This means that the structure is open in all directions, and can be extended upwards, downwards, to the right, to the left – in fact, in any direction where there is room.

In spite of this, the building has a closed character. Its monumental weight is typical of modern trends in Japanese architecture. It seems probable that such a building would not be acceptable without modification in a different age or place.

The client was the Yamanashi Broadcasting Company, a mass media concern in the newspaper, printing, and television business. In this building every department of the firm can be isolated or extended. It is also a cultural and social centre, since it has shops, exhibition rooms, a cafeteria, and other installations on the ground floor.

This building, commissioned by 3 private firms, is an open, alterable town building, in which everyone can participate.

Buildings like this Communications Centre by Tange are open structures which should be seen as part of an urban environment. This type of building will be a key feature of the architecture of the next few decades. It will no longer be possible to regard architecture in isolation from the environment, and whole towns will be conceived as integrated and indivisible units. Thus Tange's building in Kofu, the last in this book, is the beginning of a new movement in architecture which will follow the movement which has developed from 1850 to 1968, and which has been described and illustrated here.

112

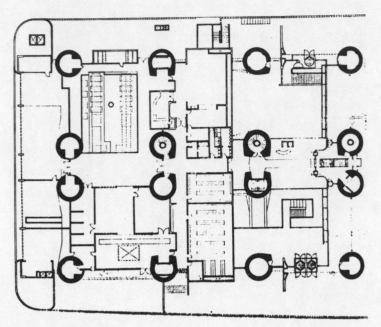

Ground plan.

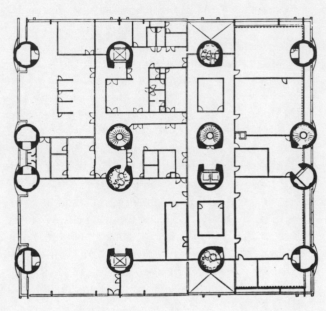

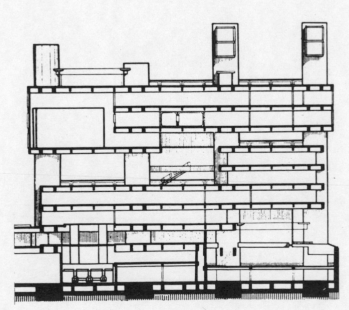

Section.

Yamanashi Communication Centre, Kofu (1964–66) by Kenzo Tange.

BIBLIOGRAPHY

Andersen, T. *Moderne Russisk Kunst 1910-1925* (Copenhagen 1969)

Andersen, S. 'Behrens' Changing Concept', *Architectural Design*, 2 (1969)

Architecture d'aujourd'hui, 1932 (special issue on A. Perret)

Architektur von Professor Joseph M. Olbrich (3 vols., Berlin 1903-07)

Argan, G. C. *Walter Gropius e la Bauhaus* (Turin 1951)

Ausgeführte Bauten und Entwürfe von Frank Lloyd Wright (Berlin 1910)

Banham, P. R. 'Sant'Elia', *Architectural Review*, CXVII (1955) 295-301;
  CXIX (1956) 343-4

Banham, P. R. *The Architecture of the Well-tempered Environment* (London 1969)

Banham, P. R. *Guide to Modern Architecture* (London 1962)

Banham, P. R. *Theory and Design in the First Machine Age* (London 1960)

Bayer, H., and Gropius, W. and I. *Bauhaus 1919-1928* (New York 1938; London 1939)

Behrendt, W. C. *Modern Building* (New York 1937)

Bergos, J. *Antoni Gaudí l'home i l'obra* (Barcelona 1954)

Besset, M. *New French Architecture* (London 1968)

Bill, M. *Ludwig Mies van der Rohe* (Milan 1955)

Bill, M. *Moderne Schweizer Architektur 1925-45* (Basle 1949)

Bill, M. *Robert Maillart* (Zürich 1949)

Blaser, W. *Mies van der Rohe* (London 1965)

Blomfield, Sir R. *Richard Norman Shaw, R.A.* (London 1940)

Boesiger, W. *Le Corbusier: The Complete Architectural Works*
  (8 vols., London 1966-70)

Borsi, F., and Portoghesi, P. *Victor Horta* (Rome 1969)

Bottoni, P. *Antologia di edifici moderni in Milano* (Milan 1954)

Brandon-Jones, J. 'The Work of Philip Webb and Norman Shaw', *Architectural
  Association Journal*, LXXI (1955) 9-21

'Building in the USSR, 1917-1932', special issue of *Architectural Design*, 2 (1970)

Casteels, M. *Henry van de Velde* (Brussels 1932)

Christ-Janer, A. *Eliel Saarinen* (Chicago 1948)

Clark, R. J. 'J. M. Olbrich 1867-1908', *Architectural Design*, 12 (1967)

Collins, P. *Changing Ideals in Modern Architecture* (London 1965; paperback 1967)

Collins, P. *Concrete: The Vision of a New Architecture* (London 1959)

Condit, C. W. *American Building* (Chicago 1968)

Cremers, P. *Peter Behrens, sein Werk von 1900 bis zur Gegenwart* (Essen 1928)

De Feo, V. *USSR architettura 1917-1936* (Rome 1963)

De Stijl, vol. I, 1917-1920; vol. II, 1921-32 (reprinted Amsterdam 1968)

Dorfles, G. *L' Architettura moderna* (Milan 1954)

Gebhard, D. *An Exhibition of the Architecture of R. M. Schindler (1887-1953)*
  (California 1967)

Geretsegger, H., and Peintner, M. *Otto Wagner 1841-1918* (Salzburg 1964)

Giedion, S. *A Decade of Contemporary Architecture* (Zürich 1954)

Giedion, S. *Space, Time and Architecture* (5th ed., Cambridge, Mass. and London 1967)

Giedion, S. *Walter Gropius* (London 1954)

Gluck, F. *Adolf Loos* (Paris 1931)

Gray, C. *The Great Experiment, Russian Art 1863–1922* (London 1962)

Gropius, W. *Internationale Architektur* (Munich 1925)

Gropius, W. *The New Architecture and the Bauhaus* (New York 1936)

Gutheim, F. (ed.) *Frank Lloyd Wright on Architecture: Selected Writings, 1894–1940* (New York 1941)

Hamlin, T. F. *Forms and Functions of Twentieth-Century Architecture* (4 vols., New York 1952)

Hammacher, A. M. *Le Monde de Henry Van de Velde* (Paris 1967)

Hautecoeur, L. *Histoire de l'architecture classique en France* (vol. VII, Paris 1957)

Herrmann, W. *Deutsche Baukunst des 19. und 20. Jahrhunderts* (vol. I, Breslau 1932)

Heuss, T. *Hans Poelzig* (Berlin 1939)

Hilbersheimer, L. *Mies van der Rohe* (Chicago 1956)

Hitchcock, H.–R. *Architecture, Nineteenth and Twentieth Centuries* (Harmondsworth 1958)

Hitchcock, H.-R. *Gaudí* (New York 1957)

Hitchcock, H.-R. *In the Nature of Materials; the Buildings of Frank Lloyd Wright, 1887–1941* (New York 1942)

Hitchcock, H.-R. *Modern Architecture, Romanticism and Reintegration* (New York 1929)

Hitchcock, H.-R. *J. J. P. Oud* (Paris 1931)

Hitchcock, H.-R., and Johnson, P. *The International Style: Architecture since 1922* (New York 1932; paperback, New York 1966)

Hitchcock, H.-R. and others *Modern Architecture in England* (New York 1937)

Hoeber, F. *Peter Behrens* (Munich 1913)

Hoffmann, H., and Kaspar, K. *Neue deutsche Architektur* (Teufen 1956)

Howarth, T. *Charles Rennie Mackintosh and the Modern Movement* (London 1952)

Hüter, K. H. *Henry van de Velde* (Berlin 1967)

Jaffé, H. L. C. *De Stijl, 1917–1931* (London 1956)

Jamot, P. *A.–G. Perret et l'architecture du beton armé* (Paris and Brussels 1927)

Johnson, P. *Philip Johnson, Architecture 1949-65* (London 1966)

Johnson, P. *Mies van der Rohe* (2nd ed., New York 1953)

Kaufmann, E. *Taliesin Drawings; Recent Architecture of Frank Lloyd Wright* (New York 1952)

Kidder Smith, G. E. *Italy Builds* (London 1955)

Kidder Smith, G. E. *Sweden Builds* (London 1950)

Kidder Smith, G. E. *Switzerland Builds* (London 1950)

Kopp, A. *Ville et Révolution* (Paris 1967)

Korn, A. *Glass in Modern Architecture* (London 1967)

Kulka, H. *Adolf Loos, das Werk des Architekten* (Vienna 1931)

Labò, G. *Alvar Aalto* (Milan 1948)

Landau, R. *New Directions in British Architecture* (London 1968)

Lane, B. M. *Architecture and Politics in Germany 1918–1945* (Cambridge, Mass. 1968)

L'Architettura di Giuseppe Sommaruga (Milan 1908)

Lauterbach, H., and Joedicke, J. *Hugo Haering: Schriften, Entwürfe, Bauten* (Stuttgart 1965)

Lavagnino, E. *L'Arte Moderna* (Turin 1956)

Lavedan, P. *Histoire de l'urbanisme* (vol. 3, Paris 1952)

Lethaby, W. *Philip Webb and his Work* (London 1935)

Lissitzky-Küppers, S. *El Lissitzky* (Dresden 1967; London 1968)

Lux, J. A. *Joseph Maria Olbrich* (Berlin 1919)

Lux, J. A. *Otto Wagner* (Berlin 1919)

McCallum, I. *A Pocket Guide to Modern Buildings in London* (London 1951)

Macleod, R. *Charles Rennie Mackintosh* (London 1968)

McCoy, E. *Five Californian Architects* (New York 1960)

Madsen, S. T. 'Horta: Works and Style of Victor Horta before 1900',
   Architectural Review, CXVIII (1955) 388–92

Madsen, S. T. *Sources of Art Nouveau* (Oslo and New York 1956)

Manson, G. C. *Frank Lloyd Wright to 1910* (New York 1958)

Meeks, C. L. V. *Italian Architecture 1750–1914.* (Yale 1966)

Meeks, C. L. V. *The Railroad Station* (New Haven 1956)

Mieras, J., and Yerbury, F. *Dutch Architecture of the XXth century* (London 1926)

Mills, E. *The New Architecture in Great Britain, 1946–53* (London 1953)

Moderne Bouwkunst in Nederland (20 vols., Rotterdam 1932)

Morrison, H. *Louis Sullivan* (New York 1952)

Münz, H. *Adolf Loos* (Milan 1956; London 1966)

Nederland bouwt in Baksteen, 1800–1940 (Catalogue of exhibition at Boijmans
   Museum, Rotterdam 1941)

Neuenschwander, E. and C. *Finnish Buildings; Atelier Alvar Aalto,
   1950–1951* (Erlenbach–Zürich 1954)

Neutra, R. *Richard Neutra, Buildings and Projects* (Zürich 1955)

Osthaus, K. *Van de Velde; Leben und Schaffen des Künstlers* (Hagen 1920)

Oud, J. J. P. *Holländische Architektur* (Munich 1926)

Pagani, C. *Architettura italiana oggi* (Milan 1955)

Papadaki, S. (ed.) *Le Corbusier: Architect, Painter, Writer* (New York 1948)

Pevsner, N. *An Outline of European Architecture* (7th ed., Harmondsworth 1963)

Pevsner, N. *Pioneers of Modern Design* (New York 1949; revised ed.
   Harmondsworth 1960)

Pevsner, N. 'Richard Norman Shaw', *Architectural Review*, LXXXIX (1941) 41–6

Pevsner, N. *Studies in Art, Architecture and Design* (vol. II, London 1968)

Pica, A. *Architettura moderna in Italia* (Milan 1941)

Platz, G. *Die Baukunst der neuesten Zeit* (Berlin 1927)

Quilici, V. *L'Architettura del Construttivismo* (Bari 1969)

Ráfols, J. *Gaudi* (2nd ed., Barcelona 1952)

Rasch, H. *Some Roots of Modern Architecture* (London 1967)

Reggiori, F. *Milano 1800–1943* (Milan 1947)

Richards, J. M. *An Introduction to Modern Architecture* (paperback Harmondsworth
   1940; hardback London 1961)

Rogers, E. *Auguste Perret* (Milan 1955)

Roth, A. *The New Architecture* (Zürich 1940)

Sartoris, A. *Gli Elementi dell'architettura funzionale* (Milan 1935)

Sartoris, A. *Introduzione alla architettura moderna* (Milan 1949)

Scheerbart, P. *Glasarchitektur* (Berlin 1914)

Schmalenbach, F. *Jugendstil* (Würzburg 1935)

Schmutzler, R. *Art Nouveau* (London 1964)

Schnaidt, C. *Hannes Meyer* (London 1965)

Scully, V. *Louis I. Kahn* (London and New York 1962)

Sfaellos, C. *Le Fonctionnalisme dans l'architecture contemporaine* (Paris 1952)

Sharp, D. *Modern Architecture and Expressionism* (London 1966)

Starr, S. F. 'Konstantin Melnikov', *Architectural Design*, 7 (1969)

Sullivan, L. H. *The Autobiography of an Idea* (New York 1949)

Sullivan, L. H. *Kindergarten Chats* (New York 1947)

Summerson, J. *Heavenly Mansions* (London 1949)

Summerson, J. *Ten Years of British Architecture* (London 1956)

Temple, E. *New Finnish Architecture* (London 1969)

Thienen, F. van. 'De bouwkunst van de laatste anderhalve eeuw', in H. Van Gelder (ed.) *Kunstgeschiedenis der Nederlanden,* II (Utrecht 1955)

Veronesi, G. *Josef Maria Olbrich* (Milan 1948)

Veronesi, G. *J. J. Pieter Oud* (Milan 1953)

Von Moos, S. *Wirkung und Gestalt Le Corbusier* (Fraunfeld 1968)

Wagner, O. *Einige Skizzen, Projekte und ausgeführte Bauwerke* (4 vols., Vienna 1890–1922)

Wattjes, J. G. *Amsterdams bouwkunst en stadsschoon* (Amsterdam 1944)

Wattjes, J. G. *Nieuwe Nederlandsche bouwkunst* (2 vols., Amsterdam 1923–26)

Whittick, A. *European Architecture in the Twentieth Century* (2 vols., London 1950–53)

Wiener Neubauten in Stil der Sezession (6 vols., Vienna 1908–10)

Wingler, H. M. *Das Bauhaus* (Bramsche 1962; English trans., Chicago 1969)

Wright, F. L. *Frank Lloyd Wright: Ausgeführte Bauten,* intro. by C. R. Ashbee (Berlin 1911)

Wright, F. L. *An Autobiography* (New York 1943)

Yerbury, F. R. *Modern Dutch Building* (London 1931)

Zevi, B. *Richard Neutra* (Milan 1954)

Zevi, B. *Storia dell'architettura moderna* (Turin 1950)

ACKNOWLEDGMENTS

Colour Plates

M. Adelmann, Zürich (88); Bavaria-Verlag, Gauting (107); Birnback Publishing Service, New York (E. Stoller 64, 76); V. von Bonin, Helsinki (39, 91, 102); Boots Pure Drug Co. Ltd., Beeston, Nottinghamshire (57); Brecht-Einzig Ltd., London (72, 90); Burda-Bilderdienst, Offenburg (108); Burkhard-Verlag Ernst Heyer, Essen (3, 4, 8, 9, 11, 13, 17, 18, 19, 20, 21, 23, 24, 25, 28, 30, 31, 32, 34, 36, 37, 40, 41, 42, 43, 44, 45, 48, 49, 51, 52, 54, 56, 58, 59, 60, 62, 63, 71, 77, 80, 87, 95, 96, 100, 105, 111, 112); F. Candela, Mexico City (110); B. Cunningham-Werdnigg, Guilford, Connecticut (104); Farbwerke Hoechst AG, Frankfurt-Hoechst (47); R. Friedrich, Berlin (84); Ford Foundation, New York (E. Stoller 106); General Motors Continental, Antwerp (70): Photographie Giraudon, Paris (1); Hedrich-Blessing, Chicago (12, 14, 26, 35, 38, 65, 66, 67, 75, 98); L. Hervé, Paris (68, 74); Holle-Verlag, Baden-Baden (29); H. Hollein, Vienna (99); Humboldt-Universität, Berlin (46, 50); Israel-Museum, Jerusalem (103); A. F. Kersting, London (2, 6, 7, 22); Dr. U. Kultermann, Leverkusen (109); F. A. Mella, Milan (5, 79, 94); A. Neumann-Z. Hecker, Tel Aviv (85, 86); Novosti Press Agency (APN), Moscow (55, 83); Orion Press, Tokyo (92, 93, 97); P. Popper Ltd., London (15); F. Rausser, Bolligen-Berne (82); J. Reeves, Toronto (101); Salmer, Barcelona (10, 27, 33); Scala, Florence (16); J. Shulman, Los Angeles (53, 73, 81, 89); E. Stoller, New York (69); Instituto Eduardo Torroja, Madrid (61); C. R. Villanueva, Caracas (78). Diagram on page 75 drawn from elevation supplied by courtesy of Yale University, pp. 92, 97 by courtesy of Professor Carl W. Condit, *the Chicago School of Architecture*; p. 139 after Thomas Howarth *Charles Rennie Mackintosh and the modern movement*.

INDEX